perspectives

Marketing
on the Internet

perspectives

Marketing
on the Internet

Academic Editor
A. Cemal Ekin
Providence College

coursewise
p u b l i s h i n g
inc.

St. Paul • Bellevue • Boulder • Dubuque • Madison

Contents

section

3

Understanding the Cyberconsumer

section

4

The New Face of Marketing

section
5

Legal and Ethical Issues of the Internet

section
6
Site Design

section
7
Looking Ahead

Topic Key

This Topic Key is an important tool for learning. It will help you integrate this reader into your course studies. Listed below, in alphabetical order, are important topics covered in this volume. Below each topic you'll find the reading numbers and titles relating to that topic. Note that the Topic Key might not include every topic your instructor chooses to emphasize. If you don't find the topic you're looking for in the Topic Key, check the index or the online topic key at the **courselinks**™ site.

section

1

The Internet has carved an indelible mark in everyone's consciousness so fast, so strong, and in such a short time we sometimes forget that it has gained such popularity in only five years. Fueled by rapid changes in computer and communication technologies, it grew in size, in content, and arguably in quality at remarkable rates. These make even the most techno-savvy person dizzy. This enormous popularity and recognition among the general public and the business sector have their roots in the new paradigm the Internet brings, with significant potential benefits to all.

The Internet has qualities that make it an exciting medium for organizations and for individuals. Marketers need to understand these qualities if the Internet is to become a significant marketing tool. Although all the readings in this book address some of these issues, the readings in the first section provide a holistic view of these qualities.

Learning Objectives

This section, with its opening comments, presents the impact of the Internet on businesses, regardless of the sector. The readings in this section will implicitly or explicitly address some of the attributes of the Internet. Try to read the articles in this section to achieve the following learning objectives and use the questions that follow to sharpen your focus on the issues.

- Identify what the Internet brings to the business world.

- Learn how the Internet is changing the business paradigm and how this may affect marketing.

- Identify the main differences between traditional business models and doing business on the Internet.

- The Internet is an interactive personal medium. For years, the dream of the television industry has been to give interactive capabilities to television broadcasts. Although some broadcasters experimented with the idea in a limited way, it did not go beyond choosing a multiple-choice answer, a very simple interaction. Whereas TV still remains a broadcast medium with no meaningful interaction, the Internet by its very nature requires personal involvement. Therefore, the Internet offers marketers an audience highly tuned to the selected content, with an intrinsic level of interest and attention.

- The Internet offers access to information on demand, pulled by users rather than pushed by broadcasters. This request-based access to information gives the ultimate in programmability of what the screen presents to the viewer. This quality, very closely tied to the previous one, presents both opportunities and challenges to marketers. On the one hand, marketers can deal with a person who *intends* to receive information and *focuses attention* on the selected content. Consequently, the quality of the communication process will increase, at least at the receiver end. On the other hand, marketers face the challenge of getting the initial attention of the individuals, as the very large number of Web sites continues to grow even more.

- The Internet delivers content that is highly customizable by either the sender or the receiver. This ability to bring specialized information to each viewer and to adjust its amount and complexity on demand brings a new dimension to marketing communications. Now marketers can present tailored content to each viewer but must better understand how to do the tailoring.

- The Internet compresses time. *Net-time* makes things happen faster, sometimes alarmingly faster. This "instant access" to information and consumers' desire to tap into it puts an extra burden on the organizations to provide timely and complete information to their constituents. Those who cannot keep up with the Net in Net-time will most likely become a Net-casualty.

- The Internet compresses space. Now everyone can go faster than a speeding bullet and jump over tall buildings in one leap. The physical boundaries around markets have been dissolving since the Industrial Revolution. The Internet has accelerated this process and has pushed the boundaries even more, thus significantly contributing to the globalization of markets. The compression of space has the potential to bring to our fingertips the goods and services we need.

- The Internet decouples the sender from the receiver in the communication process. Marketing is based on a very simple idea: exchange. This idea makes information exchange possible in the form of marketing communications and transactions as the manifestation of marketing in action. In either one of these fundamental exchanges, the sender and the receiver or the seller and the buyer usually need to engage in the process synchronously in real-time. The Internet decouples the sides in time and space and offers an asynchronous engagement in the exchange process. This gives greater flexibility to the buyer, or the receiver, to engage in the exchange process when the mood strikes.

An informed consumer awaits the marketers in the new millennium, and the Internet is strategically positioned to be the necessary intermediary. The articles that follow stress that the challenge to the marketers lies in shifting to the new paradigms in a timely way without jeopardizing the mission of the organization.

❓ Questions

1. Consider the qualities of the Internet previously discussed. Do you agree with the qualities described? Do you think there are more or others? As you read the articles in this section, try to identify some of these qualities.

2. These readings will outline how the Internet is changing the business paradigm and how this may affect marketing. Think what this paradigm shift means to you as a consumer. Consider what impact they'll have on your professional life as a marketer or in other endeavors.

3. As you read, imagine that you are the CEO of a manufacturer producing some kind of consumer goods. Identify the main differences between traditional business models and doing business on the Internet. Which differences do you think are most important? How would you change your company's marketing strategy to harness the six qualities of the Internet?

Tremble, Everyone

Ever thought of your Web browser as an instrument of egalitarianism? In the physical world, banks come in massive, marble-fronted edifices; sex shops have low, dingy shopfronts with blacked-out windows and neon lighting. Yet viewed through your browser, both are reduced to just a screen with some pictures and text. This may be worrying for the banks (how do you convey trustworthiness without the aid of marble?), but it does point to something they have in common.

Whatever industry you are in, electronic commerce will shake you up.

The Internet is affecting all businesses in similar ways. Every industry, for example, has suddenly become part of a global network where all companies are equally easy to reach. Information, once closely hoarded in many industries, is becoming a commodity. A few years ago, you might have had to pay a company such as Reuters a small fortune for a constant feed of stock quotes. Now practically all financial Web sites give them out (albeit delayed by a few minutes) free. As a result of these changes, many businesses that survived mainly because they were conveniently placed, or because they provided information that was hard to find, will soon have to find some other *raison d'être.*

But even though the forces affecting them are the same, the consequences for each industry are very different. Some are made for life online: computer equipment, for example, is a natural. Big companies have been ordering PCs online for years, using proprietary systems; now the Internet has extended that convenience to the consumer market. Leading PC vendors such as Gateway 2000 and Dell see online sales approaching 10% of their business. Last year Forrester calculated that PCs, porn, CDs—things the consultancy calls "boy-toys"—and gift items such as flowers made up a little over half of all online consumer revenues.

Consumers seem to have an open mind: in a recent survey by Yankelovich Partners, a consultancy, between 65% and 75% of people using the Internet who had not yet bought anything online said they would consider this method for making hotel reservations, paying for online subscriptions, and buying computer software, airline tickets, records, tapes, CDs and videos.

Where It Matters

Outside the technology sector, the effects of electronic commerce are being felt most keenly—for good or ill—in the following industries:

- **Financial services.** Universal access to information is hitting hard here. This is a classic example of how the Internet can open up an existing infrastructure—the financial markets' computerised information feeds—to all comers and thus transform an industry. In the past, brokers have justified their high fees by pointing to the quality of their advice. But now knowledgeable amateurs and industry experts can trade stock tips for no charge in popular personal investing sites such as the Motley Fool. Are they sometimes biased, and often wrong? Yes, just like the pros. Now that investors can get advice and market information from many sources other than full-service brokers, they are less willing to pay a premium just to trade. Discount online brokers such as e.Schwab are booming; in March the San Francisco-based firm said that about 700,000 of its accounts (one-sixth of the total) had conducted at least one online trade during the past year. Forrester estimates that assets worth $111 billion are already managed online, and that the figure will rise to $474 billion by 2000. But anything as popular as that risks being commoditised. Already more than 30 discount brokers are offering online trading accounts at rates that match or undercut e.Schwab, according to CS First Boston, an investment bank. The challenge is already clear: survive on razor-thin margins, or find some way to add value.

- **Sex.** Virtually every modern personal media technology, from photography to the videotape, has won many of its first converts from among the grubby-mac set. The big selling point is usually privacy. The Internet, which in effect brings the world's adult bookstores and video shops to home computers, is following the same pattern. Forrester reckons that erotic content accounted for sales of $52 million on the Internet last year, one-tenth of all retail business on the Web. Others think it may be three times that. One sex firm, the Internet Entertainment Group, based in Seattle, claims to have 50,000 paying subscribers online, nearly as many as the *Wall Street Journal.*

The sex industry's typical consumers tend to be avid, savvy and well-wired young men—much like tomorrow's shopper for less spicy online fare. They have become expert at hunting out the best material at the lowest price from the thousands of sex sites online. Porn purveyors, therefore, have to push Internet technology harder than almost any other industry, with video clips, customisable service, and even live video conferencing (for lack of a better term) to raise their site's profile. Their lessons for other industries? Give away lots of samples, promote your service wherever possible, and aim for international markets from the beginning.

- **Travel.** Travel agents are another group that has survived on exclusive access to information. By knowing their way around ticket prices, schedules and flight availability, they have been able to hold their own, despite the airlines' efforts to sell straight to consumers and avoid paying the agents' 10% commission. Most travellers prefer using travel agents to calling every airline themselves or figuring out how to work the flight-booking services on commercial online services, especially since using an agent costs them no more.

But the Internet, by providing an easy-to-use direct link to consumers, is giving the airlines an opportunity to erode the place of the middleman. They are doing this in two ways. The first is by selling seats on their own Web sites and together on Sabre's Travelocity, American Airlines' booking service. The second, led by Northwest and Continental, is by cutting the fees they pay to online travel agencies to 5%, on the ground that costs are far lower than in the physical world because customers find and book the flights themselves.

Yet the airlines may face an uphill struggle. Although top online travel sites such as Expedia sell more than $1 million of tickets a week, online sales still make up less than 1% of total airline ticket sales. Forrester Research estimates that this year the figure may creep up to about 1.5%. But as long as the airlines are prohibited by law from offering online bookers—or anyone else—a price advantage, most independent travellers will still prefer a quick call to their travel agent.

- **Retailing.** It is easy to see why the mall was the first image that sprang to mind when people started to think about electronic commerce on the Internet. The most obvious advantages of online shops are that their costs are lower and they are less constrained for space than their physical counterparts. Yet today less than a third of online marketers are making money, according to Activmedia, a New Hampshire consultancy.

The reason is that most of their offerings are distinctly unimpressive. Even big mail-order retailers such as J.C. Penney and J. Crew offer only a small fraction of their print catalogue online. Even those items are hard to find, slow to download, and hard to see on-screen. Where are the innovative marketing techniques, harnessing both the power of the Web and the legendary "data warehouses" of these consumer giants? Still being developed, they explain: building an online shopping site that is attractive to buyers takes longer and costs more than most of them had reckoned.

- **Music.** When Amazon's Jeff Bezos was first scouting for retail sectors in which to work his online magic, he considered music, but decided against it. Whereas the book industry had thousands of publishers, the music industry was controlled by just a few labels. He was afraid they would have the power to stifle any online venture that offered serious competition. And indeed, several online music stores that have the makings of a site as useful as Amazon's have had trouble getting record companies' permission to offer album samples, and their prices are typically little lower than those of physical music stores.

Most are losing money: online sales reached a mere $20 million last year, and industry-wide gross profits were just $200,000, according to the *Red Herring,* a technology magazine. MCI, an American telephone company, last year closed its 1-800-Music-Now site after spending nearly $40 million promoting it: its top CD sold only 400 units. Still, as Firefly is showing with its BigNote site built around a thriving community of music fans, good online music stores have the potential to outdo their physical competitors just as Amazon bests its book-trade rivals. But it could be slow going: Jupiter Communications, a New York consultancy, predicts that online music sales will increase to $186 million by

2000, still less than 2% of all recordings sold.

- **Books.** This market is no longer a one-horse race now that America's two largest booksellers, Barnes & Noble and Borders, have gone online, along with such international competitors as Britain's Internet Bookshop and a host of smaller outfits. Optimists think online book sales will reach 8% of the market by 2000. Pessimists reckon there will be a bloody battle for just the bottom 1–2%.

- **Cars.** A few years ago most people would have laughed at the idea of buying a car online. Now those who try it are more likely to sigh with relief. Instead of spending a loathsome afternoon with a salesman, customers of Auto-by-Tel, the leading Internet car-buying service, simply tell the service what kind of car they want, and wait for nearby dealerships to make their best offer. Customers report prices up to 10% lower than their best face-to-face haggling efforts could achieve, without having to step into a dealership until it is time to pay and pick up the car. The reason: it costs a dealer only about $25 to respond to an Auto-By-Tel lead, instead of hundreds of dollars to advertise and sell a car the conventional way.

Last year 2 million of the 15.1 million cars sold in America went to customers who set foot in the dealership only to pick up the car. Chrysler, which put its Internet sales last year at just 1.5% of the total, reckons that in four years' time the figure will be 25%. Manufacturers are thrilled by this trend; they

generally consider dealers a necessary evil, just as airlines do travel agents. But a creative dealership, which can set up its own Web site, can also use the Internet to expand its franchise.

- **Advertising and marketing.** These two industries, although not strictly in the category of electronic commerce themselves, are being profoundly changed by it. This is because the Internet, unlike any advertising vehicle before it, is an interactive medium, completely customisable for each viewer. The implications of this are just starting to sink in. Where they will be felt most is in the target market known as the "hard middle." Amazon's Mr Bezos defines it like this: "In today's world, if you want to reach 12 people, that's easy: you use the phone. If you want to reach 12 million people, it's easy: you take out an ad during the Superbowl. But you want to pitch something to 10,000 people—the hard middle— that's really hard."

Today's answer to the hard middle is direct mail, which is expensive and inefficient. The Internet makes it easier both to target potentially interested consumers and to communicate with them. Search services such as InfoSeek, for example, sell keywords: search for "airline tickets", and an ad banner for American Express's travel service shows up on top of the resulting list. Call it advertising or direct marketing—the distinctions are blurring. Indeed, First Virtual, an Internet commerce firm, has developed an advertisement that can act as a tiny shopfront (imagine a Nike ad that would let you order a pair of shoes from within the banner), merging advertising and direct commerce.

An Internet ad banner provides a direct link to the advertiser's site, offering interested consumers an easy way to go there for more information or an opportunity to buy. Compare that with a television ad, which has to create such an impression that you remember it days later when you are shopping. Because online advertising offers the capacity for an immediate response, it challenges the old saw that merchants know that only half of their advertising works, but not which half. On the Internet it is easy to know which half: just count the "click-throughs." Indeed, last year Procter & Gamble refused to pay for ads that people did not click on. Web sites were outraged (what if it was just a lame ad?), but one way or another advertisers will demand more evidence of effectiveness in future.

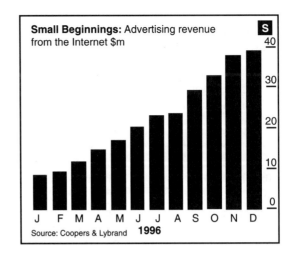

Small Beginnings: Advertising revenue from the Internet $m

Source: Coopers & Lybrand **1996**

Total Internet advertising revenues last year were just $267 million (see chart), compared with $33 billion spent on television advertising in America alone—even though top Internet sites have television-sized audiences of a million viewers a day. America Online, with 8 million subscribers the biggest Internet service provider, has more viewers than any cable television network or newspaper, and all but the world's two most popular magazines. So where is the big advertising money Internet media companies are expecting? Waiting and seeing: the market is too new for advertisers to be sure they will get their money's worth.

Article Review Form at end of book.

Is Web Business Good Business?

Although tangible returns are elusive, the first wave of Web-based companies have learned valuable lessons about how to make the most out of a presence on the Net.

Mark Hodges

Mark Hodges is senior research associate at the Georgia Tech Research Institute, where he specializes in interactive media. His e-mail address is mark.hodges@gtri.gatech.edu.

When wine buyer Peter Granoff was looking for a way out of the restaurant business, he never dreamed his future lay in cyberspace. Then one evening over dinner as his brother-in-law Robert Olson sketched out a plan for starting a company on the World Wide Web, Granoff had a vision. Olson, a former marketing executive at a Silicon Valley computer maker, wanted to sell an easy-to-distribute product with a large, passionate, and geographically dispersed buying audience. He believed the ideal product line for the Web was one whose customers needed extensive information to guide their purchasing decisions. An excited Granoff said, "You're talking about my business." Inspired, Granoff and Olson launched Virtual Vineyards, a rapidly growing online vendor of wine and one of the first of a growing number of companies that are il-

lustrating the revenue-generating potential of putting a storefront on the World Wide Web.

Companies that continue to do most of their sales through conventional channels are setting up Web sites as promotional and corporate image tools. At the same time, the Net has given birth to a rising number of Web-only enterprises.

It costs little to set up a rudimentary Web site that provides information on a company's products and services. And forecasts of the Web's business potential can be tantalizing. One often-cited source, Matrix Information Directory Services, predicts that the number of people online will expand from 57 million in 1997 to 377 million in 2000. According to a Nielson Media Research report, 2.5 million persons already have bought products or services on the Web. And Forrester Research, a market-research firm in Cambridge, Mass., predicts that Internet-based sales in the United States will jump from $518 million this year to $6.6 billion by decade's end. Over the same period, Jupiter Communications, a New York firm that studies online and

interactive technologies, projects that Web advertising will expand from $312 million to $5 billion.

Internet businesses have found that cybershoppers are attracted by the ability to research and compare products before initiating transactions—in contrast to the world of brick-and-mortar commerce, where customers often rush into purchases or must travel from store to store to compare products effectively. Web sites can offer more detailed and extensive information than a typical customer-service representative is willing or able to provide, either in person or over the telephone. The Internet marketplace also may be well-suited for customers looking for rare or hard-to-find items. Mike Schachner, managing editor of *Wine Enthusiast* magazine, predicts that a Web-based outfit like Virtual Vineyards will do especially well selling specialty or high-priced wines, as opposed to the "$10 bottle of Cabernet to have with your steak" that consumers will still buy from local shops on the way home from work.

But making money on the Web is hardly a slam-dunk. Most

early online retail ventures have failed to generate enough sales to survive, and a 1996 survey of online businesses by the market-research firm ActivMedia found that just under one-third of Internet-based firms claim to be profitable. Many consumers are unwilling to change established buying patterns, or are repelled by clumsy attempts at online marketing; people are reluctant to type their credit card number onto a Web site for fear that it will be stolen (see "Building a Bond of Trust," at the end of this article).

Right now, most companies are trying to establish themselves as major presences online and playing the game of increasing their name recognition and market share. The payoff, these companies believe, will come down the road in a year or so, when Web commerce becomes more commonplace. For example, Darryl Peck, founder of Cyberian Outpost, an online computer retailer, says his company posts $2 million in monthly sales, attracts 12,000 visitors a day, and has recorded an annual growth rate of 600 percent over the last two years. Ask about profit and loss, though, and the picture isn't so rosy. The investment in hardware, network access, and people to make a Web site efficient and attractive is substantial. Says Peck, "Our loss was under 9 percent of sales last year—that puts us a lot closer to profitability than most Web companies." At this embryonic stage of the Web marketplace, Peck maintains, strong revenue, steady growth, and high volume of traffic at the Web site—rather than net profit—are a better guide to a Web-based business's success.

Virtual Vineyards founder Granoff says that his company is growing at an average of 20 per-

cent per month and that its "trend lines are all in the right direction." Preview Travel, which provides online travel and vacation planning information through America Online and its own Web site, claims to have 1.4 million subscribers, weekly bookings of between $1.2 million and $1.6 million, and a growth rate of about 20 percent per month. Hot & Spicy Foods of Morgan Hill, Calif., opened a Web site in November and saw an immediate spurt in business; sales during the first quarter of this year were double what they were during the same period of 1996, according to president Jeffrey Marcil. These and other successful sites emphasize transaction efficiency, rapid response, and tools for customizing the customer's visit. They frequently allow visitors to make contributions to the site or talk with each other in a way that makes them feel like members of a community.

These cybermerchants are learning that even in a medium as exotic as the Web, all the rules of traditional business still apply. Companies need to get strong financial backing, find customers, offer high-quality products, process orders efficiently, and win repeat sales. But to survive the early shakeout period, Web-based enterprises must also do more than simply master these fundamentals of Marketing 101. Merchants need imagination to design shopping environments tailored to the Web's unique strengths and weaknesses.

Judging from the business climate on the Web, many companies have made rapid progress toward learning the craft of Internet marketing. Online retailers provide entertaining and informative sites that customize shopping for the individual consumer and

even anticipate consumers' buying preferences. Despite such developments, the financial prospects of Internet commerce are hard to gauge. Information that has been released focuses on the cheeriest statistics the companies can muster, such as the number of visitors to their online stores and the rate of revenue growth. While this is an appropriate mentality for a start-up business, it can carry a company only so far. Eventually, costs must be covered. And as the novelty of the Web wears off, the challenge of offering a distinct and customer-friendly site becomes ever tougher—and more essential.

Tapping the Web's Wonders

Many early-adapting businesses have struggled with how best to use the new medium. Commonly, companies fail to exploit the capacity for interactivity, offering static sites that serve as electronic versions of brochures. Successful companies, in contrast, have developed dynamic, information-rich sites that create an informal, often whimsical atmosphere that consumers enjoy searching whether they buy products or not, and that take advantage of the Internet's unique attributes. Good Web business sites offer visitors a wealth of useful, diverting information in addition to detailed product descriptions. Virtual Vineyards, for instance, publishes a "tasting chart" that helps shoppers learn how to judge wines by intensity, sweetness, body, acidity, tannin oak, and complexity. It also provides a glossary of frequently used terms and tips on how to mix wine and food and an archive of menus, including recipes and wine choices, for a variety of holidays and special occasions.

Online booksellers are also employing innovative ways to use free information to stimulate sales. Amazon.com devotes a Web page to each book that the cyberstore sells, and many of the more popular offerings feature links to author interviews and reviews by professional critics. Another Internet bookstore, PureFiction in England, not only reprints snippets of critical reactions to its featured offerings but also publishes sample chapters and offers five-minute audio excerpts of its books on tape.

Early-adapting companies have found that too much visual sophistication can be counterproductive. Frustrated shoppers bail out of business Web sites quickly when detailed renderings of products or other images take too long to load on their computer screens. ReadMe.Doc, a computer-book retailer in Chambersburg, Pa., recently scaled back on the number of graphic images on its site because "it was taking too long for someone with a 14.4-kilobit-per-second modem to get a page up," says president Christopher Kendall.

In a similar vein, Perry Lopez, creator of Hot Hot Hot, a hot-sauce retailer in Los Angeles, stresses the importance of easy navigation. He has tried to create a Web site where customers have to click only once from the home page to get to key information in any given category. But such an approach is a matter of personal taste; some Web users prefer pages with small amounts of information and frequent links.

Internet business experts caution would-be cybermarketers that good Web site design takes time. It is deceptively easy to throw together a quick-and-dirty Web page in a few hours. But a high-quality site that customers will feel comfortable visiting and revisiting requires planning and maintenance. Successful electronic merchants make detailed studies of commercial Web sites before designing or opening an electronic business. For instance, Darryl Peck says he "spent 16 hours a day checking out Web sites" before formulating a business plan for Cyberian Outpost. Similarly, the founders of Amazon.com spent a year learning the business before going online, according to Scott Lipsky, vice-president of business expansion.

Web business veterans recommend bringing in outsiders or customers to evaluate a new site before launch. AMP, one of the world's leading manufacturers of electronic and electrical connectors, took a year to develop a Web site allowing online parts purchase. For almost six months before the site officially opened, major customers piloted the new system and offered comments on its usability, according to Robert Orendorf, project manager for AMP eMerce Internet Solutions. And Virtual Vineyards took nine months to develop a product inventory system to support the company's Web site, accommodating more than 75 wineries and 45 specialty-food companies.

Attracting and Keeping Customers

There's nothing so forlorn as an unvisited Web site. Companies that want to attract people to their online storefront use a variety of channels, both on and off the Internet, to attract potential customers. One approach is to send marketing offers to customers through electronic mail. Such efforts need not be the kind of unsolicited junk mail, or "spam," that so enrages many recipients. Many Web sites ask visitors to register, a process that offers the option of signing up for e-mail from the company announcing product news.

One technique that universally attracts customers to a Web site is visualizations of products. When engineers search the AMP Connect Web catalog, for example, they can navigate among 70,000 choices by part name or number, or by using a menu of product pictures. Once customers have found products meeting their specifications, they can view detailed line drawings, and in some cases, download three-dimensional renderings. At Toyota's Web site, customers can not only read text screens with detailed product specifications and dealer locations but can see what a variety of colors look like on a car model, view new automobiles from different vantage points through photographic "walkarounds," and look at interiors through a special "photo-bubble" view like that provided by a fisheye lens.

Granted, such attempts to visualize cars are primitive compared with what consumers see when visiting an automobile dealership. And shoppers often have to go through an involved process of downloading free software to use such effects. But car buying on the Web has proven surprisingly popular, especially in the form of online brokering services that gather product information and handle transactions. The Auto-By-Tel site, for example provides access to financing and insurance information as well as an electronic form for requesting no-haggle, no-obligation price quotes on specific car models. Since starting up in 1995, the company has processed 325,000 requests for quotes from a network of 1,500 accredited dealerships. One participating dealer—Atamian Honda-Volkswagen of Tewksbury, Mass.—credits Auto-By-Tel for initiating as many as 25 percent of its sales.

In the San Francisco Bay area, the 12-dealership Tasha Automotive Group has sold several hundred cars through another Web-based buying service, Autoreach, according to Jon Fisher, director of operations. Although those represent less than 5 percent of total sales, Fisher expects more than 20 percent of his company's sales to come from the Internet within five years, based on recent growth trends. Fisher is particularly excited about the potential of Web sites to alleviate consumer disgust with the high-pressure sales and marketing tactics common in the automotive business.

Building Electronic Communities

Surfing the World Wide Web can be an adventure, but online users are often eager to relieve the loneliness of the ride. Many Internet businesses are trying to tap into the desire for interpersonal connection by establishing hospitable sites. People need to feel that someone is listening and responding on the other end of the modem.

While fast and consistent response is a basic of good business in any case, entrepreneurs have found its importance magnified on the Web. Shoppers want some

confirmation other than a message box on a Web site that their orders have been processed. The rapidity of e-mail transmission has accustomed Internet users to expect responses to their questions and concerns within hours instead of days. Scott Lipsky of Amazon.com says that the company strives to answer every e-mail note—usually within hours. With the site's business growing by 30 percent each month, this task has become more daunting with each passing week, and the bookseller has continually beefed up its staff to meet this demand.

Business Web sites also gain by fostering a sense of community among their visitors. The first prerequisite of community-building is to offer a place "where people want to hang out," says Lee McKnight, a specialist in Internet economics and a lecturer in MIT's Technology, Management, and Policy Program. One way to do so is to address visitors in an informal, often humorous tone that encourages customers to have fun while making purchases or gathering product information. Visitors to Van den Bergh Foods' Ragú sauce site, for example, enter a cozy dining room dubbed "Mama's Cucina" where a grandmotherly woman waits at a table set for two. A dialogue bubble over her head says: "You're buying a new computer? What's this new new all the time now? I've got pots and pans older than you." In similarly colloquial language, Mama offers visitors recipes, Italian lessons, a free vacation contest, and advice on one's love life, along with information about Ragú products.

Some online businesses encourage a sense of community by allowing customers to contribute

information to their sites. Virtual Vineyards publishes consumers' favorite ways to marry wine and food while offering the "Cork Dork"—a column that answers customer questions about wine. Amazon.com invites readers to post their comments about books it sells alongside those of professional critics.

Another tactic for building community is to emphasize interaction among customers. An excellent illustration of this approach is Onsale Inc., which conducts several virtual auctions a week of refurbished computers and home-electronics products. Shoppers can not only follow the progress of the auction and enjoy the pleasure of the hunt but can also include personal comments with their bids—and read those of other buyers. "They often get into competitive interactions, making comments like 'No way, MP of Mountain View, it's mine!!'" says marketing director Michelle Pettigrew. Onsale also stirs the pot by soliciting comments from bidders on topics not directly related to the purchase, posing questions such as "What's your favorite personal-computer game?" These interactions, says Pettigrew, help ensure that the auction is "not just a static online catalog or order-taking mechanism."

Onsale's strategy of combining entertainment with retailing appears to be paying off. The company says it has attained profitability with monthly sales exceeding $4 million. And according to PC Meter's recent audience rating reports for the World Wide Web, the online auction house often attracts visitors for more time each month than any other Internet shopping location. Between August 1996 and January 1997, Onsale shoppers spent an average of 30 to 48 minutes on the site each month.

Businesses gain further important advantages by maintaining strong electronic-mail contacts with customers. "A lot of times all you have to do is ask your customers for their opinions and feedback and you get a statistically reliable sample in a matter of hours," says Onsale's Pettigrew. "We use our customers as a sounding board whenever possible." Rosalind Resnick, president of a Web-site design company called NetCreations, considers the three hours a day she spends answering mail from customers as time well spent. "Customers are thrilled to get a response from the president of the company," she says. "The more interaction the better."

Indeed, Hot & Spicy Foods president Marcil says that what he likes best about adding an Internet component to his business is the rapid access it gives him to customers. He can make a change in product offerings and get the word out immediately to customers—both on his Web site and through targeted electronic mailings to regular cybershoppers at his store. The response rate to e-mail specials is around 5 to 7 percent, he says, in contrast to the 3 to 4 percent response elicited by traditional targeted mailings.

Customized Shopping

Successful online businesses have even found ways to tailor the shopping experience to individual buyers. These innovators give consumers tools that ease product searches or profile individuals' buying preferences and offer information tailored to their needs.

A good example is Preview Travel, where consumers have access to a powerful engine for customizing their trip plans. A would-be shopper enters a destination and preferred dates, times, and airline. An automated flight-planning system then displays a selection of flights that match the desired itinerary—including fare, seat availability, type of airplane, meals, number of stops, and the flight's on-time record.

Preview also offers best-fare options, reflecting the fact that the difference in cost for relatively small changes in plans can be significant. For instance, a recent request for a round-trip quote from Atlanta to Sydney, Australia, came in at slightly over $3,000 for the preferred times. The best-fare quote reduced that price nearly 50 percent by shifting the departure time for the Los Angeles-to-Sydney leg of the flight from late afternoon to early evening, and by changing the trip home from Sydney from around noon to mid-afternoon. While the same services are available from traditional travel agents, booking air tickets over the Web lets the consumer transact business at any hour of the day or night, and do comparative shopping.

Other Internet-based businesses are taking customization into a new dimension with software that digests information from consumers and then responds to their buying preferences. The Vertigo Group, for example, recently introduced One-on-One Banking Center software, which banks can make available for their customers to download from Web sites. The software leads consumers through an "interview," eliciting basic personal information as well as details about their assets, debts, and investments. One-on-One then generates an "action plan" with recommendations for investing a specific amount of money in an equity mutual fund, opening a tax-deferred annuity at a given dollar level, or purchasing an individual retirement account.

One-on-One then identifies products offered by the sponsor bank and provides screens on which customers can get more specific information—for instance, they might ask to see certificates of deposit that earned given rates of return over the past 10 years. If consumers cannot get all of their questions answered through the One-on-One interface, they can send an e-mail message to the bank. When they are ready to make purchases, the software provides a means of doing so online.

Intelligent-agent technology promises to offer an even more ambitious means of customizing online shopping. Now in its infancy, agent software allows business Web sites to ask participating customers questions or track their buying preferences and use this information to anticipate future needs. The agent for an online company can then send product announcements or news that consumers might find interesting. Eventually, individual shoppers may maintain their own intelligent agents that would continually scan the Web for information or carry out specific shopping assignments.

One early example of intelligent-agent technology at work can be found on The Firefly Network. New members fill in forms on the screen, rating their preferences for musical groups and movies. Armed with this data, Firefly—a free service—will give them information about music and videos that matches their expressed preferences, and inform them when members with

No matter how hospitable a Web site, consumers often remain reluctant to part with money through the Internet. Before the 1996 Olympics, for example, Nancy Davis of Atlanta dialed up an online sales site to purchase event tickets. But she almost gave up when a dialogue window asked for her Visa number and her mother's maiden name. Davis was hesitant about releasing such information casually—and certainly not over a telephone line, at the request of a machine. Her reluctance highlights the fragile bond of trust between buyer and seller in the depersonalized setting of Web commerce. Consumers also fear that online transactions will not remain private and that their purchasing habits will become a matter of record.

The situation is getting better. CommerceNet, an industry association of online businesses, is collaborating with the Electronic Frontier Foundation on a project called eTrust to address this concern. The eTrust system accredits Internet companies according to transaction security and their willingness to protect customers' personal information. Complying companies will be allowed to display "trustmarks" that indicate several levels of customer-friendliness. A pilot project involving as many as 100 companies and organizations is now under way, with global launch expected later this year.

Financial institutions, meanwhile, have established new types of payment schemes to enable the electronic equivalents of anonymous cash purchases on the Web. For example, a consortium of major communications and financial firms, including AT&T, Chase Manhattan, Dean Witter, and Wells Fargo, late last year created Mondex USA, a company that will offer a "smart card" for electronic-cash purchases on the Internet and in conventional stores. Consumers with the Mondex software first go to their regular bank's Web site to load their cards with cash value, which they can use to make anonymous online purchases. Merchants receive payment within seconds of the sale. Mondex USA has installed features that protect its "smart card" from theft, including encryption, digital signatures, and the option for password protection.

Proponents of this virtual currency believe that the ability to make micropayments at prices as low as fractions of pennies will stimulate the Internet economy. For example, consumers who are unwilling to spend $50 a year to receive a periodical online might happily part with a few cents for a single article—or fractions of a cent to look at a small part of one article, or just to peruse the table of contents.

While advocates see micropayments making purchase of low-price items easier, skeptics contend that any scheme that rewards the vendor adequately would require steeper prices, inhibiting the kind of frequent, casual use of Web sites that surfers now take for granted. They argue that most customers who buy information on the Web will probably still find subscription-based or advertising-supported products more economical than products priced à la carte. In all likelihood, the pay-per-view and subscription-based systems will coexist, offering consumers more choices

and strengthening the versatility of the Internet as a marketplace.

Beyond the psychological barrier of uncertain privacy, Internet commerce may founder over a technical obstacle: the lack of compatibility between methods of processing Web transactions. Approximately 20 companies have developed software offering proprietary payment or security solutions, and these systems do not necessarily speak the same language. The inability of merchants and customers to readily authenticate one another's identity or agree on a type of payment threatens the free flow of Internet commerce, contends Jay M. Tenenbaum, chairman and chief executive officer of CommerceNet, an industry association of online business. "We're well down the path to digital anarchy," says Tenenbaum. What's needed, he maintains, is "a universal protocol between any wallet and any merchant."

Toward this end, CommerceNet collaborated with the World Wide Web Consortium (the group of organizations that sets standards) to create a common method for software to handle Internet payments. This effort has spurred development of eCo System—a translator that helps incompatible software used in Web business transactions to "talk" to each other. The eCo System framework provides a way for a variety of commercial processing software to communicate the basic information needed for a financial transaction. Tenenbaum believes eCo System will evolve into a common business language for automated transaction-processing on the Internet.

similar interests are available for conversation in the Web site's chat rooms.

When Pull Comes to Push

In the first heated year or so of Web business, most of the action has revolved around efforts to tap the consumer market. More recently, as the Web proved to be more than a fad, companies have started to buy and sell products and services with one another. Such business-to-business sales make sense because businesspeople typically know what product they're looking for, according to Joseph Bailey, an MIT doctoral student who has written extensively about Internet economics.

Nonetheless, many companies still hesitate to use the Web because of doubts about its reliability. "Businesses need to feel they can trust the pathway between them and the supplier," says senior analyst Blane Erwin of Forrester Research. Some companies are limiting the risk by conducting online transactions only with established business partners who are given access to the company's private intranet.

Another major shift in the model for Internet commerce concerns the technology available for marketing. Until recently, Internet marketing activities have focused on strategies to "pull" customers into sites. In the past year, however, software companies have developed tools that allow companies to "push" information directly out to consumers, transmitting marketing messages directly to targeted customers. Most notably, the Pointcast Network uses a screen saver to deliver a continually updated stream of news and advertise-ments to subscribers' computer monitors. Subscribers can customize the information they want to receive. By clicking on intriguing advertisements, they proceed directly to a company's Web site. Companies such as Virtual Vineyards are already starting to use similar technologies to push messages to customers about special sales, product offerings, or other events. But push technology has earned the disdain of many Web users. Online culture exalts the notion that the information flowing onto the screen comes there by specific request. Once commercial promotion begins to fill the screen unbidden, the distinction between the Web and television fades. That's a prospect that horrifies Net purists.

But it is hardly inevitable that companies on the Web will need to resort to push strategies to make money. The examples of Virtual Vineyards, Amazon.com, and other pioneers show that a Web site selling the right kind of products with the right mix of interactivity, hospitality, and security will attract online customers. And the cost of computing power continues to free fall, which bodes well for any enterprise setting up shop in silicon. People looking back 5 or 10 years from now may well wonder why so few companies took the online plunge.

 **Article Review Form at end of book.**

New Rules for Net Entrepreneurs

Mario Morino turned $600 of seed capital into an $80 million fortune. Now he's teaching a new generation the rules of success.

Eric Matson

Mario Morino has blue-chip entrepreneurial credentials. In 1973 he invested $600 and founded a company, Morino Associates, to develop management software for mainframe computers. He took the company public in 1986, then engineered a merger to create Legent Corp. in 1989. The new company took off; six years later it was a $500 million organization with 2,800 employees. In 1995, Computer Associates International bought Legent in a deal worth $1.7 billion—at the time, the largest software acquisition in history. Morino's $600 had turned into a personal fortune of $80 million.

Today, Morino, 54, teaches other entrepreneurs how to apply his experiences in the Age of the Net. The Morino Institute, based in Reston, Virginia, is building a community of "netpreneurs" through a Web site (http://netpreneur.org) that maintains databases of Internet innovators, hosts online discussion groups, and links businesspeople with potential mentors, investors, and partners.

"There's an entirely new model of entrepreneur being created around the Internet," explains Morino. "We're trying to create a social fabric for this new entrepreneur."

The Institute also works to repair the social fabric of the country. Its public-service mission includes creating computer networks and Web sites for neighborhood centers and helping industry professionals identify nonprofits that need their skills.

In an interview with Fast Company, Morino explored how the Net has changed the logic of building companies.

Build Products with Other People's Money

A sound business model is still the most important part of any startup strategy: What's the product, who's buying it, and at what price? But once you've developed a compelling idea, you should try to sell it in advance. Let other companies fund your product development for you.

At Morino Associates, companies like US Airways and Boeing were our "homes" for years at a time. We developed products in the context of what those companies needed, but we always kept the intellectual property rights. Too many entrepreneurs spend too much time screwing around internally. Go find a customer! These early customers don't just provide cash flow; they also provide tremendous insights about how to improve what you're doing.

Hire Part-Time Networks, Not Full-Time Staffs

Today finding the right people is more important than securing the best financing. That wasn't true 10 years ago, when a company could make it with a good idea and solid funding. But now you need so many different skills to get things done. The scarcity of good people with the right skills is very real.

How do you deal with this scarcity? One approach is to assemble networks of part-time people rather than a staff of full-time employees. I know a startup that provides travel-planning services for companies. It needed management talent, travel-industry expertise, information-technology skills, and high-level graphics personnel. But rather than hire six full-time people—which would have taken forever—it created a partnership of six part-time people. Everyone got a piece of the business but none of them left their other jobs. It was much easier.

Also, recognize that valuable people come from unexpected places. In the PC era, most entrepreneurs were engineers with hardware or software expertise. The Internet era draws from a much wider talent pool. You don't have to master the technology to be a player.

Someone who used to work at the Federal Election Commission created a business that packages and resells FEC information. He's not a technical guy, he's a content guy, but he created a technology business around that content. There are thousands of people with deep knowledge about databases in government, education, and business. They can create valuable products, and they don't have to be engineers.

Partner Early and Often

Great entrepreneurs exude persistence and doggedness, which means they will never be great collaborators. But they simply must get better at it. On the Net, the window of opportunity to turn ideas into products is so short that you have to start partnering from the day you start your company.

There's a group in Washington, DC called Cross Media. It spun out of MCI and is developing a "1-800" email service. One of the founders is a technical manager, the other is a marketing person. But they've outsourced all software development and have already signed distribution agreements with companies like Microsoft and AOL. That's the way to do it.

To Learn Faster, Ask for Help

The pace of change is accelerating, so entrepreneurs need to learn faster than ever. Which means they have to change how they learn.

I was always a great networker. I knew the "right" two or three people to call about a particular technology or market segment. That doesn't work anymore. Things move so

quickly that the odds of knowing just the right person are remote. Today great networkers know the right routing point—people who are going to know the 10 or 20 best people in the world in a specific space, and who can route you to them. You don't learn by searching for answers; you learn by asking for help.

Bootstrap Until It Hurts

Equity is like gold. You should hold onto as much equity as you can for as long as you can. It's not just about maintaining control; it's about demonstrating commitment. The ability to hold onto equity convinces people in a very distrustful world that you're for real.

We never used outside funding at Morino Associates or Legent until we went public. We bootstrapped everything. We'd sell some contracts, develop products for other companies, pay our expenses, build up our capital. Over time, we managed to generate very significant cash flow. Bootstrapping is tougher than ever today. But great entrepreneurs can still do it.

 Article Review Form at end of book.

Internet Kamikazes

Interview with CNET's Halsey Minor

The CEO of CNET has created one of the most popular news sites on the Web. He's also taking on Yahoo and America Online, and partnering with Internet service providers. UPSIDE talked to Minor on October 22, the day CNET announced a larger-than-expected loss for the quarter.

Richard L. Brandt

Richard L. Brandt is editor of UPSIDE.

UPSIDE: **So, let's talk about earnings!**

Minor: Oh, God, can't we—we'll talk about that after a while!

What elements do you want to know about? The central focus to our company for the past three and a half years has been to identify the niches where we wanted to be and go as fast as we could to build services around those niches. If you believe that the Internet opportunity is enormous, you spend more money for a longer time, and if you believe that the Internet opportunity is smaller, it means you pull back sooner. So we went out and invested heavily.

In the CNET-branded area, there's technology news, software downloading, software and hardware reviews, gaming and then different niches, like ActiveX.com

and Browsers.com, which are really software downloading but specific. Also Builder.com, a Web builder, but really reviews. We've tried to go as fast as we could to lay claim to each of these areas.

Along the way, we also decided to go after the space occupied by AOL, Excite, Yahoo and other guys. We sort of didn't talk about it, but we were quietly building a way to compete there. We wanted to be in this other business, Snap Online [a Web-based service that competes with America Online].

It all boils down to the fact—and I've said this to investors for a year—that for most of '97 we were building. As of November, we will have launched our last site, Computers.com.

Now, everything's out there, all the services are launched, and it's time to figure out how to best organize our company and match expenses with either revenues or potential revenues.

Do you think that was the right approach?

I don't think that we've made the wrong trade-off in doing that. For a stretch as long as six months, I had four engineers working on CNET. I had about 55 working on Snap. I moved the whole engineering staff over to Snap. It was a bet that, even if I did that, Ziff-Davis wasn't going to catch us. And so far it's panned out. According to the statistics, whether it's ad revenue or numbers from RelevantKnowledge or PC Meter, we're still bigger and ahead of 'em, and now I've got a lot of resources back.

Probably, in hindsight, I would have hired more senior managers faster. I would have done it two quarters ago instead of this quarter.

You also announced a revenue shortfall. What was that from?

Computers.com was originally scheduled to launch Sept. 1. We had to push it back—first, because it took longer than we thought, and second, because we didn't have the resources to get it out. This is going to be a huge service from a revenue standpoint. Because of the delay, we aren't getting the advertising we expected from Dell or the other direct computer sellers. That's like the single biggest category in *PC Magazine*. Because it was pushed to November, we're not going to hit our numbers next quarter, either.

Now, if we weren't running a million miles an hour, it wouldn't even have been close.

Fighting Those Yahoos

Yahoo aggregates content from other sources and considers itself a media company. You do more original content. Do you consider yourself a publisher, a media company or what?

We're a media company. If you sell ads and you are in the business of getting ratings and building an audience, you're a media company, irrespective of whether you're an aggregator.

The most confusing thing about us for investors is Snap Online, where we're doing more aggregation than original news. What I say is that they're not as different as they look. Ted Turner is in the business of building cable networks. He built CNN around an original global news-gathering operation, and he built the cartoon channel around aggregating.

How do you strike a balance between being a content creator and an aggregator?

When we started linking News.com to places like UPSIDE and Ziff-Davis, everyone thought we were crazy. I had investors

calling me up asking, "Why are you doing this? I just went to UPSIDE and turned four pages there, and you sent me. You could have had those four pages!"

This may sound like a bunch of pap, but to serve the interests of the people who are coming here, you have to do whatever it is that you as a user would want. That means pointing to competitors. The Web is this interlinked medium. Let's make sure we're the place that everybody wants to come to because we're single-mindedly focused on delivering the best experience we can. For traditional media companies, it's the hardest thing in the world to do. CNN is not used to saying, "Hey, we've got good coverage on Lady Di, but on ABC at 9 o'clock they're going to have a special." I still don't think Ziff-Davis does it.

But aggregation requires an editorial sensibility in and of itself. In Snap, we have editors in the news, money and sports areas who are trained to recognize an important story, issue or Web site. We're not producing stories there, but it's not just links. It's edited.

Yahoo, which started as an aggregator, now gets some 50 million page views per day, compared with your 4 million—which is not bad either! But does that indicate that the aggregator is the more important role? Yahoo even turns a profit.

The role of helping people find information on the Web is important. I don't know if you can necessarily say that it's a more or less important role. I don't know if *People* magazine is more profitable than *PC Magazine*, but if it is, would people say that *People* magazine is more important than *PC Mag*? Probably. It probably is! Is it, long-term, a better business?

Maybe, maybe not. That's unclear right now.

A lot of the traffic you get is people coming in searching for sex. We know that from Snap. Yahoo caters heavily to that. It accepts a lot of sex advertising. There are a lot of pages turned that aren't terribly valuable. Of that 50 million, there's a lot of stuff that's not salable. Their sell rate is extremely low. If you're more targeted, particularly in our categories, technology news or computer gaming, you're highly valuable. People pay a lot of money, particularly as transactions come online and we become a feeder directly into transactional services.

America Online is also both a content creator and an aggregator. So whom do you see as your primary competition?

Ziff is clearly competitive, on the CNET side. On the aggregation side, it's a broad list of companies. You do have to include Microsoft because you always have to include Microsoft. We run into Excite and Yahoo on the Web. But our model is built around helping the ISPs compete with AOL.

Explain how those partnerships will work.

We'll probably announce next week that we're MCI's online service. [MCI will send out] CD-ROMs with all our tutorials and stuff. The Web site you come to will be mci.snap.com. The same thing will probably have happened with Sprint by the time this article comes out. We're announcing that we're Compaq's online service. The idea behind Snap is not to go out and try to compete with Excite and Yahoo for all the existing people on the Web. We want them, and over time we'll try to get some percentage of market share. But we'll really go out to the new users coming onto the Web, or people who are churning out of their ISP. We'll be the default portal through which they pass.

In a sense, then, you are a Web-based competitor to AOL.

Correct. That's the best way to think about this.

That's also a direction that Yahoo is moving in.

Absolutely. Ironically, Yahoo has always seen itself that way, but they didn't want to say it because they thought they'd sneak up on AOL. As soon as we said we're going after AOL, they said "Yes, we are too!" It's really funny.

In the world of commercial online services, there are four components: navigation, content, access and software. In the old days, everyone thought you had to provide all these. Prodigy and AOL did, although AOL was smarter and partnered with other content companies.

Then the Internet comes along and all of a sudden online access is really part of a larger telecommunications business. Companies like AT&T or MCI say, "You know what? This is part of what we do." And on the software side, Microsoft says, "You know what? The browser is part of an operating system." And Netscape, which started as Internet software, says, "You know what? Really we're an enterprise software company." For Netscape, the browser is just part of an enterprise e-mail solution or communications switch. In the content area, CNN says, "You know what? We do content for TV and online," and the *New York Times* says, "You know what? Our content works in newspapers and online."

This becomes a problem for everybody who started out in these quadrants—PSI, NetCom, and on the software side, Netscape. Is it an Internet access business or is it a telecommunications business? Is there an Internet software business or is all software Internet enabled?

Everyone thought that there were going to be a million new content companies on the Internet, and there aren't. There's like one. That's us. And we do television programming, too.

Few companies have been successful in the content quadrant. This is highly competitive, with a lot of existing content players moving online.

Navigation is the only place where there wasn't a logical set of companies that could move into it. So you had an explosion of new companies: Excite, Lycos, Infoseek, Yahoo, LookSmart. This doesn't exist in the analog world. This is a fundamentally new business.

So if you're me and you're thinking about building a big business, where do you go? There's nothing in access or software. The only quadrant that's left for you to go to is navigation. And Yahoo's moving into content. This is sort of the semipermeable membrane of the Internet.

Old Journalism, New Journalism

Why did you choose television as your other medium?

When I started in 1992, writing the business plan I noticed that there was no television program about computers and technology, but it was clear that it was becoming a consumer phenomenon. The way I sold the idea to VCs was to buy like 100 computer magazines and lay them on their desks and say, "This is a big opportunity." But it was a well-saturated market. So the idea was to do television programming and tie it into online services. At the time, the online services were Prodigy, CompuServe and then this dinky company called AOL. I trademarked a phrase, which I guess we still own: "We're not just a television network, we're networked television." CNET's mission is to redefine television in the age of interactive media.

And then the Web came along and made the online side much bigger?

I always thought that online would be a big business for us. The Web came along and it happened faster than I ever thought. We were originally going to do a 24-hour cable channel, and the Web came along so fast that, in many ways, it obviated the need for us to build out an analog 24-hour channel filled with lots of junk.

What do you think about some sort of merger between the television and online services through something like WebTV?

The Web will come to television through WebTV, or whatever, as a supplemental resource to television. I'm not a big believer in the idea that full-scale Web surfing is going to happen through a television set. The reason I saw TV and online working together is that TV is a medium that does not support a great deal of granularity of information. The idea was top-level entertainment, skim the surface with television, then have all your real depth searchable and available online. We didn't try to blend the two. People who watch television don't want to hold a mouse. But people who are online don't want to sit still.

Some people have speculated about a different storytelling approach with an interactive medium. Do you see that?

There's nothing I see that tells me that online is going to be a good medium for storytelling. Everything has been tried and hasn't really worked. It doesn't mean there won't be isolated examples of people who do innovative things, but if you want to look at where most of the traffic is going, even five or 10 years from now, it's going to revolve around people retrieving information, buying parts and services, doing research of some form or another. All the other stuff will be spice.

What's the difference between online journalism and print or television journalism?

There's been a lot of snobbery from print journalists about online journalism. Some of it is warranted. There's been a lot of bad journalism on the Web. Frankly, a lot of the good journalists were snobs and didn't want to move over. It wasn't the medium, it was just where the talent was. We were pioneers in getting good journalists to come over. Now more are going to come over.

The other difference in online journalism is that speed is always going to be important, and stories will build. You will report stuff that sometimes is not going to have even the depth of television. On television, they start relaying information and say, "This is what we've heard," and two hours later they come back and say, "Well, we've actually found that the lady who died was in the car with four other people." The Web has that same kind of phe-

nomenon. You can constantly update it, you can constantly add to it and rebuild stories throughout the day. We don't have the luxury of spending two weeks on a story, so you just kind of put it out.

People online don't want a whole lot of in-depth stuff, particularly around news stories. It's harder to read on the screen. That doesn't mean that you can throw something out there without fact-checking. Some people do, and they do the whole medium a disservice.

The Web is also seen as an equalizing force. Anybody can post information. There's a backlash against the organized press, so people are turning to this grassroots movement for getting information from the Internet. But the difficulty is, there are also not those journalistic standards.

Exactly right. And rumor and innuendo travels fast over the Net.

Is that changing the nature of the news business?

No, because I think the people who have high standards of editorial credibility will do the best on the Web over time. Quality will always win in the long run.

The number one thing that turns people off is that a lot of journalists did not like the egalitarian nature of the Web. They did not like the fact that somebody could publish information and not have to attend the Columbia School of Journalism. They said this entire medium is flawed because anybody can do it.

At the same time, there is something of a mistrust of the mainstream press. A lot of people see it as elitist.

But it is. There's a lot of elitism in the press.

Doesn't that leave room for some of these grassroots news movements to take over?

None of these groups individually are going to be very big. There will be people who have all sorts of causes and agendas who will publish information, and sometimes they'll label it news and sometimes they won't, and sometimes they'll label it as fact and sometimes it won't be.

I don't think any individual one will be big, although in toto it will be relatively large.

Where the Money Is

Is a transaction-processing model part of your future?

Yeah. We're going to start closing the loop everywhere. We've talked a lot about Comuters.com because it's the reason our expense number was high. I had a lot of people over on Snap that I couldn't move over to Computers.com, so we hired a lot of outside contractors.

This was a year-and-a-half-long effort. I'm obviously highly biased, but I think it's going to be as big a breakthrough for Web editorial as News.com was.

We're harvesting data about computers for sale directly from PC manufacturers, from [distributor] Ingram Micro, from PC Order, and from tons of different resellers. We're bringing it in, lining it up by skew and by editorial.

You can click on desktop computers, drill down, and just get reviews that are related to PC desktops. Or you can see all of our reviews, our buying guides, see the top 10 business desktops.

You can drill down further and say, "I want to buy a PC." We then drop you into the database, and you can sort and refine your search by price, processor, etc., or you can sort by whether we actually have a review of the product. You can sort them by just CNET reviews, by the date that the machine came out, by suggested list price and so on.

When you've chosen a product, like the Compaq Presario, you click on it. We bring up a picture and some information. We let the manufacturer have a little ad area where it can provide further information. We aggregate tons of specification data, more than you'd ever want to know about the product. We aggregate support information—organized by manufacturer, Web address, days that their tech support is open—from a variety of sources. Then we have reviews, either CNET reviews or reviews from around the Web, from our competitors.

You can then add machines that you like to your list of picks. Then you can bring up a list of all the machines you selected as you were going through and compare them.

By price and performance?

You can do head-to-head comparisons on any data. So when you decide you want to buy the Presario, you click on "Where to Buy." That aggregates information from another database of people who want to sell you this product. You can sort them by such things as whether they have the product in stock, by whether they support international sales, or by price.

When we launch, we'll have 10 to 14 resellers already plugged in. You can link to their Web sites, directly to their product purchase pages. Or you can put in your zip code and find the store closest to you and get a map and driving instructions.

Do you make your money from transaction fees or advertising on this service?

This is advertising. At the top are ads from companies that want to build brand preference. As I'm going down trying to choose what kind of PC I want, we want Compaq screaming, "We're the best, we're the best, click me and find out why." Then, after you decide to buy a Compaq, there are a bunch of people who say, "I want the transaction, I want the transaction!"

Do you get a fee for selling a qualified lead to a reseller or do you get a cut of the transaction?

Not the transaction. I'm not going to take a risk on how good they are at fulfilling orders. Somebody may click on the ad and their server's down. It's their job to convert the lead. What I may do is sell them shelf space.

How do you sell them shelf space? Just by putting them in this listing?

Yeah.

Do you charge by the number of click-throughs?

Some people will get tons of clicks, others none. When Michael Dell runs an ad in *PC Magazine,* he gets more people who call than you and I would if we started Bob's Computer Store. Unfortunately, it's survival of the fittest. And unfortunately, it favors the big brands. I'm not trying to create an egalitarian environment on the Web. I'm following a tried-and-true media model, which is setting a price. Some people are successful and can pay it and generate the requisite number of leads to make it work. Some can't, and they will go away.

There is a scenario that says, if you end up clicking on an ad and going through and becoming a qualified lead, the advertiser ought to pay you more. The way I look at it is, you're either going to be good or bad. If you're bad, then you can't pay it. I set that bar so that I maximize my revenue. That means some people can't play.

The whole pay-per-click model of the Internet doesn't work well because it penalizes people who gets lots of clicks.

Any subscription plans for your sites?

No.

The Web advertising business seems to be developing more slowly than people expected. How soon will advertisers figure out how the Web works and divert advertising there?

They're coming on en masse now. E-commerce is going to be the catalyst. Now that people are generating revenues in the medium, they're going to start spending money in the medium to drive more revenues. You're seeing it in travel, you're seeing it in CDs, you're seeing it in books. You're going to start seeing it in hardware and software soon.

What's the trick to selling ads on the Web?

Back to the early days of CNET, we were good at generating revenue. We didn't have the luxury of just building a bunch of services, so we hosted the first conference on site tracking because we wanted tracking to happen, and we wanted to be perceived as a leader. We were the first to introduce tracking for Web advertisers. We were the first people to do dynamic delivery of advertising based on who you are, the browser you had, Mac vs. PC platform, all that stuff. We launched the Crusader program to educate advertisers about how Web advertising worked. It wasn't revenue-generating. It was a service to get them more comfortable spending money.

But my key belief is that if you do not generate traffic and are not a leader in your category, you have a hard time generating revenue. Ultimately, you just have to build an audience. Later you can come back and figure out how to [exploit] the audience, but you have to build an audience.

When do you expect to turn the corner to profitability?

That's a hard question because it's one you should never answer. But it will definitely happen next year. Most of the analysts have us at third quarter of next year.

But there are a couple ways of looking at it. One is: When will CNET turn profitable and when will CNET plus Snap become profitable? We're going to push pretty damn hard to make CNET profitable in the first quarter.

How do you see the mix of revenues between CNET and Snap in the long term?

I would think in '99 they're going to be equal. It's hard to say. CNET could generate a ton of revenue. We've done a pathetic job of getting revenue. I personally have met with about two advertisers in the past six months. We had to sign 100 content deals for Snap, 20 distribution deals, because the writing is on the wall. Everyone knows you've got to move fast now to lock up distribution.

But we're a giant category, and we're targeted. I'm all about product. We're about buying stuff. And we're going to get real good at it real quick.

 Article Review Form at end of book.

WiseGuide Wrap-Up

Because of its unique qualities, the Internet has become the darling of many business and nonbusiness organizations. There is plenty of hype in this fascination with the Net as we experiment with the new medium and try to understand its intricacies.

Successful online marketers apply the technology where its strength lies, on information-rich products and information-enriched products.

Information-rich products, such as books, music, software, and financial services, intrinsically contain "information." The physical form of these products exists solely to contain the information in them. Focusing only on "information-rich" products may cause one to miss some opportunities by creating *information-enriched* products by placing them in *information envelopes*. Information-enriched products will likely include those for which the buyers would like extensive information before making their purchase decisions. As Internet marketing matures and evolves, we will see more products being put in information envelopes as consumers become more accustomed to using information extensively in their important purchases.

R.E.A.L. Sites

Site name: Cyber-Retail: The WWW Storefront

URL: http://newsweek-int.com/archive/netpro/archive_body_frame_netp1219.html

Why is it R.E.A.L.? This article looks at the potential of cyber-retailing in 1996, a good reference point in time when the web was being considered for marketing and commerce.

Key topics: retailing, commercial online transactions, profitability, security, authentication, online storefronts

Site name: Selling Wine Without Bottles: The Economy of Mind on the Global Net

URL: http://www.eff.org/pub/Publications/John_Perry_Barlow/HTML/idea_economy_article.html

Why is it R.E.A.L.? A thought-provoking, abstract view of online transactions and how they differ from physical ones as digital technology separates information from the tangible world. It is long but worth the time spent reading it.

Key topics: virtual world, intellectual property, copyright information, payments in cyberspace, cryptography

section 2

Learning Objectives

When reading the articles in this section, try to think about commercial transactions, no matter how small or large. What and who are involved in making these transactions possible? Also ask whether the process can be replicated on the Internet. When you study the readings and integrate them with your class notes, you should

- Explore and understand the critical issues of electronic commerce.

- Learn the challenges posed by e-commerce and the efforts to resolve them.

- Learn and appreciate the complexities of this new commerce environment.

Electronic Commerce and Marketing Exchange

Commerce involves the buying and selling of goods and services by bringing buyers and sellers to engage in the ultimate goal of any business: transaction. This simple concept has been around for ages, pumping resources in and out of economies, allowing for the creation of possession utility for consumers, and fulfilling the revenue-generating mission of business enterprises.

A smoothly working commerce environment requires more than just buyers and sellers. A wide range of supporting and facilitating organizations offer services that make commercial systems function and create value for all involved. A consumer walking into his or her favorite store to purchase a single item triggers the involvement of many participants in a commercial transaction. The seller has the store for the customer to walk into, where goods coming from many sources via some form of transportation await selection. To handle the payment made with a credit card, a bank enters the picture, promising payment to the merchant. The credit card company authorizes the transaction, using the services of a telecommunication company probably arranged by a consortium of banks, other financial institutions, and technology providers.

A monetary system facilitates the exchange process and holds a vital role in commerce. In domestic commerce, a local monetary system becomes the basis, while proxies for this system may make the whole matter more convenient for both sides. The most common proxies for money are checks and credit cards. In any of its forms, money is nothing more than information that "trusted" agencies control. These agencies include governments, which issue money, and banks, which issue checks and credit cards.

In traditional commerce, buyers and sellers have been using such systems for a long, long time and implicitly trust the system. Any change in the system required building trust for the new method of payment and a new way of verifying the trustworthiness of the parties involved. The Internet brings a new set of questions to commercial transactions. Fundamentally, the issue still remains one of trust. The nature of the Internet and the way it operates make these issues very challenging, at least in the short run.

Today, commerce on the Internet operates as an extension of the traditional commerce model and resembles mail-order or catalog-based operations. In this hybrid environment, some real and some perceived obstacles to electronic commerce, e-commerce, exist. Three technological, procedural, and perceptual concepts—authenticity, security, and confidentiality—encompass the issues that need to be resolved.

Questions

1. Systems have been used in which value is created and used in nonmonetary ways. Will there be a new, Internet-based "monetary system," in which value is created and used on the Internet?

2. Why are different payment systems needed for large and small transactions on the Internet, while one monetary system seems to work in traditional commerce?

3. Does a single form of payment work in traditional business transactions? What do you use to make payments for different product purchases? Why?

Risks vs. Rewards

If electronic commerce is to flourish, buyers must believe that patronizing a cyber-storefront is at least as safe as shopping at a suburban mall.

Robert Mueller

Robert Mueller, a freelance writer from La Grange, Ill., has covered information technology for more than 20 years.

Stephen Schilling is the kind of online voyager that companies setting up shop on the World Wide Web long for: a consumer with disposable income who isn't afraid to send charge card information over the Internet. Whether he's buying a box of cigars or a case of chardonnay, the Manhattan Beach, Calif., business executive seeks out Internet sites that let him put down plastic virtually—so to speak.

"I've seen so many TV reports and read so many newspaper articles about overall credit card fraud that I figure using my credit card on the Internet is no riskier than using it to pay for a meal at a restaurant," Schilling maintains.

That message—that patronizing a cyber-storefront is at least as safe as shopping at a suburban mall—is one companies hoping to make money on the Web need to promote if electronic commerce is to flourish.

"When you look at Internet security, you have to look at the risk/benefit ratio and spend your security dollars where they'll do the most good," points out Peter Tippett, president of the Carlisle, Pa.-based National Computer Security Association (NCSA). From his perspective, credit card fraud isn't even on the top 10 list of Internet security issues for consumers.

Serious hackers are more interested in attacking servers for access to sensitive information. If someone wants to get your credit card number, he says, it's a lot easier for most people to fish a receipt out of the trash than to collect it on the Internet.

Cyndy Ainsworth, director of marketing for Virtual Vineyards, the Palo Alto, Calif.-based retailer from which Schilling purchases wine, agrees that such a threat is greatly overblown. Indeed, 75 percent of the thousands of Virtual Vineyard customers ordering from the website provide credit card information over the Internet. Skeptical customers provide credit data by phone or fax.

Still, some prominent Web retailers warn their customers against sending credit card information online. Some experts feel that stance could cost them sales.

Take Schilling. He ignores websites that require him to phone in his credit card number to place orders. "It's more convenient to just process the order myself online," he says.

Merchants that do use secure Internet servers to accept credit payments express satisfaction with their security. Virtual Vineyards, for example, uses Netscape Commerce Server, which deploys a communications convention called secure sockets layer (SSL). That, in turn, uses mathematical encryption techniques to code sensitive information.

Customers know they're on a secure server because they see an icon on their SSL-enabled browsers (a key in Netscape Navigator, a lock in Microsoft Explorer).

Similar encryption technology is at the heart of a new, open standard for secure credit card transactions known as secure electronic transaction (SET). This standard is being championed by American Express, MasterCard and Visa, and supported by such Internet hard-hitters as GTE, IBM, Microsoft and Netscape. It uses a form of certification—an assurance from a third party—that the operator of the server is what it says it is. SET requires that the credit card user also be certified.

Under the SET scheme, certification will be handled by the banks or other firms that issue the credit cards. Each digital certificate will be unique, a so-called electronic signature that guarantees that only the legitimate credit card holder can make purchases.

SET, NCSA's Tippett says, is an improvement over SSL in one respect: Credit card information remains encrypted all the way through the transaction. Even the Web merchant doesn't see it. On the other hand, unlike SSL, other information the Web shopper provides to or gleans from the website (including inquiries, surveys, products or services, shipping address and so on) is not necessarily encrypted.

Large Amounts, Greater Risks

When you move out of retailing and into financial services, the stakes for consumers can be a lot higher, and the tolerance for risk correspondingly lower. That's why First Union National Bank in Charlotte, N.C., has taken steps to secure its Internet transactions. At the lowest level are account queries, which are protected by passwords. One level up is electronic bill-paying. For that, the bank uses SSL encryption and VeriSign certification.

First Union, the nation's sixth largest bank, also uses multiple firewalls to protect its cus-

Defining Cyber-Vandalism

While credit card fraud is a major concern of online merchants, it's just one of the ways cyber-crooks can interfere with Internet commerce. Some of the more common fraud and vandalism problems, according to Peter Tippett, president of the National Computer Security Association, include the following:

Hacking: Hackers look for weaknesses in website security, then use those weaknesses to get at proprietary data such as customer information and passwords. The first lines of defense against hackers are firewalls that separate the site from the rest of the organization's IT resources.

Jamming: Jammers use software routines to tie up a website's server communications, which prevents legitimate visitors from entering the site. Jamming—also known as denial of service—isn't common, but an attack on a New York Internet service provider last September drew national headlines.

Lax security: Poor internal security—uncontrolled access to computer hardware, poor protection of passwords and lack of formal security policies—is probably the biggest threat to information security of all kinds, including Internet security.

Malicious software: Cyber-vandalism is becoming a big problem on the Internet. Viruses are probably the best-known form of online vandalism, though they are also among the easiest to defend against. Trojan horses posing as legitimate software can cause the host to divert confidential information to an unauthorized third person.

Sniffing: Sniffing is electronic eavesdropping. Sniffers use an easy-to-produce piece of software that sits somewhere between the website user and the site provider's server and intercepts passing information. This information may include credit card numbers and other confidential data. Sniffing can be prevented by encrypting information.

Spoofing: Spoofers fraudulently represent themselves as other organizations. The spoofers set up false sites and collect confidential information from unsuspecting Web users. Spoofing can be prevented with certification programs.

—R.M.

tomers. The bank's Internet servers reside in an informational no man's land that's characterized as the DMZ by Peter Browne, senior vice president for corporate information security. On one side of this demilitarized zone sits First Union's internal network; on the other side, sits the public World Wide Web.

Guarding the frontiers on both sides are firewalls: A Sun Microsystems SunScreen SPF-100 protects the network from access obtained through the Web, and a SunSoft Solstice FireWall-1 prevents unauthorized bank personnel from viewing Internet transactions.

"We need to think about security over the Internet in exactly the same way we think about se-

curity at the bank's branches," says George Capehart, vice president of technology and strategic planning, customer direct access. "There have to be degrees of trust and security, and different security models for different levels of transactions."

For higher-value transactions, First Union is considering even more elaborate fraud-defying techniques. The bank is trying out a system from VASCO Data Security that generates a bar code on the customer's screen. The customer uses a handheld device that reads the bar code and generates a one-time password that identifies him or her to the bank.

Obviously, security is a major concern of banks and their

Hot Sites

With the proliferation of websites, businesspeople do not have the time to search haphazardly for the information they need. Ken Leebow, president of Atlanta-based Professional Solutions (http://this.is/norman), recommends this list of useful business sites:

If You Seek It . . .

The Big Page lists almost 600 search engines grouped by categories, including general search engines, multiple engine searches, media, software and technology.
http://www.beaucoup.com/engines.html

Wall Street Index

Streeteye, the index of Wall Street Internet resources, has links to news, market data, exchanges, brokers, banks and investment managers. The site also links to personal finance resources and has a search function.
http://www.streeteye.com

Trade Show Central

This site is a trade show director that lists shows around the globe. One section lets organizers spread the word about their show by including it in the directory or by designing a home page that will link to Trade Show Central. Organizers can also search more than 2,000 facilities by specialty, square footage or location.
http://www.tscentral.com

Additional Sites

Suitable for all users: This National Multimedia Association of America site helps users select the best software for their needs and improve communication between users and developers. Individuals who have first-hand experience can rate specific software applications on 10 questions ranging from ease of installation to quality of features. Ratings and additional comments are instantly added to the database and made available to the general public and developers.
http://www.ratings.org

Online library: More than 1,000 full-text technology, health and science books can be found online at the National Academy Press website. Specialty titles can be selected from 15 categories.
http://www.nap.edu

customers. That's the reason 15 banks joined with IBM to create the Integrion Financial Network, which will deliver secure electronic banking services over the Internet.

What's Ahead?

In the near future, financial service companies will develop so-called smart cards, credit and payment cards with embedded chips that carry significantly more information than the magnetic strips they now use. Credit card companies talk about integrating card readers into devices such as PCs, phones, interactive TVs and automated teller machines.

Eventually, the entry of big-name retailers and mail-order houses into Internet merchandising could do as much to reassure reluctant shoppers as the improved security measures that persuaded the stores to set up shop on the Web in the first place.

 Article Review Form at end of book.

The End of Cash

James Gleick

Cash is dirty—the New Jersey Turnpike tried to punish toll collectors recently for wearing latex gloves (thus giving the driving clientele a "bad impression"), but who can blame them? Cash is heavy—$1 million in $20 bills weighs more than you can lift, and drug dealers have been disconcerted to note that their powdered merchandise is handier for smuggling than the equivalent money. Cash is inequitable—if you are one of the 50 million Americans poor enough to be "unbanked," you pay extortionate fees to seedy, bulletproofed check-cashing operations (even more extortionate than the fees charged for automatic teller machines, often up to 1 or 2 percent and rising). Cash is quaint, technologically speaking—unless you're impressed by intaglio-steel-plate-printed paper with embedded polyester strips (meant to inconvenience counterfeiters). Cash is expensive—tens of billions of dollars drain from the economy each year merely to pay for the printing, trucking, safekeeping, vending, collecting, counting, armored-guarding and

general care and feeding of our currency.

Cash is obsolete.

So here come Bitbux, E-Cash, Netchex, CyberCash, Netbills, and DigiCash—through the Patent and Trademark Office and into the marketplace. A frothing mix of public, private, semipublic, bank and nonbank institutions are rushing in with new forms of money. As the Internet booms, those experimenting with commerce at an electronic distance are struggling to perfect the sending of cash over wires.

The credit card companies have realized that their products are no longer about credit but rather about convenient payment for goods and services; they are entering the cash game with "smart cards" making heavily marketed debuts in Atlanta this month and New York at year's end. A British-based project called Mondex is promoting a global standard for digital cash at sharp odds with the Visa and MasterCard approach. Like their competitors, the Mondex people have noticed that cash changes hands 300 billion times a year in the United States alone, and they want their cut. They believe that

electronic money has reached the stage of a classic emerging market and that the test for every participant will be to survive the next two years.

The big players are not alone. Internet startup ventures, overseas telephone companies, universities and city transit systems are all experimenting with digital payment schemes with extraterritorial ambitions. A battle has begun for market share—and also for a quintessential modern commodity, sometimes overlooked but always coveted: float. Float is wealth in transit—money that has been parked temporarily in a place where someone, probably not you, can earn interest on it. If the issuer of a traveler's check or subway token or smart card can grab a piece of your money and collect interest for days or even hours, it gains an edge. No wonder everyone seems to wants to mint money—except the Mint, which is carefully standing aside, for now.

But are these new creations really money? When money cannot be touched, when it turns to electrons, when it dematerializes, some people start to worry about what they really have. Will it be enough for a bank, or a credit-card company, or even the Government to validate some chip as "money"—can it ever be as real as a dollar bill? The nightmare parable of digital cash goes this way:

You check your favorite leather jacket in a restaurant and get a receipt. On the way out, you present the receipt to the attendant. He sniffs it, rubs it, holds it to the light, cryptanalyzes it and—relief!—confirms its authenticity. He hands the receipt back and assures you: "That is your jacket."

Digital money is perfect money, flawless money, intangible money. It is money that has been robbed of its substance—the opportunity to get scuffed, worn, dirty and perhaps lost. It is networked money, and point-of-sale money, and money on a card, and money on a computer. It is money that weighs nothing and moves at the speed of light. It is money incarnated, finally, as pure information.

That comes as a shock; yet information is what money has always been. It is information about value and wealth. Let's say you go on line and buy a bottle of Martelli Vineyard Puncheon Select Gewürztraminer from Virtual Vineyards, an Internet site. The wine is real—the parcel service burns jet fuel to get it to your door. You are obliged to become $14 poorer and Virtual Vineyards is entitled to become $14 richer. You could send dollar bills by mail—those little green symbols of wealth acquired in past transactions. Once perhaps you could have sent a sliver of gold bullion—a symbol in its own way, now stripped of its special legal status. Only the information need change hands, so now you can send an experimental form of electronic payment called CyberCash. Does it matter? This

long-distance commerce becomes the ultimate extension of a process that began a century ago, when the Western Union Telegraph Company—a communications company, not a bank—jury-rigged a way to turn cash into bits flowing across wires. The wiring of money means something different now, when the transport medium, the Internet, is decentralized, international and uncontrolled.

In a real sense, money has already gone digital—or virtual, or notational. The creased bills in your pocket are a language as outmoded as Morse code. The money supply of the United States amounts to more than $4 trillion dollars. Every business day more than half that amount sloshes about among banks and other institutions in purely electronic form: signals flowing over wires. These accounts are reconciled by transfers not of actual dollar bills but of mere bits—the information is the be-all and end-all. "People today do not put $5 billion in a truck and drive it from one bank to another—that's just irrational" says Kawika Daguio, a specialist in payments technology for the American Bankers Association.

In fact, of the broad American money supply, only a small fraction—less than one-tenth—exists in the form of currency. All the bills and coins in consumer pockets, bank vaults and elsewhere amount to about $400 billion. And most of that currency, as much as two-thirds, has long since departed the country, probably forever, mainly in the form of $100 bills. They belong to overseas money launderers and other enterprises that for one reason or another prefer not to keep their wealth in local denominations and local banks.

The vast daily traffic in money across the interbank network is not backed by dollar bills. Nor of course is it backed by the stores of gold at Fort Knox and elsewhere, the gold standard having long since gone the way of ducats and pieces of eight. "Money is the current liability of a bank," asserts Sholom Rosen, Citibank's electronic-cash guru. "It's as simple as that: it's not gold, it's not silver, it's the current liability of a bank."

You believe in banks, don't you? That's good, because ultimately money is backed by nothing but your own confidence, habit, and faith—a form of faith as powerful and essential to modern life as any religious belief. The coming digital era will make this plain to everyone, as never before. Still, the stock of old-fashioned cash out there is growing, not shrinking. About $1,400 in bills exists somewhere for every American. "That's a lot of paper money," says Lawrence Summers, the Deputy Treasury Secretary. "The question isn't why it's so small. The question is why it's so big."

Cash is growing, yet it is dying. You will carry some around for years to come, and perhaps barely notice when you stop using it in grocery stores, at gas stations, in vending machines. But the first forms of digital money to hit the market will not be the best forms; the rules that lawmakers have developed for managing paper money will not be the best rules.

For everyone who uses cash, everyone who stores it and everyone who regulates it, a challenge is nearing. The challenge will be to make choices. Some kinds of electronic currency will protect privacy, and some will violate privacy. Some will make crime easier, and some will make it extraordinarily difficult. Some will tax commerce parasitically, and some will catalyze it. The new minters of money will have enormous power to choose—unless consumers, on the one hand, and Government officials, on the other, decide to make their own choices.

"Digital *cash*—the stuff that circulates—isn't the only winner on the horizon, if it's a winner at all," says Daguio. Alternatives will be emerging from within the banking system and from the on-line world.

"If you didn't have to dig in your pocket for a coin and could drive by a tollgate at 65 miles an hour, everybody benefits from that," he says. "If you can send money to your children, or send money to someone you've never dealt with before, it opens up new opportunities and eliminates obstacles to electronic commerce. With credit cards there's always the risk that somebody isn't going to pay; with electronic cash that risk is done away with, and transaction costs can come down significantly.

"And people wouldn't have to pay those abominable fees to check-cashers. It's amazing what can happen, *if* the technologies are deployed correctly and the regulatory structure makes sense."

Brother, Can You Spare a Chip?

Vice presidents of Visa International, Visa U.S.A., and an assortment of associated banks have been thick on the ground in Atlanta over the past month, trying out the new cash card. It works in the Visa company cafeteria. Mastercard has already rolled out the equivalent in Australia and begun advertising it on American television. About 5,000 Atlanta merchants have agreed to install networked card-reading devices and accept the card in lieu of cash. Visa hopes to have "several million" cards in the marketplace before the Olympic Games end this summer—an ambitious number, considering that the Olympics expect to draw barely 2 million visitors.

The card is a chip embedded in plastic: a wafer-thin computer with, in this year's version, 2 kilobytes or 4 kilobytes of memory. The memory lets it store about 80 times as much information as the typical magnetic stripe on a credit card or fare card, and the processor makes possible the use of cryptographic methods to secure the data.

Using the card is supposed to be fast and easy. Unlike the cards that persuade automated teller machines to spit out cash, these smart cards require no PIN or password. Cardholders do not sign the cards; nor do they show any identification to merchants. They just insert the card into a small terminal. The card and terminal engage in a quick electronic conversation, validating each other's tiny identities, and if all goes well, a carefully recorded transaction takes place. The tally of cash on the card goes down, and the tally on the terminal goes up. If you lose the card, you have lost the money (don't come crawling to Visa—this is cash, or so the theory goes).

Visa and other credit-card companies have adopted a technology that requires physical contact between card and card reader, but contactless technology is also available. You can wave your card in the vicinity of a turnstile or speed through a highway tollbooth, and a transaction can take place wirelessly. A card-reader debits your card from a distance of a few inches or a few feet. (Convenient—then again, the next generation of pickpockets may need to do no more than brush on by you wearing the right card reader inside their raincoats.)

Considerable thought is being given to the question of where your cash goes—something like $2 trillion a year changes hands in amounts of $10 or less—and how to take slices of ever-smaller transactions. A Visa promotional video shows a motorist, having been caught speeding, cheerfully handing over his smart card to the trooper for instant justice: "Good afternoon, sir," the trooper says. "You have the option to take care of that right here on the spot." ("Is that his personal card reader or the county's?" Elliot Schwartz, analyzing digital cash for the Congressional Budget Office, says laughing.) Children's allowances are a very real sliver of the money supply, and the Tooth Fairy is still believed to deal in cash. Mondex points out, euphemistically, that cash is "an important mechanism for spontaneous charitable donations"; it is certainly hard to imagine beggars trading cups for card-readers.

At first the cards will be used until empty and thrown away; soon they will be reloadable. Next winter Visa and MasterCard plan a joint test in one of the world's most consumer-driven neighborhoods, the Upper West Side of Manhattan. The experiment is designed to make sure their competing cards will work in the same machines. And will New Yorkers use them? Smart-card manufacturers know that many people dislike anything resembling computers. They know that cash has a magical aura for some—that in movies, for example, we love it (crassly) when bundles of cash glow from inside suitcases or piles of cash provide an aphrodisiac bedding material. Then again, in cooler moments we despise cash, too, so perhaps it is just as well that there is nothing romantic about a stored value card. Whatever the emotions at play, Visa cites studies suggesting that consumers tend to spend 5 or 25 or 40 percent more with a cash card than with cash—perhaps because they are lulled by the unreality of it all.

These spinoffs of credit cards will be the first big, mainstream digital cash, but this does not mean that they will succeed in dominating the market or—a separate issue—that they are ideal from the point of view of public policy. Still, the ultimate shape of electronic money will depend enormously on who wins the early market-share battles. Money, as a product, will offer a perfect example of the Law of Increasing Returns. The more people use any given type of money—the closer it comes to universal acceptance—the more useful and attractive it will become. Just like fax machines and Microsoft Windows, any particular form of electronic money will take off when, and only when, it achieves a certain level of penetration in the marketplace, a critical mass. By then it will have required a huge investment in the infrastructure of card readers and other associated technologies; that will raise the barrier for potential new competitors.

It seems natural to the credit-card companies to divide the world between buyers and sellers. In their system, an extension of the credit-card model, you are either a consumer or you are a merchant. Only merchants have the hardware and the authority to accept electronic money. Visa and MasterCard have made enormous investments in creating a payment-clearing infrastructure, all the millions of linked card-reading hardware around the world and the decades of consumer habits that make it all work, and their smart cards are meant to build on the power of that infrastructure.

The Mondex experiment is different. It imagines a world where everyone's telephone and everyone's computer can read money from smart cards and write money back. A trial has been running since last summer in the town of Swindon, England—Mondex cards loading and unloading in hundreds of stores and through street telephones with special screens. "I was able to give my 6-year-old daughter a pound," says Tim Jones, Mondex's chief executive. "If we were both talking on Mondex phones, I could pop my card in, and you could pop your card in, and we could exchange funds. That for me is the core notion of a product that wants to call itself money."

Those hoping to ride the wave of commerce on the Internet agree that the distinction between merchant and customer is breaking down, along with the distinction between reader and publisher. Everyone on the World Wide Web suddenly seems to have information to sell, or advertising space. If only those Webmasters could conveniently collect a bit of your cash each time you drop by their sites! "It goes back to preindustrial society," Jones says. "Economies are brought alive by markets where everybody goes along as a producer of goods and everybody also goes along as a consumer. People can purchase information from their peers and sell information to their peers, just as if they were taking clothes or food to the agricultural market." With a difference: this marketplace is global.

These are expensive experiments—all those chips, all those terminals, all that marketing. The card-issuing companies presumably intend to make money, though they speak in slightly vague terms about just how. There are ways. They can take a slice of a few percentage points from every transaction, from the merchants' side. That way it is invisible to consumers; it is a kind of tax nonetheless. Issuers can sell advertising space on the card itself; residents of Singapore, for example, are already accustomed to using what look like miniature Calvin Klein billboards to pass through transit-system turnstiles. The credit-card companies may be able to profit from information sifted from the vast mass of purchase records—information that could be of use in marketing. They may profit in a small way from one of the weird psychological side-effects of anything to do with money: people like to collect it. Visa is already working with companies that specialize in marketing "commemorative" coinage, in hopes that customers will buy smart cards and set them aside, more or less forever, on the mantelpiece. And issuers of digital cash hope to profit generally from lost cards—telephone companies and transit systems already figure gains ranging from 1 percent to a phenomenal 10 percent—but there may be a surprise lurking in state escheatment laws, which require banks to turn over unclaimed accounts to the government after some period of time.

And then there is the little matter of float. "I've got a card for $50 in my wallet, and it'll probably take me a month to use that up," says Doug King, a vice president of Wachovia Bank, one of the partners in the Visa project. "You multiply that out by millions of people, and there'll be some float there."

The ability of financial institutions to earn interest on your electronic money may not mean much now. When cash goes truly digital, it may mean everything. It is seldom recognized that the Government benefits directly from the float on the cash in your pocket, the cash on your dresser, the cash waiting inside parking meters, the cash roaming around in armored trucks, the cash resting in the dachas of the Russian mafia, and all the rest of the $400 billion in cash outstanding. Holders of cash lend their wealth to the United States, interest free, just as holders of American Express traveler's checks lend their money to American Express. The Federal Reserve is required to buy and hold Treasury securities in an amount equal to that cash, and every year it turns over the interest it earns, currently about $20 billion. This income, known as seigniorage, represents revenue the Government stands to lose as cash gives way to privately issued electronic currencies.

As, of course, it already is. At grocery stores and gas stations, ATM debit cards have an early head start; in Europe, gas stations now operate during some periods with a staff of zero. As cards wax, currency wanes: $100 bills are legal tender, in theory, but in real life many merchants will no longer take them—there is too much counterfeiting and too much plain uneasiness, as the Mint switches over to the odd-looking new-style bills. Certainly there is nothing to stop smart cards from replacing cash in stores, subway systems and taxicabs, or at pay telephones and vending machines. Nothing, that is, but confusion, warring standards, business anarchy and, perhaps, a loss of faith.

Whose Currency Is It?

Once upon a time, American commerce was bursting across a new frontier so explosively that the technology of cash could not keep up. Coins and bullion were too awkward to handle and too slow to move. In the early 19th century a multitude of banks, large and small, began issuing private notes instead: money made of paper. Immediately there were standards problems. Notes that were trusted in one state traded elsewhere at discounts that varied with distance, if the notes were accepted at all. By the outbreak of the Civil War, 10,000 brands of paper money were circulating, and as much of a third of it was phony. Only then did the Federal Government step in, creating a national paper currency and deliberately driving the competing forms of money out of existence through the imposition of a 10 percent tax.

This was controversial. The Supreme Court held that Congress has the power to restrain "the circulation as money of any notes not issued under its own authority." To a few officials, most notably the Director of the Mint, Philip Diehl, there may be an interesting analogy here. "Coins are a declining second-wave technology of commerce," he has said. "What we are wrestling with here today are the implications of these emerging electronic third-wave substitutes for coinage." If smart cards are a new form of money, shouldn't they be issued by the one true minter of money, the authority with the power to cut through a war of confusing, conflicting standards—the Government?

"Government-issued electronic currency would probably stem seigniorage losses and provide a riskless electronic payment product to consumers," Alan Blinder, then vice chairman of the Federal Reserve, told a recent Congressional hearing. But he and most of the Federal Reserve and the Treasury have taken the view that direct government involvement in the roiling digital-cash business would be hazardous and stifling.

In the "current climate," as those in Washington tend to say, anything that smacks of an expanded role for the Government is anathema. Policy-makers at the Treasury are reluctant even to talk about electronic money on the record. "It's easy to go in and say, 'oh, we're going to regulate everything,' without knowing what everything is," says a senior Treasury official. "We want to know what everything is." He adds: "There are very serious policy issues—seigniorage, money laundering, financial stability issues, there are consumer issues that are genuinely important that we must address and look hard at. It may be sensible for the Government to issue a card—that's conceivable—but what if you issue it and nobody uses it?"

A task force headed by the Controller of the Currency is considering these policy issues, at a deliberate crawl. The many private institutions getting into the money business agree, with all their hearts, that the Government ought to just stay out of their way. They are not quite so worried that no one will use their products.

DigiCash, an Amsterdam-based company run by an American cryptography expert, David Chaum, is experimenting with money in varying degrees of reality. One version cannot be converted back to dollars or any other national currency, yet thousands of Internet users have begged to have some to spend in slightly whimsical Internet shops. The Ecash Shop of Internet Lining sells six on-line images of Japanese scenery, for one-and-a-half cyberbucks (c$1.5). For c$5, the American Book Center Grand Lottery Extravaganza will offer you the chance to win an actual, tangible, material object: a hardback copy of John Grisham's potboiler, "The Rainmaker"—"delivered to your home, for FREE!!" But real commerce is available, if not quite convenient, with another version of DigiCash's technology, issued through the Mark Twain Bank of St. Louis. This lets users store dollars in tightly encoded form on the hard disks of their computers. CyberCash, an altogether different operation based in California, issues digital "wallets"—items with no more or less tangible reality than the digital dollars they contain—for use in Internet commerce. At the moment, you have to open bank accounts with old-style cash, or at least turn over your credit-card number, to get any of these digi-cyber-electro-dollars.

To bankers, this looks like anarchy. The one place they would like the Government to take action is the place where nonbanks start to step on their toes: banks are subject to many regulations and safeguards that, so far, their less orthodox competitors remain gaily free from.

Over at Citicorp, the Emerging Technology group is creating (and fighting patent battles over) what the bankers hope will be the most securely based of all these systems. Their vision encompasses not just cash, but also the huge portion of the payments system that runs, almost as archaically, by check. Millions of people have begun paying bills electronically, tossing into the trash the little windowed envelopes that come each month. Nevertheless, nearly all company-to-company transactions today are by means of checks, expensive to process and highly vulnerable to counterfeiting. The average American signs 270 checks a year, according to Citibank, compared with 10 for the average German. This is a burden of which Citibank would love to be relieved.

"We're going to have to go to this technology for reasons that have nothing to do with consumer convenience," says Colin Crook, senior technology officer of Citicorp. "This is profoundly important long term. It will change the entire infrastructure of banks. It takes $150 billion a year just to run the U.S. banking system. That's a crazy number at the end of the day."

Meanwhile, guises of money continue to multiply. The post office issues 200 million money orders a year. Traveler's checks, food stamps, even frequent-flyer miles are becoming tradable and convertible to merchandise. Ersatz private monies have always existed—tokens, tickets, and chits of all kinds. But these are blending in the mainstream economy as never before, just as real cash comes to seem less and less distinctive. When so many objects can serve as money, currency loses its special status.

Inflation and technology have conspired, anyway, to make American currency seem ill-configured as never before. The dollar bill of 1996 buys about what a dime did in 1941. The 1941 dime was more convenient. But the Government has not seriously considered a dollar coin since the debacle of the poorly designed Susan B. Anthony dollar nearly two decades ago. Because we use paper money for amounts as small as the 1996 dollar, a whole vending-machine technology has sprung up to cope with dollar bills; still, your chances of straightening, un-crimping and stuffing any particular bill successfully into a machine are frustratingly small.

To return the currency to its 1940's condition, the smallest bill would have to be the $10; the smallest coin, the dime. At the bottom of the ladder, pennies are an expensive nuisance, blatantly disrespected. Take one, leave one. Billions of them simply vanish from the economy each year—another hidden cost of money. Oft-cited polls by Gallup and others that purport to show a continuing fondness for pennies—made mostly of zinc—are commissioned by, of course, the zinc industry. Many people do believe that eliminating pennies would lead to sneaky rounding-up price increases, but logic suggests this is not so: a two-dollar toy that now goes for $1.99 would likely drop to $1.90 rather than rise to $2.00. The Treasury believes officially that the currency is fine and popular as is. Americans are conservative about their dollars and cents. They may not want it to change, but it has changed and is changing: shrinking, fading, stepping back into a crowd.

Could a host of new monies undermine our collective confidence in Money—in the mass delusion that has made the United States dollar such a bedrock? Does the Government have the responsibility, or even the standing, to take action? Federal officials are watching and waiting, hoping that dollars will always be dollars and trying to let many flowers bloom. "I think we should maintain an enormous presumption in favor of letting people participate in markets and compete and do all those things, while insisting on a whole set of regulatory safeguards that insure that electronic money is not marketed by people who are then going to default," says Summers at the Treasury. Neither the Government's traditional monopoly on the minting of money, nor the threat of lost revenue from seigniorage, persuade him that the Government should act.

"I don't think that setting up the Government Electronic Money Corporation is particularly attractive," he says. "That is the philosophy that brought you the world's state-run airlines, the world's state-run telephone companies and the world's state-run electric companies, and by and large it hasn't been very successful."

True—but by standing aside, the Government risks abdicating its responsibility for deep policy decisions. Consider, for example, the unanticipated rise of credit cards over the past two decades. Credit cards are no longer, for most of their users, a significant source of credit. They are simply payment devices—money at a distance. As a practical matter, it has become difficult to buy an airplane ticket or rent a car without a credit card. The vast bulk of mail-order and phone-order commerce depends on credit cards—or, more precisely, credit-card numbers, for merchants no longer need see or touch the actual card. The credit-card companies not only handle the payments conveniently; they have also come to serve, day in and day out, as a sort of shadow judicial system. You can trust a mail-order house with your credit-card number as you would never trust it with cash, because you know that the credit-card company will hear your complaints, examine parcel-service records, and back you if the merchandise fails to arrive. The days of C.O.D. are over. You pay for this system, of course, in the form of higher prices for everything sold by merchants who accept credit cards. In fact, because the credit-card companies have mostly succeeded in forbidding merchants to offer discounts for cash purchases, you pay for this system even if you do not use credit cards—for example, if you are poor.

In effect, the economy has spawned an enormous privately managed payment system, financed by a hidden sales tax. A completely distinct, equally private system is the network of automated teller machines that has sprung up over the past two decades. These, too, carry high charges in percentage terms and are mostly unavailable to the poor. Electronic cash could evolve in the same way—public policy made without public debate.

In its quiet way, the Government has contributed to the decline of cash. Many people believe that, if they wanted to, they could get a $1,000 bill or even a $10,000 bill. Not so—the United States has long since discontinued bills in denominations greater than $100, even as it has added new laws making it harder and harder to make big payments in cash. It has imposed ever-tighter restrictions on your ability to drop off a secret suitcase stuffed with cash at your bank or at your lawyer's office. Cash, the Government believes, has become largely a tool of criminals. This is true.

Laying Golden Eggs

Whether or not you think you're ready for a smart card, surely you could be tempted by the not-so-smart card known in digital-money circles as the Evergreen Card. The Evergreen Card is digital cash with one flaw: the counter in its built-in chip gets stuck and fails to deduct the charge. In other words, it is the legendary magic purse, always ready with another coin.

Does it exist? Only in a cloud of speculation and myth, though a rumor swept a meeting of cryptography aficionados recently that Daguio, of the American Bankers Association, had actually seen one.

"Oh, God, I didn't say that, I really didn't," Daguio says. Not exactly, anyway. He merely pointed out that, no matter how good the design, technology always has implementation problems. Smart cards rely on software, and software always has bugs. "These things are so, so complex that just a little defect in a card in the wrong place on a random basis in a large batch could produce really interesting stuff," he says. "You know how hard it is to program software. Some of these bugs might not show up until you debit 60 cents, credit 40 cents, and then debit $1.50. If it becomes widely known that that's what you have to do . . . "

Visa officials are fairly sure that none of their Atlanta cards will be evergreen. "We'd never say never, but we haven't experienced that kind of a problem," says Gordon Howe, senior vice president. They also know that some people will not wait for the flaws but will try to create their own. "The chip is a physical thing; anything physical, the security people will tell you can be attacked," Howe says.

As money enters a new age, so does counterfeiting. The ultimate threat is the perfect copy—the virtual coin that proves mathematically identical to the real thing. If money is a string of bits, then someone, somewhere, can make a perfect copy . . . and another . . . and another . . . An arms race is already raging between those working to armorplate digital cash with doubly and triply secure cryptography and those working to pierce the armor. Security experts assume that nefarious characters, in search of an unending stream of money, are already investing millions in the next stages of research and development.

At first, issuers of smart cards with chips will be relying in part on how much easier it is to counterfeit smart cards with magnetic stripes. No sooner had New York's subway system virtualized its fare tokens in the form of magnetic-stripe cards than a few ingenious citizens discovered that they could throw together some cheap circuitry and heads from an old tape recorder and produce their own Metrocards. "You can reproduce cards ad nauseam—it's magnetic data," says Jerome Page, general counsel and vice president for business development at the Metropolitan Transportation Authority. At least the payoff is just a ride on the subway, for now, though the M.T.A., like so many other semi-public agencies, has wider electronic-money ambitions for its product. When counterfeits are detected, turnstiles can be reprogrammed by the central computers in a matter of hours, blocking the bad cards. Some users are shameless. "This is New York," Page says. "People come in to customer service and say, 'Joe sold me this $80 card for $30 and it doesn't work—I want my money back.' " The credit-card companies, too, will be able to invalidate counterfeit or defective smart cards from a distance—if they detect them.

For every new idea in tamper-resistance, there is a new idea in tampering. Any chip can be cracked open and examined with an electron microscope—at least in theory. Manufacturers can put extra layers of oxide and metal over the silicon. Attackers need to etch these layers away carefully. Manufacturers can inject caustic agents that become active when exposed to oxygen, destroying the chip before it can be inspected. They can make some cells light-sensitive, programming them to erase critical data. Attackers can crack open cards in oxygen-free chambers or in the dark. Manufacturers can encase the chip in an epoxy containing diamond or carbide dust, to dull machine tools. . . . "At least you can cause people to have to spend a lot of money," says Eric Hughes, a cryptography expert who is founder of Simple Access, an Internet services company. "But doing the second chip is far, far less money than the first. And if you could make a master chip that spoke the right protocol, you could make a little money mint for yourself."

He and others believe that the best strategy for a would-be latter-day counterfeiter is to work now, invest, and wait—resisting the temptation to attack the new systems in their embryonic stages. They also suspect that the biggest vulnerabilities will come from laziness and carelessness, not from inherent flaws in the technology. In the hot competition for early market share, companies may just cut corners.

"Information warfare is going to make people very worried downstream," says Crook at Citicorp. "We have an immense paranoia about how dangerous it's going to be. I think that the security requirements in our industry are going to be more severe than at the Department of Defense."

Follow the money, as Deep Throat once said.

No one knows how much of the economy is still underground, in the sense of untraced by banks, credit-card companies and Internal Revenue auditors. But if someone says, "You understand, I have a cash business," you do understand: a cash business today means an operation that evades taxes by concealment and deceit, keeping double sets of books and laundering money. If you learn that your city councilman has been putting cash into his safe deposit box, you are rightly hard-pressed to imagine a noncriminal explanation. If your painter demands payment in cash, you will not assume that he is paying his taxes in full. When small contractors routinely offer discounts for cash payment, it is not because cash is convenient, or because they enjoy the smell of old-fashioned greenbacks.

So a world where all money has gone digital could be a world where honest plumbers and restaurateurs, accounting for all their income and paying all their taxes, would not have to feel like schlemiels. Eliminating cash would free the world of the single biggest form of tax fraud. It could also wipe out a host of other crimes: bribery, kidnapping, extortion, and even robbery. All these depend on the existence of cash as an anonymous and untraceable means of payment.

Yet this could also be a world where vast computer databases keep track of every magazine you buy, every bus you ride, every hot dog you eat, every beer you drink, every video you rent, every sawbuck you borrow. If the network can follow the trail of all your spending, it can become more omniscient than a private detective who follows you around with a camera. In the money business, knowledge is power: your spending habits, your likes and dislikes, are valuable to marketers. That is not necessarily bad. Many smart-card issuers have plans for including clever extraneous information on their chips: credit-card companies imagine storing your vital health data, for example; transit systems imagine storing trip histories that would make possible frequent-rider discounts or special rates for bus-to-subway transfers. Still, the possibilities are chilling to anyone who cares about privacy. Separate information sources are becoming linked, letting your various watchers compare notes, and the detail in their dossiers is becoming finer and finer.

"The granularity of information that's revealed about payments is going to explode,"

says Chaum of DigiCash. In cryptographic circles, Chaum is the best-known advocate of a form of electronic money that could preserve anonymity, using advanced encoding techniques to create protective envelopes. Cryptography is as close as modern mathematics comes to magic. Banks could, for example, register every digital dollar they issue and verify the dollars when they return, while remaining unable to trace the spending trail in between. Chaum's scheme is not symmetrical: it preserves the anonymity of the buyer while recording the identity of the merchant. And by a clever mathematical device, if the buyer tries to spend the same digital dollar twice, his cover is blown.

He fervently believes that this is a flavor of money that consumers will want. "Privacy is inherent in the notion of a free market," he says. "If we don't get the national currencies in electronic form properly, then the market will route around them and make other currencies."

It's simply a design choice. Smart cards, or their on-line equivalents, could function as blindly as raw cash. They could be even less traceable than in Chaum's system. That is a frightening prospect to law-enforcement authorities. Having finally made life difficult for drug smugglers with heavy cash suitcases, they will not casually allow the manufacture of half-ounce chips that could make possible blind transfers of hundreds of millions of dollars: the money launderer's dream. Even if the Government takes no other action in the electronic-money arena, it will surely move to extend its restrictions on cash to cover digital equivalents. And so far, the large institutions entering the

electronic-money arena are leaning toward less anonymous, less private approaches than Chaum's —betting that most of us will be willing to sacrifice more pieces of privacy for, say, convenience. Chaum could prove right, but only if the marketplace is willing to cast its votes for privacy.

To a degree that is little appreciated, the Government and financial institutions have already succeeded, mostly, in eliminating the anonymity of cash in bulk quantities. By making it difficult to move large sums of cash in secrecy, they have tightened a net. Most Americans will say in public-opinion surveys that they worry about their financial privacy, that they do not want to give anyone the ability to follow the cash trail they leave every day. Then, they go ahead and leave that trail without giving it a second thought.

Most of our economic life is already networked: every check, every credit-card payment, every telephone call exists in a computer somewhere. Sure, you can sneak out anonymously and purchase a copy of Penthouse, but if you order a dirty pay-per-view movie from your cable company, you probably do not worry that the information finds its way to a data base somewhere. Meanwhile, more than one adulterer has been revealed, more than one murderer hunted down, because they could not avoid leaving a trail of credit-card receipts. If nothing else, the heightened fear of counterfeiting in the digital-cash world may drive banks, rightly or wrongly, to make sure that all money is networked money. "It's arguable," Daguio says dryly, "that banks have a right to determine whether somebody spent the same coin a thousand times."

We have private money: cash. We have networked money: everything else. Digital money is inherently neither private nor networked. The technology can go either way. Ultimately someone will make a choice—the marketplace, or the Government, or the credit-card companies or the banks—and the technology will support it.

In 1996, virtually no one in or out of Washington thinks that the Government should step in, take charge, and issue an electronic currency. There is a case to be made: That money is not just another product, best left to the vagaries of the market, but the irreplaceable underpinning of society. That confidence in money requires *one* currency, not a multitude. That only the Government, after public debate among contending interests, can set standards equitably, rather than leaving the critical choices to, say, the credit-card companies.

But the Treasury does not want the responsibility of guessing the future and maybe guessing wrong—creating an Edsel or Susan B. Anthony. It is just too soon. "There's this race," says Philip Webre, a principal analyst with the Congressional Budget Office. "We're at the gate. We don't even know how long the race is or how many horses are in the race." We do know that the computer industry does not want lawyers and Congressmen imposing judgments about technologies of which they have proved famously ignorant. The old-line banking industry, and the nascent digital-cash industry, want the chance to sell their own products.

And, of course, they are all fighting for the float. Will you fight as hard for the right to earn interest on your cash? Will you decide that you want that last shred of privacy that comes with dollars that do not have your name and Social Security number built in? Or will someone decide for you? While you still can, why not reach into your pocket for a few last vestigial dollar bills, make sure you have exact change for the bus, and buy yourself a secret, nonnetworked hot dog.

 Article Review Form at end of book.

Can Digital Change Balance of E-Commerce?

Dave Kosiur

Dave Kosiur is a freelance writer and consultant. He can be reached at drkosiur@ix.netcom.com.

Tech Analysis

Web-based catalogs generated booming sales during last year's Christmas season, but other businesses, particularly content providers, are still looking for a way to make a profit from the Web.

Still missing is an accepted micropayment system that lets users pay for small bits of timely content. Digital Equipment Corp. has thrown its hat into the e-commerce ring with MilliCent, which in January was released on the Internet for public trials after two years of in-house development.

To keep transactions inexpensive and secure, the MilliCent system uses "scrip," which users buy ahead of time for use on the Internet.

In MilliCent, scrip is an electronic token that represents a prepaid value and is valid only for purchases from a specific vendor.

Scrip can represent any currency denomination and even other forms of tender that are of value to the vendor, such as reward points in a loyalty program or membership in an online community. To reduce the hassles associated with storing a number of different types of scrip in a customer's electronic wallet, MilliCent uses brokers, which produce scrip on behalf of multiple vendors.

Once customers have purchased broker scrip—through a credit card transaction, for example—they can trade the broker scrip for vendor-specific scrip as needed. The scrip is protected against unauthorized use by a cryptographic hash function.

For additional security, the tokens are serialized to help guard against double-spending—a customer (or hacker) sending the same scrip to a vendor at two different times.

In many digital cash schemes, such as Digicash Inc.'s ecash and Carnegie Mellon University's NetCash system, the vendor maintains the account balance. With MilliCent, the customer maintains the account balance, which is encoded in the scrip held by the customer.

Shopping with MilliCent is straightforward. Customers buy scrip from a broker, visit vendors' sites and use scrip to pay for items. The scrip representing the purchase is later redeemed by vendors at the broker's site.

Scrip exchanges are transparent to the user when a series of vendors are serviced by the same broker. When multiple brokers are involved, the process is still smooth, because brokers will have automatic methods for redeeming each other's scrip.

In the initial MilliCent public beta, only Digital acts as a broker, but other brokers are expected to participate as the beta testing progresses.

A Three-Way System

The MilliCent system consists of three parts: an electronic wallet for the customer, a vendor server and a broker server.

The wallet, which is available for Windows 95 and Windows NT, can be downloaded at www.millicent.digital.com. Once installed, it works in the background of the user's computer, in conjunction with Version 3.0 or higher of Netscape Communications Corp.'s

Navigator or Microsoft Corp.'s Internet Explorer.

The wallet performs basic accounting and purchasing procedures for customers, including obtaining scrip from a broker, converting broker scrip into vendor scrip and tracking all scrip uses. Users can check balances and list purchases by date or amount. Purchases are recorded by URL, document title and document description.

The wallet lets users configure a spending policy to help prevent overspending. For example, a policy could require the user's permission for all purchases above 10 cents but automatically approve smaller purchases. The policy can include warnings when spending at a vendor's site exceeds a given amount in a given time.

The second component of MilliCent's system, the vendor server, is the processing gateway that works alongside the vendor's Web server. The vendor server handles per-click purchases (for a given Web page or image, for example) and can process subscription-based purchases.

To keep purchase disputes to a minimum, MilliCent includes a reload option that vendors can set for each item. If a customer loses a connection with the vendor's site and does not receive the purchased content, the customer can click the Reload button on a browser to obtain a new copy.

The vendor broker tests each piece of scrip received for double-spending, tampering or theft, using the unique ID number of each scrip and the hash function used to generate it. Transactions are logged by URL, category, date sold, price charged, money tendered and change returned.

The broker server converts money into scrip and adjusts for different forms of broker and vendor scrip. Brokers can accept credit card payments through SSL (Secure Sockets Layer) or SET (Secure Electronic Transaction).

Brokers must establish contractual relationships with vendors to sell their scrip. The contract includes the right to sell vendor scrip within a certain range of serial numbers—the same numbers the vendor uses to check the validity of any scrip a customer uses.

To make money on penny-size transactions, the MilliCent system must keep transaction costs as low as possible. MilliCent does not issue receipts for purchases, letting the content serve as its own receipt. Security is also less strict than the policies in many other digital cash systems. The value of scrip is relatively low, so it's not worth stealing unless someone steals lots of it. Stealing large amounts would be difficult, however, because customers hold small amounts of scrip at a time and spend even smaller amounts at a site.

Hash functions are used to authenticate scrip, eliminating the need for computationally expensive digital signatures. Scrip is also verified locally at the vendor's site, reducing the need to talk to the broker. Finally, because the balance of the account is kept in scrip, transactions can be quickly verified by the customer and the vendor; the final transfer of funds from the broker to the vendor can take place offline.

 Article Review Form at end of book.

E-Commerce Standards

Some $ and sense

Kevin Jones

Intraspection

Another set of initials entered the electronic commerce playing field this month with the introduction, after a 10-month gestation, of OTP.

OTP, which stands for Open Trading Protocol, joins a crowded alphabet soup of ambitious and evolving standards for transactions over the Net proposed by various consortia.

Yes, standards are important. They establish a lingua franca for commerce; a means by which the vendor and the buyer can agree on what constitutes a transaction. But if this were the evolution of the earth, we would be in the bubbling ooze phase—lots of promising linkups, but nothing that's come to life.

OTP, backed by MasterCard International Inc. and Mondex International, a U.K.-based smart-card company, in a consortium

that includes Hewlett-Packard Co. and IBM Corp., promises to provide things no other transaction standard yet supplies, such as handling taxes and receipts. But it's already crippled.

Standards need the agreement of the major players. And Visa International (www.visa. com) is conspicuously absent from the OTP effort. One source said the rivalry between Master-Card (www.mastercard.com) and Visa is the reason.

Visa, for its part, is the chief proponent of Secure Electronic Transaction (SET), another payment standard with its own challenges.

There are competing versions of SET—which IBM (www.ibm. com), HP (www.hp.com) and others are trying to iron out—and it offers a kind of branded security the market may not be demanding. SET is viewed as so tailored to banks that there's little incentive for merchants to adopt it.

As Peter Roden, executive director of the Open Buying on

the Internet (OBI) consortium, says of the e-commerce standards: "They are pretty much Jell-O," still in flux with organizational and niggling technical difficulties slowing development.

Indeed, OBI, a business-to-business transaction standard aimed at trading partners, is six months behind schedule, and public trials have been delayed until June.

One of OBI's failings is its focus on single-vendor catalogs, while corporations setting up extranets want to be able to buy from multiple vendors. OBI also decided to encapsulate the functions of electronic data interchange (EDI) in a browser, but now is thinking of using the Extensible Markup Language (XML)—more delay. XML is a format that lets Web developers control and display data the way they control text and graphics.

And then there's EDI itself. Often dismissed as a dinosaur, EDI has, perhaps, as much potential as any of the newcomers to become an e-commerce standard. Several vendors, including Harbinger Corp., IBM and GE Information Services, offer services that hide the complexity of old-style EDI forms inside a friendly Web-based front end.

So which standard will emerge?

"[It's] too early to say," says Erica Rugullies, a Giga Information Group Inc. analyst.

There likely will never be just one standard. But we need an orderly marketplace and the proposals need to be close enough to each other in order for the standards to make sense and businesses to make dollars.

 Article Review Form at end of book.

WiseGuide Wrap-Up

The critical issues of authenticity, security, and confidentiality are at the heart of the success of electronic commerce and, to a large extent, marketing on the Internet. What exactly are these that present a significant challenge to e-commerce and marketing?

We use personal signatures as indicators of authenticity of the documents containing them. Methods exist to verify the authenticity of hard-copy documents containing a signature. The same is not necessarily true on the Internet. The sellers would like to verify that the buyer ordering an expensive gift is really who she says she is. Likewise, the buyer would like to know whether the merchant at the other end is the one it pretends to be. This requires verifying the authenticity of both sides by a "trusted" third party. This verification needs some technical and some procedural issues to be resolved before it gains widespread use.

The second issue, security and integrity, refers to several different but closely related concepts. First, the users do not want the information they submit falling into the wrong hands.

Part of this concern is perceptual, while a good part remains quite real. People do not think twice before handing their credit card to a waiter after a good meal in a restaurant. He disappears into the back room for several minutes and returns with the card tucked inside the leatherette folder containing the check. No one knows what happens in the back room, but the guest does not question the integrity of the individual. Likewise, people are equally willing to give credit card numbers to a person at the other end of the telephone taking an order for a product they order from a mail-order retailer. However, many are concerned about typing their credit card number to a form presented by an Internet marketer. The image of a hacker sitting in a basement room, watching the computer screens of the people on the Internet scares consumers, although the probability of the credit card number falling into the wrong hands is fairly slim. Another issue related to security is the integrity of the transaction. Not only does the information need to travel in a secure environment, but the sides must not be able to deny engaging in that

transaction. This concerns more sellers than buyers. The sellers would like the consumers to be bound by the order to maintain the integrity of the transaction.

Confidentiality is the third concern of the parties engaged in e-commerce. Using cash in a physical world detaches the personal information of the buyer from any purchase. In real life, cash purchasers are anonymous. In a digital world, where buyers must submit detailed information about the purchase and themselves, maintaining the same level of anonymity may not be attainable. However, companies are working to develop technologies that will either offer the same level of anonymity or ensure very high levels of confidentiality to the information submitted by online buyers.

The challenges are not trivial, and their resolution requires transparent technology to users and full compatibility across vendors' technologies. Interestingly, these very solutions are presenting business and marketing opportunities to many facilitating firms.

R.E.A.L. Sites

Site name: ACNielsen Internet Survey Raises Questions about Future of E-Commerce

URL: http://www.acnielsen.com/acn/press/canada/971124.htm

Why is it R.E.A.L.? A. C. Nielsen shares information regarding the obstacle to e-commerce.

Key topics: Internet users, access, buying behavior online, concerns over online payments

Site name: E-Money (That's What I Want)

URL: http://www.wired.com/wired/2.12/features/emoney.html

Why is it R.E.A.L.? A discussion of "cash" and why it may disappear as digital technology permeates the world of commerce.

Key topics: Money, cash, intangible money, credit cards, smart cards, value creation, electronic cash

section

3

Although they come from all parts of the world, consumers in cyberspace may have different behavioral characteristics from the behavior they manifest in the real world. In the virtual worlds of cyberspace, consumers may have stopped at their favorite MUD (Multi-User Domains) and engaged in a round of Mighty Morphin Power Rangers on the way to the virtual shopping at a cyberauction. What will be the dynamics of such an auction, where bidders do not see each other and have different contextual references about their virtual worlds?

"We build our ideas about what is real and what is natural with the cultural materials available," says Sherry Turkle.[1] Thus, in a different contextual world, a different approach to studying the behavior of consumers will be necessary. Those who form communities on the Internet will manifest behavior in the context of their new world. Although the Internet was once the exclusive domain of scientists and academicians, the composition of the population on the Internet is quickly changing. The question for the marketers might be "As the netizens of those communities walk down the 'Main Street Internet,' will their responses be similar to what we may observe on 'Main Street USA'?"

On-the-fly customization capabilities of the Internet will take advantage of its ability to collect information offered by the consumer and present different content and advertising based on each user's profile. Collecting this information is difficult and important. The methods used by behavioral scientists in traditional markets will be neither sufficient nor suitable to this task. Additionally, the information-collection process needs to be essentially continual. This will allow dynamic alteration of marketing efforts based on changing user profiles.

Analyzing the large amounts of data collected on an ongoing basis will also require developing new analytical techniques and enabling technologies. Data mining has already gained strategic importance, and the quality of the data mining engine used may make substantial differences in gaining strategic advantages over competitors. The Internet bookstore, Amazon, for instance, offers customers additional suggestions based on the title they intend to purchase, and the suggestions are quite sensible. The instant analysis of patterns of behavior at Amazon is one of the fine examples of information-based marketing on the Internet.

Learning Objectives

The virtual worlds that exist on the Internet are populated by virtual people, netizens. Their computers have become portals that transport them into places where no one has gone before (and probably never will), yet their presence in these virtual worlds has real consequences, since, unlike Tron, the movie character that gets sucked into a computer, netizens are very real people. As you read the articles in this section, keep in mind that online consumers are real people exploring virtual worlds. Do they have any reason to behave differently? If so, what reasons can you think of that may compel them to act differently? Can we explain their behavior using classical consumer behavior models? When you critically examine these issues through these articles, you should

- Explore and develop an understanding of the behavioral dimensions of the Net surfers.

- Learn how and why people form communities on the Internet and how this may affect marketing.

- Learn the qualities of the Internet that may, ironically, bring a more personal touch to marketing.

[1]Sherry Turkle, *Life on the Screen* (Simon & Schuster, 1995), p. 237.

Questions

1. When people surf the Net and particularly when they engage in some form of communication on the Internet, they tend to be more spontaneous, less careful in some ways, and they manifest behavioral patterns different from those of their real life. What makes people behave differently when they are on the Internet?

2. What activities are more likely to be affected by this change in behavior? How do you think it might influence marketing?

3. Visitors to many sites come from many different parts of the world with different cultural values. Many leave without offering any information about themselves or may hold back some information. With such fuzzy information, how can marketers approach segmenting these markets, the composition of which may change with great fluidity?

Internet Communities

Forget surfers. A new class of Netizen is settling right in.

Amy Cortese in New York and Robert D. Hof in San Francisco

With Seanna Browder in Seattle, Peter Elstrom in Chicago, and bureau reports

After her marriage broke up, Bonnie Sakadales ventured onto the Internet for advice on raising her son and daughter alone. Last June, the University of Maryland administrative assistant landed at Parent Soup, a World Wide Web site plastered with parenting information and online "bulletin boards" where visitors swap solace and tips. Within days, Sakadales struck up an online conversation with Al Cole, an Oswego, N.Y., security guard, who was struggling with custody issues. After two weeks of long phone calls, Al drove to Damascus, Md., to meet Bonnie—and they fell in love. Last Valentine's Day, they were married, and Bonnie is still singing the praises of Parent Soup: "It gave me a world to be in besides work and the kids. I can't imagine what my life would be like without it."

Neither can millions of other Web surfers who are approaching the Internet in an altogether new way. Instead of flitting from site to site dabbling in the gobs of information and latest news flashes, this new class of Netizen is settling in, staying put, making a home away from home. Oh, they're after the info, too, but they seek far more than that. They want a sense of community—the cyberspace equivalent of the bar at TV's "Cheers," where everybody knows your E-mail address.

To these Netizens, content is no longer king. They're not necessarily plunking themselves down on barstools at uptown Web sites laden with splashy content like Time Warner Inc.'s Pathfinder or the oh-so-hip online lofts of HotWired Inc.—both hemorrhaging big bucks in search of visitors who will stick around. Nearly every walk of life can chat it up, from Tripod for twentysomethings to Utne Online for New Age intellectuals to GolfWeb for Tiger Woods wannabes. Says Tom Rielly, CEO of the online gay community PlanetOut: "It's not the content. It's the people, stupid. Content may be why people visit a site. But community is why people stay."

"Next Wave"

Call it the colonizing of cyberspace. Forget surfing: Today, people of like minds and interests are establishing Internet communities faster than any construction company in the brick-and-mortar world. According to a new BUSINESS WEEK/Harris Poll, 57% of those hopping on to the Net today go to the same sites repeatedly instead of wandering like nomads from one to the next. And of the 89% of Netizens who use E-mail, nearly one-third consider themselves part of an online community. "We're at the beginning of an explosion," says Andrew Busey, chairman and chief technology officer of ichat Inc., an Internet startup in Austin, Tex., that makes software for online chats. "Community and communications is the next big wave on the Internet."

What's behind this new geography of the Web? Experts say the biggest factor is the changing demographics of its users. There are now some 40 million people on the Web, up from 1 million in December, 1994. As that number grows, the online population begins to look more like the mass population. The BUSINESS WEEK/Harris Poll, for example, found the Web is no longer a stomping ground just for the young: 67% are now 30 years and older, including 19% over the age of 50. And, today, women account for a bigger portion of the Net population than ever before—41%, up from 21% a year and a half ago.

As Mr. and Ms. Mainstream venture into cyberspace, they often find it a dizzying place, what with hundreds of thousands of Web sites to choose from. So, just as in the physical world, Net newbies are gravitating to Web sites where they can find friends and feel comfortable. "To most people, the Internet feels like jumping out into the ocean," says Douglas Rushkoff, author of Cyberia, a book on cyberculture. "Online communities provide the lifeguards."

Early signs show they may also provide the profits. Netrepreneurs are finding they can turn the intrinsic cultural appeal of communities into a real business proposition. The numbers tell the tale. According to a study by the University of Minnesota, if a site doesn't capture Web surfers' interest within eight seconds, they're gone—off to another one with a click of the computer mouse. Even if they stay, the average visit is only seven minutes. That leaves precious little time for Web publishers, advertisers, and merchants to promote or sell anything.

Not so inside Net neighborhoods. Simply adding a way for Web surfers to chat, for example, consistently boosts traffic on any Web site by as much as 50%. It also calms those itchy index fingers: Chat visitors hang around a half-hour, three times the aver-

age—a big lure to advertisers. And a little communication can go a long way toward wooing those wallets. A new study by Yankelovich Partners Inc., a marketing research firm, found 63% of people online say they won't buy anything over the Web until there's more human interaction involved.

Garden Escape Inc. found that out fast. CEO Clifford A. Sharples launched the Web site in March, 1996, primarily as an online nursery with everything from 294 different kinds of roses to heirloom cherry tomatoes. But Sharples was soon inundated with E-mail and questions. Three months ago, he did something about it, adding chat and forums on regional gardening issues, such as one for the Pacific Northwest. The result: Visitors spend twice as much time on the site now—20 minutes. And sales? They're growing at 40% a month, boosted by orders from chat participants, who spend an average $100 an order, vs. $60 from others. "We thought of ourselves as more of a store," says Sharples. "We underestimated how important community would be."

So just what is a Web community? For now, most of these online gatherings are still in their formative stage. Like Rome, they are not being built in a day but are evolving as people gather and establish, week by week, their interests and their needs. That makes their nature as eclectic and varied as the neighborhoods in Brooklyn and Bombay.

There are some constants, though. All communities are built around a common interest or passion, whether it's playing piano or being a parent. But the ideal community site does more than just focus on like interests. It encourages lots of communication

and interaction, whether through chat rooms, bulletin boards, or discussion forums, which can stretch out over a period of months. "In the chat rooms, people essentially become the content," says Sony Online Vice-President Matt Rothman.

But most important of all, the creators of these communities don't try to play the role of benevolent dictator. Sure, they provide a framework and guidance along the way, but then they step back and let the members shape the community. On 3DO Co.'s Meridian 59 site, for example, the Redwood City (Calif.)-based company put together a medieval world of sorcery and swordplay, then opened the doors. Very quickly, a group of people formed bent on killing other players, and just as quickly, a group sprang up to protect the innocent. Now when "killers" are spotted, members of "protector" groups stalk and do them in. "The successful communities stand back and let nature take its course," says Chip Morningstar, co-founder and chief scientist at Electric Communities, a Cupertino (Calif.) builder of virtual communities.

For many inhabitants of online communities, that course is a direct path from their work lives. According to the BUSINESS WEEK/Harris Poll, 42% of those involved in an online community say it is related to their profession, while 35% say their community is a social group, and 18% say it revolves around a hobby.

Farm Belt

One of the more successful work-related sites is Agriculture Online (@griculture, in geekspeak). Launched two years ago by Meredith Corp., this site offers the latest farm news, Global Positioning Satellite data, commodity prices, and bulletin boards galore. Visit the Electronic Coffee Shop and jump into a discussion on how to control soybean cyst nematodes or offer up a down-on-the-farm joke. "Interactivity is the linchpin of this whole thing," says @griculture Online editor John Walter. "But the chemistry of good discussion groups is mysterious."

Baffling or no, it's working. The site has mushroomed from 83,000 "hits," the number of times a site is accessed, in August 1995, to 5 million hits last month. And now it's on track for profitability by yearend through a combination of advertising revenues and $10 monthly subscriptions for its Blue Ribbon premium services, which include up-to-the-minute weather reports.

While such communities are new to the Web, they spring from the very roots of the Internet. In the early 1970s, the Internet emerged as a tight-knit community of Defense Dept. scientists exchanging research data. Soon, as universities and private research labs hooked in, more and more participants began forming subcommunities. In 1979, so-called Usenet groups, which allowed computer users to post messages in bulletin-board fashion, developed and blossomed into thousands of "newsgroups" focusing on everything from Apple Computer Inc.'s Macintosh software to "The X-Files" TV show.

Online communities have a rich tradition outside the Net, too. The WELL, for instance, started in 1985 in Sausalito, Calif., as one of the first community-oriented "bulletin-board systems," so-called BBSes—private computers reached via the telephone system rather than the Net. In late 1995, the WELL made itself accessible via the fast-growing Web. Others, such as New York's East Coast Hangout (ECHO), still operate thriving BBS communities.

America Online, however, was probably the first to get it right for the masses. In the early 1990s, AOL popularized chat, which allowed people to exchange messages live. Today, AOL boasts some 14,000 chat rooms accounting for about one-third of its members' time online. Recently, AOL introduced another innovation—"buddy lists," which alert members when friends are online so they can exchange instant messages. "Community is the Velcro that keeps people there," says AOL Studios President Theodore Leonsis.

Now the Web is laying out the www.elcome mat for communities. When the Web surfaced in late 1993, most sites focused on their newfound ability to publish graphics-rich documents. But in 1996, software makers began developing Web-based programs for discussion forums and chat. These programs are in hot demand now, creating a booming business for startups such as ichat and eShare. And some sites, such as LiveWorld Productions Inc.'s Talk City, are devoted exclusively to chatting.

Today the push is to turn the age-old appeal of communities into cash—especially on the profit-starved Web. Just last month, for example, the popular political site PoliticsNow closed amid rumors that it is losing money in the low seven figures. CMP Media Inc., unhappy with how little revenue its NetGuide Live site was generating, cut most of its staff. Time-Warner's Pathfinder is losing at least $5 million a year.

And American Cybercast, which is producing The Spot and The Pyramid cybersoaps, filed for Chapter 11 bankruptcy protection in January. The problem: These early Web efforts have not taken full advantage of interactivity.

It's early, but there are tantalizing signs that cybertowns could fulfill the early promise of profits on the Web. For one, these sites are alluring to advertisers, who will gladly pay to reach an audience that stays put long enough to absorb their ad messages. Moreover, communities have common interests and more defined demographics, say a group of gardeners or antique-car buffs, that make it easy for advertisers to target buyers. "You're reaching more qualified eyeballs," says Seth Goldstein, president of SiteSpecific Inc., a New York interactive advertising agency.

That's already translating into higher ad rates for some Net neighborhoods. Women's Wire, for example, is a Web community for career-oriented women that commands ad fees of $50 per 1,000 "impressions," or ad viewings. That's up from $20 last summer and considerably more than the average $30 for mainstream Web sites. Firefly Network Inc. does better yet. The Boston software maker runs a site to showcase its filtering software, which can track the likes and dislikes of members—say, what movies they enjoy—and then recommend similar films. The site has attracted 2 million registered users, who spend an average 32 minutes each visit. Firefly's ad rates: $70 to $100 per 1,000 impressions.

Now, some cyberhoods are getting even more mileage out of advertisers. Just as consumer-products giants hawked laundry detergent by sponsoring the old

TV soap operas, many merchants today see a big plus in being linked to an online community. Sponsorships are particularly suited for community sites since they are less intrusive than banner ads and "they integrate the sponsor into the neighborhood," says David Bohnett, CEO of GeoCities, a Santa Monica (Calif.)-based startup. Bohnett ought to know. GeoCities helps Web users set up their own home pages and then arranges them in preferred communities—Napa Valley for oenophiles and Silicon Valley for gearheads. The site now has 500,000 Web pages, drawing some $500,000 a month in advertising and sponsorships. VISA USA Inc., for example, sponsors a restaurant review area called Restaurant Row, while Microsoft Corp. sponsors the Programmers' Pavilion.

Safety Tips

Parent Soup is taking sponsorships a step further. It is working with advertisers to set up "bridge sites"—complete companion Web sites closely linked to Parent Soup (box). Take the one Parent Soup has with ParentsClub.com, a site for the kids' cough syrup Triaminic. This site has scads of parenting info, including child safety tips, and because it offers more than just info on Triaminic, "people feel we're more credible," says Barry Cohen, senior brand manager for the cough medicine. The result: "Traffic to our site has been enormous," Cohen says. For Parent Soup, such sponsorships work so well that 80% of advertisers come back.

The biggest cash coup of all for Net neighborhoods may be the ability to charge admission. Subscription fees have long been out of reach for most Web sites.

Microsoft's highbrow online magazine Slate, for example, has delayed charging for a subscription indefinitely, and even Playboy can't seem to command monthly fees. Yet online communities are making a go of it. The WELL, for instance, charges 11,000 members $10 a month for access to 260 ongoing conferences. 3DO's Meridian 59 collects $9.95 a month from its members. And WebGenesis Inc.'s The Globe chat site, which lets people yak about TV, music, and other topics, is bringing in $75,000 a month from its annual $25 subscriptions, a third of total revenues.

Of course, there's no telling whether any of these communities—or the hundreds of others in various stages of construction—will succeed in the long run. It's unlikely there will be any Netscape Communications-style quick killings. "There aren't going to be any overnight successes," says Forrester Research Inc. analyst Emily Nagle Green.

Indeed, considerable challenges lie ahead. Internet communities could reshape the way buyers and sellers conduct electronic commerce. Consumers will naturally gravitate to communities offering a wide choice of information or product suppliers—not those run by one merchant. Auto buyers, for example, won't flock to a General Motors site if all it offers is GM cars. That means consumers will wield much more power over vendors than ever before, says John Hagel, co-author of the new book *Net Gain: Expanding Markets Through Virtual Communities*. Consumers, for example, could play vendors off one another to get the lowest prices. But merchants and advertisers may also balk at being lumped together and choose

not to do business with those communities.

That also puts Web communities at the mercy of what advertisers think is marketable. One community already is changing its stripes because of a paucity of advertising. Howard Rheingold, author of *The Virtual Community*, envisioned a new advertising-based community for people interested in the collision of computers and culture. But now, after not garnering enough ad support, his Electric Minds site is shifting to building communities for others, such as IBM, though it will maintain its own site. "This is very early," says Rheingold.

Lack of Control?

Virtual villages may also find themselves unprepared for the forces they will unleash. Chat rooms, for instance, are often appallingly juvenile, even hostile places, where you're as likely to be insulted as you are to be enlightened. In that environment, advertisers can be subject to ridicule. "Advertisers worry about the lack of control," admits Bayard Winthrop, vice-president of business development for chat site WebChat Broadcasting System.

And there's a flip side to community loyalty: Members demand a say in the community's direction that may not always jibe with the intentions of the site's owners. But publishers and merchants who want to be associated with a Net neighborhood may have to live with it, say online community veterans. "Any community you try to control will quickly dissolve," says Maria Wilhelm, president of The WELL.

Will all this pay off in the long run? Will people really feel part of a community built around, say, pantyhose—as Sara Lee Corp. is trying to do for its L'Eggs products? For some long-time community builders, steeped in the pointedly noncommercial roots of the Net, the answer is no. People need an emotional attachment to feel part of a community, and a narrow product focus won't do the trick. Says Rheingold: "Any company that thinks they can go out and create a community in 30 days to sell a lot of pantyhose is going to be disappointed." Indeed, he says, no matter what the type of neighborhood, it takes time—probably years—to form a lasting community.

Some communities are already finding it tough on the cyber frontier. Last October, for instance, iVillage acquired parenting site ParentsPlace.com, which still operates as a separate site. Moms Online recently tapped New York-based online department store CyberShop to take over its online store. "We just don't have the cash resources," says Moms Online Business Manager Rob de Baun. Why is this consolidation happening so early in the game? Says Hagel: "Many of the early efforts have had overly optimistic business plans."

For all the challenges to creating true communities online, it's clear that once people get a taste of them, they don't want to leave. Take Ellen Remily, a mother of two young children in rural Shelton, Conn. She found such a friendly community on AOL's Moms Online that she's now a volunteer chat host. "There is always someone who understands where you are coming from," she says. "This is my cyber neighborhood."

If builders of online communities can't figure out how to

The Internet Today: By the Numbers

More women are on the Internet than ever before. Today, women make up 41% of the Net population, compared with just 23% in September, 1995.

One quarter of online users—some 10 million people—have purchased something online.

The number of Americans using the Net has nearly doubled, to around 40 million adults, over the past year.

The Net is not just for the young. 45% of adults surfing the Net are age 40 or over. 32% are between 18 and 29.

Adult Net users are more affluent and better educated than the population as a whole. More than 42% have household incomes greater than $50,000, compared with 33% of the overall population, and 73% of Net surfers have attended college, vs. 46% of the total population.

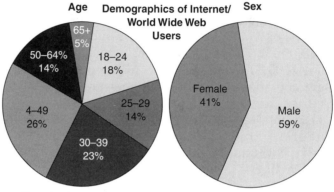

Look Who's on the Web

Demographics of Internet/World Wide Web Users

Age / Sex

Data: Louis Harris & Associates, Baruch College   © BW

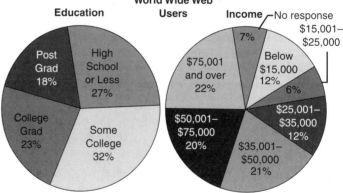

Demographics of Internet/World Wide Web Users

Education / Income

Data: Louis Harris & Associates, Baruch College   © BW

make a buck out of that kind of loyalty, maybe they should ask the experts: their members. For instance, when members of Tripod, a community for twentysomethings, started requesting space for personal home pages, CEO Bo Peabody asked them if it would be O.K. to place ads on

their pages to defray the cost. To his surprise, 96% said yes. Now, Peabody expects 1997 ad sales to top $3.5 million, or 70% of overall revenues.

A few more examples of that kind of economic democracy, and Netizens may feel as if they've found Home Sweet Internet.

Who's Doing What Online

Computer Users

Do you use a computer, or not?

Yes, use computer	43%
No, do not use computer	57%

Where They Go

Do you use your computer to

	Use	Do not use
Access an online service such as America Online or CompuServe	27%	73%
Access the Internet or World Wide Web	48%	52%

What They Do

Thinking about what you do online, how often do you use the Internet, World Wide Web, or an online service for:

	Often	Sometimes	Rarely	Never
Research	50%	32%	10%	8%
Education	37%	38%	15%	10%
Entertainment	31%	30%	16%	23%
News	30%	39%	14%	17%
Hobbies	18%	34%	17%	31%
Game-playing	14%	18%	18%	50%
Obtaining information about computers or software	13%	32%	31%	24%
Socializing	13%	12%	24%	51%
Investing	12%	16%	18%	54%
Shopping	1%	9%	26%	64%

Who 'Surfs'

When online, are you more likely to "surf" or do you visit the same group of sites regularly?

Surf	39%
Visit same sites	57%
Don't know/refused	4%

Who They Talk To

Do you use your computer to interact with other people via . . .

	Use	Do not use	Don't know
E-mail	89%	11%	0%
Chat groups	26%	74%	0%
Conferences or forums	20%	80%	0%
Listservs or E-mail lists	21%	75%	4%
MUDs/MOOs	5%	88%	7%

Where They Find Them

When you interact with others online, do you most prefer: E-mail, chat groups, conferences or forums, listservs, MUDs/MOOs, or something else?

E-mail	83%	MUDs/MOOs	0%
Chat Groups	9%	Interactive games	0%
Conferences or forums	3%	Other	2%
Listservs	3%		

Who's Doing What Online (*Continued*)

Expert Opinions

When you interact with others online, who do you prefer to interact with: subject experts, nonexperts who share your interests, people willing to chat about a broad range of topics, or someone else?

Subject Experts	27%	Someone else	36%
Nonexperts	15%	Don't know	3%
People w/broad range	19%		

To Chat Or Not To Chat

Do you prefer sites where you can interact with other people or do you prefer sites where you obtain information without interacting with other people?

Prefer interactive sites	18%	Don't know	5%
Prefer noninteractive sites	77%		

Community Feeling

If you interact via chat groups or listservs, do you think of yourself and others who participate in your listserv or chat group as members of an online community, or not?

Yes, part of community	57%
No, not part of community	43%

Social Or Professional?

What term best describes the community you participate most in?

The community is a social group	35%	None of above	2%
The community is a professional group	42%	Some of above	2%
The community is a hobby group	18%		

What They Talk About

When you interact with others online, how often do you choose interactions about:

	Often	Sometimes	Rarely	Never
Computers or software	14%	29%	23%	34%
Education	18%	42%	17%	23%
Entertainment	15%	30%	23%	32%
Game-playing	12%	12%	20%	56%
Hobbies	13%	36%	17%	34%
Investing	10%	12%	22%	56%
News	18%	35%	19%	28%
Research	26%	38%	17%	19%
Shopping	1%	7%	23%	69%
Socializing	18%	25%	22%	35%

Most Don't Buy

Have you ever used the Internet, World Wide Web, or online service to purchase anything, or not?

Have purchased	24%
Have not	76%

Ads Catch The Eye

Thinking of when you are on the Internet, World Wide Web, or online service, have you seen or noticed any advertising for products or services, or not?

Have seen ads	83%
Have not seen ads	17%

Survey of 1,003 adults, including 259 Internet/World Wide Web users, with a sampling error of +/–3%. Interviews were conducted April 11–16, 1997, for BUSINESS WEEK by Louis Harris & Associates Inc. and Baruch College of the City University of New York

Business Week/Harris Poll: A Census in Cyberspace

Edited by Keith H. Hammonds

Since the World Wide Web sprang into life on the Internet three years ago, it seems this is all we've heard about. Mostly, the talk has been about the future: how the Net will revolutionize communications, create a global electronic marketplace, and open up business opportunities. But before the Internet can fulfill its potential and make good on the hype, there needs to be a critical mass of Netizens—the "eyeballs" and wallets to attract the advertisers and commercial ventures that support the Net.

According to a new Baruch College-Harris Poll commissioned by BUSINESS WEEK, we're almost there. The poll, which surveyed 1,000 U.S. households, found that 21% of adults use the Internet, the World Wide Web, or both. That's 40 million people—half of all computer users and double the number of folks on the Web a year ago. An additional 12% of respondents use commercial online services, such as America Online or CompuServe.

The demographics are shifting, too. As more and more Americans find their way onto the Net, it's only natural that the cyberspace population is beginning to reflect the population back on terra firma. The gender gap, for one, is steadily closing. The Net population is now 41% female, up from 23% in September, 1995. And it's not all whippersnappers. Forty-five percent of those surfing the Net are 40 or older, with baby boomers—those in their 40s—making up the largest group of all Web surfers, at 26%. When looked at as a percentage of their age group, 30% of those 25 to 29 have access to the Net, compared with 25% of the 18-to-24 and 40-to-49 groups.

One area where the Net still trails the general population is race. The Internet remains a medium dominated by whites, who make up 85% of Internet and Web users, according to the Harris Poll. Blacks and Hispanics each account for 6% of Net users—up just slightly from a year ago.

Critical Mass

The Net population is also still skewed toward the affluent: 42% of Internet and Web users have household incomes of more than $50,000 a year, while only 18% take in $25,000 or less. But since the lower-income category probably includes many students, it may overstate Net participation by the country's poorest households.

The Net may be reaching critical mass—but what are the masses doing? In general, they're using it as a giant electronic library. The most common activity on the Net across all demographic groups is research: 82% of those who use the Net or an online service scour it for information, either sometimes or often. Education ranked second, with 75% of respondents saying that's why they head for the Net. News and entertainment are other big draws, with 68% and 61% of respondent respectively, citing those activities.

The least popular pastime? Online shopping. Only 1% of cybercitizens frequently shop online, while 9% do so sometimes. But the news for Web merchants is not all bad. Nearly one-quarter of online users have purchased something either on the Internet or an online service.

Playground

That's the broad brush, but on closer look, there are distinct differences in how people approach the Web. Age, more than education or income, seems to be the prime determinant of Internet behavior. From the poll results, a sometimes surprising picture emerges of how the young and the old spend their time in cyberspace.

Young people are more likely to use the Net for entertainment and socializing, while older folks spend most of their time on more serious matters. For example, 24% of 50-to-64-year-olds and 19% of those 65 and over say they use the Net often for investing purposes. That compares with just 6% of 18-to-24-year-olds and 3% of those 25 to 29. And a striking 92% of 40-to-49-year-olds use the Net for education. Older Net surfers also visit the same sites more regularly, while their younger counterparts appear to be more flighty: 47% of those 18 to 29 say they surf, compared with just 30% of those 50 and over.

Younger people tend to view the Web as a sprawling playground. Some 51% of 18-to-29-year-olds use the Net often for entertainment—two or three times as much as those 30 and up. Young people are also avid players of Internet games and participate more in chat groups and discussion forums. And for those who see the Internet's gaming sites full of adolescent males, here's a jolt: 21% of women surveyed said they play online games often, compared with 9% of men.

Rather than chasing Gen-Xers, Net merchants may want to aim their efforts at older folks. The typical online shopper is predictably affluent but surprisingly advanced in age. Although the sample size of online shoppers is low, the Harris survey suggests that senior citizens are most likely to buy online: 42% of those 65 and over have purchased something online. Those savvy seniors are followed closely by the 50-to-64-year-olds, 39% of whom have made an online purchase.

 Article Review Form at end of book.

Web Marketing Gets Personal

Personalization tools and the Web pave the way for one-to-one marketing.

Steve Alexander

Steve Alexander is a free-lance writer in Edina, Minn.

If the visions of today's one-to-one marketers come true, visiting your favorite Web site will be like going to Cheers, the bar where everyone knows your name. Rather than sifting through standard Web pages in total anonymity, the Web site will actually recognize your profile, the products you like, and your personal preferences. This means that IT strategists and Web marketers need to become familiar with the technology that will enable corporations to better target customers, experts say. But because of the immaturity of the market, the technology silver bullet in the one-to-one marketing world, as well as the rules of engagement concerning privacy, is still up in the air.

Although the paths to more sophisticated customer service may be many, the goals are clearer. In the era of one-to-one marketing, visiting Web sites promises to be a much more interactive experience.

You may be asked to rate products to establish what you'd like to buy, or you may be offered information about a product because previous Web page visitors with your tastes said they liked it. Banks may offer customers visiting their Web sites different financial products based on the amount of money in their bank accounts.

At other Web sites, a profile of you may be created based on the items you click on, whether they are text, advertising, or searches for information on the Web. For example, that Web site where you looked at cars is likely to remember that you liked sport utility vehicles. And every time you click on a new ad, the profile the Web page has of you will be adjusted slightly to fit your latest interests. The next time you visit, you'll be shown content, advertising, or products that fit that adjusted profile. And in the near future, personal information you choose to store on your hard drive may be automatically delivered to a Web site that wants to know more about you, such as your address or hobbies.

Because of the potential in improving customer relations, particularly online, analysts are predicting dramatic growth for one-to-one marketing. So far, the customer base consists of a handful of early adopters that include banks and Web pages devoted to marketing various products via the Internet. About one dozen vendors are serving up many different technological approaches, but Forrester Research, in Cambridge, Mass., says the market is still in its infancy and it is too early to know which technique will win out.

It's also too early to know whether the pending "open personalization standard"—which would allow customers to permit disclosure of certain personal information to Web sites via next-generation Web browsers—will be important in one-to-one marketing.

Another unanswered question is how much the issue of personal privacy will affect the use of one-to-one software, which in effect gathers information on individuals even though the information is intended to be used only to create anonymous categories of customers.

First Step: Profiling

Perhaps the biggest problem one-to-one software vendors face is the uphill battle to promote their concept. Today most Web site marketing isn't nearly that sophisticated. Forrester analysts say most Web marketers are still putting ads where users might be presumed to find them, such as placing banner ads for cars on Web sites devoted to car enthusiasts.

"Profiling is the next step, but precious few people are doing it yet," says Bill Doyle, senior analyst at Forrester.

"There are very few one-to-one marketing applications on Web sites today, maybe 30 or 40," says Neerav Berry, director of product management at Broad-Vision, a one-to-one software vendor in Los Altos, Calif. "But by a year from now we see that growing pretty rapidly to about 100."

Berry sees three main Web markets for one-to-one software: banks, retailers, and company intranets or extranets that could use the software for knowledge management in which different employees would see different Web content.

Forrester analysts see big growth as well. They predict that direct marketing will soon outweigh banner advertising as the best way to reach customers on the Web, and that by the year 2000 nearly 80 percent of Web advertising dollars will be spent on direct marketing. At the same time, total dollars spent on online advertising are expected to sky-rocket from less than $1 billion this year to more than $8 billion by 2002. All this is good news for one-to-one software vendors, and it could be equally good news for customers who factor the new technology into their marketing plans now.

Customer Retention

Although much of the discussion of one-to-one marketing revolves around tailored advertising pitches based on customer profiles, the real concern of marketers may be retaining customers.

"It's a lot easier to keep people as customers than it is to get them," Doyle says. "Smart direct marketers often acquire customers at a loss because they can make a lot from someone who is a lifetime customer. I think the huge opportunity for one-to-one software is in retention; as customers are tied ever more closely to a marketer, the marketer learns more about them and serves them more efficiently."

But some vendors see the software as nothing short of essential for serious marketing on the Web.

"There is so much choice on the Web that personalization will be the key differentiator for businesses," says Saul Klein, senior vice president of brand and strategy at Firefly Network, a one-to-one software vendor in Cambridge, Mass. "It's currently impossible for most companies to generate this kind of customer preference information. Credit card companies spend a fortune on data mining to get preference information from transactions. So a new Web technology that throws off this valuable data gives data miners great new information to work with."

Behind the Curtain

The two main technologies underlying one-to-one marketing on the Web are "rules-based matching," which creates user profiles based on user preferences and information requests, and "collaborative filtering," which sorts previously created profiles into "affinity groups" in the hopes of inferring what products a customer might be inclined to buy.

Edify, in Santa Clara, Calif., sells software that enables banks to show different Web pages—each offering different types of advice or financial services—to different types of customers. Each time a customer buys a bank service, the Web page information that person will see in the future is altered somewhat to fit the person's new profile.

William Soward, Edify's director of financial applications marketing, says banks are looking to one-to-one software for help because banks play an increasingly small role in the financial markets and hold 20 percent or less of the nation's assets.

"The more customized and personalized the Web banking experience is, the more likely a person is to come back to the bank's Web site," Soward says. "That means the bank is more likely to get more information about that person and use that data as the basis for selling additional products and services."

Busey Bank, in Champaign-Urbana, Ill., invests in one-to-one marketing software to keep its competitive edge. The bank relies on a simplified user profile that shows users different banner ads and informational Web pages based on data about the user's bank account balances and type of bank accounts, says Lisa Courtney, senior vice president.

"People with higher bank balances or certain types of accounts will see a banner that says, 'Saving for your future' or 'Make money work for you,'" Courtney says. "Clicking on that will take them to a part of the site where they will find financial planning calculators. For example, they can calculate how much they need to save for retirement. Then they can find out about our investment services, and how much interest they can earn on certain types of bank deposits."

Neural network technology can also be used to create user profiles based on the relationships of key words. Aptex Software, in San Diego, offers a variation on rules-based matching software for marketing or customer support applications.

"We look at current and recent user behavior—the content that people view or the content of what they type in an e-mail or a query on a web site," says John Gaffney, marketing vice president at Aptex. "We then use that information about their current interests or behavior to select the appropriate advertising, products, coupons, or frequently asked questions documents."

For example, if a visitor to a Web page sends an e-mail requesting product literature, the Aptex software reads the e-mail, understands the request and responds by sending the appropriate document. The software then updates that person's user profile based on the product literature request.

"Whenever that user communicates with me by e-mail, Internet chat, or Web page, I update the user's profile," Gaffney

says. "The next time a user visits that Web site, the new information in the profile will affect what advertising or other material will be delivered to that user."

Infoseek, a Sunnyvale, Calif., company that operates a Web search engine, uses Aptex's technology to deliver advertising campaigns to selected Web users based on individual user profiles. When created, a profile is stored in a Web browser cookie file and retrieved by the Aptex software each time the user visits the Infoseek Web site.

As a result, a Web page visitor who used Infoseek to search for topics such as "outdoors," "camping," "hiking," or "mountains," would automatically be shown an advertisement for a sport utility vehicle rather than an ad for a car, says Marv Su, senior director of advertising operations at Infoseek.

The technology helps Infoseek demonstrate to advertisers and advertising agencies the effectiveness of its advertising campaigns. After showing ads to users, Infoseek counts the number of users who respond to ads by clicking on them—something marketers call "click-through rates." Sites with higher-than-average click-through rates are more desirable to advertisers, Su says.

"By using real user behavior in our profiles, we certainly exceed industry standard click-through rates by at least 50 percent," Su says.

Rules-Based Matching

Firefly Network does both rules-based matching and collaborative filtering with different products. Klein says the two technological

approaches are complementary rather than competitive, as shown by the fact that both are used by one of Firefly's customers, bookseller Barnes and Noble's online marketing arm.

"Rules-based matching allows you to apply traditional business logic to targeting content or advertising or products at an individual," Klein says. "The rule might go like this: If a user is male and in the following age group and in the following zip codes, show him the following content. It allows you to take a fairly simple approach toward personalization based on profile information."

"Collaborative filtering uses that same profile information, finds other people who are like you based on your profile, and creates 'affinity groups,'" Klein adds.

Although the two technological approaches can be complementary, currently there appears to be more rules-based matching software packages in use on the Net. The important distinction seems to be that rules-based matching can be customized by nontechnical users while collaborative filtering takes a more automated, "black box" approach.

"Rules-based matching puts control in the hands of nontechnical business managers, and allows them to change the rules on the fly without changing the application logic or writing code," Berry explains. "Collaborative filtering is a black box engine running an algorithm, and you have no control over what it's doing."

BroadVision uses rules-based matching, but it also markets collaborative filtering software from another company, Net Perceptions, in Minneapolis.

"We definitely believe that both will exist, but I believe the rules-based market is much bigger," Berry says.

The open personalization standard (OPS), sometimes called the open profiling standard, has yet to be agreed upon by the industry. Under OPS, users could choose to store personal information, hobbies, and interests on their PC hard drives and then decide whether to disclose that information to a particular Web site.

Klein says that OPS will become widely used next year when new browsers from Microsoft and Netscape take advantage of it. He estimates that the total market for one-to-one software probably will be a little more than $250 million in 1998.

Privacy Minefield

However, privacy concerns could affect the rollout of one-to-one marketing based on OPS.

A recent study showed that consumers who go online "hate junk e-mail, steer away from data gathering sites, and worry about child exploitation. New technolo-

Stages of Personalization

One-to-one marketing hinges on personalizing the end-user experience. Web sites will become most compelling once a user profile is established and shared among several Web sites.

	Basic	Advanced	Compelling
User profile	Manual update	Manual, with some automatic update	Automatic, dynamic update
Richness of experience	Low	High	Extreme
Span	One site	Multiple sites in bounded communities	Universal

Source: Forrester Research

gies will not solve the problem." In a survey, Forrester analysts found that 80 percent of consumers believe the Internet needs policies or legislation to protect privacy.

One-to-one software vendors and users see no such privacy problems.

"Privacy is not an issue for us," says Aptex's Gaffney. "I don't want to know your name. I don't want to store an audit trail of the places you've been and the things you've said. But, if the customer wants to disclose additional information to a Web site, the marketer can do a better job of personalizing."

"The key concept of Firefly is informed consent," Klein adds.

"A user only gives up profile information when a business is clear what it will be doing with that information."

Although the one-to-one software market encompasses several approaches, not all of today's dozen or so players will survive, Doyle predicts. "Some approaches will dominate and others will fold. But it's so early in the game, and so few marketers are really capable of using these tools to their full extent, that the winners can't be identified."

 Article Review Form at end of book.

Segmenting the Internet

Thomas E. Miller

To hear the press tell it, youth dominates the Internet. Hip publications like Wired magazine and popular columns like Newsweek's "Cyberscope" project a cyber-youth image rife with rebellion and iconoclasm. One might conclude that no one over age 30 ever goes online.

Not so. Although twenty-somethings are more likely than average to use the Net, those aged 18 to 29 represent only 31 percent of the total adult audience in the U.S., according to Find/SVP's recent American Internet User Survey. Baby boomers in their 30s and 40s are nearly as likely as younger adults to use the Internet, and they make up 53 percent of the estimated 8.4 million adult users. Those aged 50 and older account for 35 percent of all adults, but just 13 percent of Internet users. An additional 1.1 million Internet users are under age 18, based on parents' responses.

Although the Internet reaches a tiny portion of the population today, its reach is growing rapidly. The number of adult users of the World Wide Web tripled from 2.2 million in 1994 to 6.6 million in 1995, confirming press reports of exponential growth. Moreover, between July 1995 and January 1996, the number of commercial host computers (.com) grew from 1.7 million to 2.4 million.

The Internet signifies different things to different people. Those who "surf" view the Internet as an end in itself and a valid use of time, while those who are seeking specific information often find it a frustrating time-waster. Understanding how various groups navigate the Net and how their behavior may change in the future is crucial for those who hope to use the network as a delivery medium for products, information, or services.

Many businesses can usefully segment their customers by education or income, two of the strongest predictors of consumer behavior and spending. However, the Internet is still in its infancy. Most of its current users are early adopters, people with high levels of education and income who are likely to try new technology before it becomes mainstream. This means that education and income are not always useful ways to segment this particular market, at least not yet.

Other ways to classify Internet users include the manner in which they use the network—for business, personal, or academic purposes—and their level of experience. The latter approach clearly differentiates various types of behaviors, but can be tricky to measure. Someone who has used the Internet for more than a year might be an occasional and relatively inexperienced user, while a recent enthusiast might have both logged more hours and gained a greater understanding of the Net's intricacies.

As it turns out, most users tap the Internet for more than one purpose. Sixty percent of adult respondents to the American Internet User Survey say they employ the Internet for both business and personal activities. Of users who report that more than half their Internet activities are "personal," 30 percent tap the Internet at work, including 8 percent who use it exclusively from their workplace. Similarly, 16 percent of such personal users go online at academic locations, including 7 percent who do so exclusively. Alternatively, over half of all adult users who say their usage is predominantly for business indicate they go online from home, including 19 percent of business users who go online exclusively from home.

One way to divide Internet users into mutually exclusive and easily identifiable groups is by age. The stage of life at which people are introduced to the Internet has a lot to do with what they want and need from it. For example, young adults are likely to have begun using the Net as students, while many older users first encountered it at work. These differences, along with the reality of people's lifecycles, dictate age differences in Internet use.

Younger users communicate more online and are nearly three times as likely as older users to have published their own personal Web sites. Half of under-30 users and 44 percent of 30-to-49-year-olds use e-mail daily. Younger users are also most likely to visit Usenet newsgroups, the closest equivalent to chat rooms on the Internet. Of younger Webheads who also use commercial online services, 36 percent spend the majority of their online time with e-mail and chat.

Clearly, younger users exhibit a heightened proclivity to socialize online. Those aged 30 to 49 communicate less frequently online. Nearly half of boomers who use e-mail say that most of it is for work, versus 25 percent of those under age 30. Those aged 50 and older are about as likely as young adults to use e-mail on a daily basis, at 49 percent, but they are more like boomers in their emphasis on work-related usage. Mature users are less likely than

boomers and Generation Xers to visit newsgroups, but those who do are frequent users, nearly matching those under age 30 in hours logged. Overall, mature Internet users resemble young adults more than middle-aged users in their preferences for communicating and socializing online.

Differences in how people of different ages view their time partly explain the use patterns. Younger users have more discretionary time than those in their 30s and 40s, according to focus groups conducted as part of the Find/SVP study, and they are more likely to put a priority on socializing. Those aged 50 and older also have more free time than the middle-aged and a greater interest in meeting people online, especially if they are singles or empty nesters. Meanwhile, Internet users in their busy midlife years, nearly two-thirds of whom have children, typically complain about lack of free time. Chatting online is not what they want to do, although they will participate in special-interest groups that can help their careers or address family-related information needs.

Younger users do not identify as strongly with the idea of actively seeking out information. They browse more Web sites than older people, but they are less likely to describe what they do as "searching for information." They tend to see their Internet activity as experiential rather than as simply a means to retrieve information. Not only do younger users typically have fewer household and family demands than older users, they have more freedom to turn their online time into a personal lifestyle experience.

People aged 30 to 49 typically report peak usage relative to

other ages of many categories of online information content, ranging from special-interest groups information to education and training, health and medicine, investment information, and customer services. Boomers and Xers are equally likely to report that they use the Internet to learn about news and hobbies, download software, and retrieve product information, but boomers are twice as numerous.

Those under age 30 are significantly more likely than average to make use of one information category—music and entertainment. They are also more likely than older users to download photos, video clips, and music clips. Surprisingly, younger users are also most likely to access bank-account balances online, although only 14 percent do so, and they typically use specialized online services rather than the Internet proper.

Users aged 50 and older do not lead usage in any single category of information retrieval, but they score well in use of online news, special-interest groups, product information, and health and medical information. Older users are less likely than average to tap most types of investment information online, not because they don't need it, but evidently because they have already established other ways of acquiring such information.

Online shopping peaks among the middle-aged. Among current online shoppers, nearly 60 percent are aged 30 to 49. Young adults have less money, and are less likely to shop online, although they lead in CD purchases and also score well on hardware and software purchases. Baby boomers are more likely to book travel reservations and buy food via the Internet.

Over-50 Net users are most likely to buy software and books, as well as some travel-related packages.

People tend to see the future of the Internet largely through the same color glasses they wear today. However, their actual future use will undoubtedly shift as their lifestyles change. True to their current patterns of use, middle-aged users are most likely to say that the Internet is a great medium for information retrieval. As boomers age, it seems likely that they will retain an interest in the Internet as an informational resource. As they move beyond their working years, however, they will increasingly use the Internet as a research tool for leisure and social pursuits, as well as for health-care information.

Advertisers and marketers will probably grow their business among mature Internet users as boomers age, but they should continue to focus their efforts on the middle-aged. When dual-income Generation X couples reach their late 40s with two teenagers at home, they'll be glad to take advantage of Internet grocery shopping services.

For vendors intent upon converting the Net to an entertainment medium, the prime target today and in the future is likely to be younger adults with free time on their hands. Parents will be a solid secondary market. Midlife users today who express interest in entertainment options may be thinking of their children

rather than themselves. Focus-group participants in their 30s and 40s express substantial interest in tapping into online "edutainment" activities for their kids.

Despite the large number of college students present in the under-30 Internet audience, this is not the segment to target for education-related services. People are more likely to value online services to maintain and retool work-related knowledge and skills, and such interest rises steadily with age. Those who provide continuing-education services and target working-age Americans probably have the brightest future on the Internet.

Today's young adults will continue to view the Internet as a social and communications medium as they get older, but as they reach their time-pressed middle years early in the next century, the Net's informational value will probably supersede its entertainment value. At the same time, today's children may use the Internet as a research tool long before they hit middle age, since their parents are already emphasizing its educational virtues. They will also enjoy the company of "Web-pals" via the Net.

Even so, just 2 percent of American children under age 18 use the Internet today. These privileged youngsters may be bridging national and cultural barriers by joining a global online community. But they also run the risk of increasing the distance between themselves and their more

numerous peers who currently have no access to the information highway. One avenue to expanding the reach of the Net in the U.S. is through public schools. Another possible route for bringing the Internet to the masses is currently a topic of feverish debate in Silicon Valley—the introduction of low-cost, low-end access devices to link the Internet to those without computers or computer skills. It's not clear that the Net will ever become as ubiquitous as color TV. But it is clear that its ultimate success will be only as broad as the diversity of people who use it.

Behind the Numbers Find/SVP's Emerging Technologies Research Group conducted the American Internet User Survey in November and December 1995 as part of an ongoing effort to measure consumer interest and use of interactive services. To qualify, respondents had to be aged 18 or older and cite at least one Internet application other than e-mail that they personally use. They could access the Internet by any means, including commercial online services such as America Online or CompuServe, and from any location including workplace, school, and home. In-depth telephone interviews were conducted with 1,000 qualified Internet users. For more information, call (607) 275-9590.

 **Article Review Form at end of book.**

Competitive Shopping

Cyberauctions are turning the Web into a vast Oriental bazaar, complete with haggling and excitedly competitive bidding.

Julie Pitta

"Not so fast, TR, you overweight lardo." That not very polite message appeared recently on OnSale, an Internet Web site that auctions everything from computer gear to Omaha steaks. Why the flame mail? TR had outbid Madog in a pitched battle over an exercise contraption, one of many being auctioned off that week, and the loser was letting off steam.

On-line auctions make blue-light specials at Kmart look downright civilized. Sotheby's it ain't. Civility takes a back seat to acquisitiveness as Net-surfers wrangle over everything from personal computers to livestock, using a mouse for a paddle.

"People are bidding on nose-hair trimmers," says a bewildered Kirk Loevner, president and chief executive of Internet Shopping Network. "It's just bizarre."

Online auctioning is hot. There are flea-market auctions of individual items, and auction-style mass marketing of baubles like Ginzu knives and exercise machines. This isn't just shopping. It's competitive shopping, and Web users are a competitive bunch.

Loevner's Internet Shopping Network is a wholly owned subsidiary of the Home Shopping Network, run by former movie mogul Barry Diller, who is also the network's majority shareholder. It falls into the Ginzu knives category. The operation recently ran a half-hour auction that persuaded 100 on-line buyers to part with between $20 and $28 apiece for knife sets. That pales in comparison with the thousands of gizmos that the Home Shopping Network can sell in a half-hour of televised excitement, but it's not bad for electronic commerce.

"I don't know that anyone can predict how this is going to evolve," Diller says. "But I wouldn't have said that we could go from a standing start six months ago to where we are now." Internet Shopping Network is auctioning $1.5 million worth of merchandise a month, a figure that Diller expects to double within a year.

For all the promise of E-commerce, few consumers have rushed to the Net to do their shopping. Most of the $12 billion in Internet sales rung up last year were by businesses buying from each other.

Earlier Net retailing schemes, like on-line catalogs and malls, made the mistake of replicating in cyberspace a physical-world experience, with poor results. Electronic catalogs offered no more convenience than their print counterparts. Internet malls, while more convenient than suburban shopping centers, lacked their variety.

But unlike these nascent formats, on-line auctions are entertaining. They get the juices flowing. They breed excitement from competition.

Check out Ebay, the San Jose, Calif. auction site that is the on-line equivalent of the neighborhood flea market, selling everything from vintage jewelry and pottery to antiques of questionable value. Recently Ebay auctioned off a carved wooden cane purportedly of Civil War vintage, for $38.50. For its middleman role

Just a Sampling of Web Sites Hosting Auctions. Web Users Are Flocking to Internet Auctions, to Wrangle Over Everything from Ginzu Knives to Livestock.

What's Available	
ebay.com	Antiques and collectibles like vintage jewelry, pottery and beanie babies.
firstauction.com	New stuff: computers, consumer electronics, costume jewelry and more.
onsale.com	Computers, consumer electronics and sporting goods.
philatelists.com	Old and rare stamps.
usaweb.com	A listing of over 1,000 Internet auctions.

Ebay collects a fee of up to $2 plus 5% of the final price. The rest of the money goes to the owners of the goods. Ebay does several thousand transactions a day.

In a way, the cyberage retailing is a harking back to the haggling that used to characterize all sales in local dry-goods stores and farmers' markets. Fixed retail prices date only to 1872, when Aaron Montgomery Ward got into the mail-order business.

Nowadays, a national retail chain doesn't haggle, because the process is too labor-intensive. But the Internet may change the economics of haggling. The Internet drops the cost per transaction, so it becomes practical to auction an item for dollars rather than thousands of dollars and still make money. A mass merchandiser like Internet Shopping Network, for example, can program its computers to accept the 3,000 best bids higher than $2.10 for 3,000 pieces of costume jewelry.

There are other attractions to Internet auction shopping. The Net's global reach can make the variety of merchandise appear seemingly limitless. Collect stamps? Philatelists Online has a collection that would take years of prowling stamp shops to find. Looking for a used computer? OnSale auctions off refurbished computer gear usually sold by liquidators to businesses, but rarely available to consumers.

"People are bidding on nose-hair trimmers."

Here's how cyberauctions work at outfits like Ebay. After filling out a brief form you become a registered member of the auction. Click onto an intriguing listing to view a description and, in most cases, a scanned photograph of the item. Also listed will be the highest previous bid; some auctions will also list a bidding history, which includes the number of bids, the amounts and the cybernames of the bidders.

Compared with walking into a Montgomery Ward store, it's something of a Wild West out there. What's to protect the seller from a bad check—or a buyer from a crook? While Internet Shopping Network acts like a store, taking title to the merchandise it auctions, outfits like Ebay don't. At an Ebay-style auction you mail off a check to the individual who is selling—and pray that you don't get stiffed. In most cases, buyers pay the freight, too.

But the medium is evolving some means of keeping players honest. At Ebay, clicking onto a seller's or bidder's name links you to comments from others regarding previous business dealings with the buyer or seller in question. Ebay posts a star next to sellers with a particularly good reputation. Those who amass too many complaints are banned.

It's still a bit like an Oriental bazaar—but that, after all, is the oldest form of marketing.

 Article Review Form at end of book.

WiseGuide Wrap-Up

The qualities of the Internet make reaching and targeting smaller groups or individuals easier while reaching mass audiences remains tougher. Segmenting the markets on the Internet will still be highly relevant but quite different from the practice in conventional markets. The variables used for this purpose need to be modified or developed for online users. Will traffic at a site be as important as the buying power of the visitors? This depends on the marketing strategy of each company and the way it deploys the Internet as part of its overall marketing strategy.

R.E.A.L. Sites

This list provides a print preview of typical **coursewise** R.E.A.L. sites. There are over 100 such sites at the **courselinks**™ site. The danger in printing URLs is that web sites can change overnight. As we went to press, these sites were functional using the URLs provided. If you come across one that isn't, please let us know via email to: webmaster@coursewise.com. Use your Passport to access the most current list of R.E.A.L. sites at the **courselinks**™ site.

Site name: ACNielsen

URL: http://www.acnielsen.com/

Why is it R.E.A.L.? Searching this site for "Internet consumer behavior" reveals related information.

Key topics: Online markets, online consumer, buying behavior, brand loyalty, panel data, online shopping, spending patterns

Site name: Traffic

URL: http://newsweek-int.com/archive/netpro/net_prop2.archive.html

Why is it R.E.A.L.? Audience measurement efforts on the Internet.

Key topics: Terminology of Internet audience measurement, hits, views, Web audit, need to understand visitors

section

4

Learning Objectives

This section contains the bulk of the readings pertaining to many aspects of marketing. Depending on one's interests, they can be read in any order, as long as the related ones are kept together. As you read the articles in this section, try to get outside the box of marketing and start asking "why not" instead of "why." Marketers might have struggled to learn to use television as they tried to apply what they knew about radio. In time, they developed an enormously potent marketing tool in television. Now, as we experience a major change in marketing, the best stand we can take is one of flexibility.

After critically evaluating the messages in these articles, you should

- Develop a sound understanding of the need for a paradigm shift in marketing.

- Learn the current uses of marketing on the Internet.

- Be able to put together a marketing plan that integrates the Internet into a total marketing strategy.

- Develop and deploy a marketing Web site for a selected organization.

The New Face of Marketing

Companies engage in marketing to facilitate exchanges that will satisfy consumer needs and will bring the organization closer to its goals. Marketing must not be confused with selling, advertising, or retailing, for they constitute only a part of it. In developing marketing strategies or managing daily marketing activities, decision makers try to gain a sustainable advantage and maintain that advantageous position over their competitors.

Marketing has gone through several evolutionary stages and has entered a new one with the advent of the Internet. Currently, the changes in marketing are subtle and small as marketers try to understand the new tool at their disposal. As new technologies emerged in the past, they brought with them major social changes, and the Internet will do the same in the years to come. The automobile gave us the shopping malls and suburbs, and telephone changed the way we communicate and even shop for goods and services. As the Internet matures and the bandwidth increases, it, too, will bring social change and, consequently, changes in marketing.

Even while we wait for the technology to mature and some barriers to e-commerce to disappear, the Internet has already made its presence known to marketers. Only a short while ago, in the early 1990s, the mere mention of marketing on the Internet would have been enough to make many users start fuming and flaming brash marketers or advertisers on the Net. The Net was not yet a commercial environment for the benefit of marketers. In less than five years, marketing has become alive and is now doing well on the Internet. Today, users can access information from the Web sites of many organizations from AAA to ZUZU, marketing a large variety of goods and services.

As marketing tries to create the four basic utilities of form, time, place, and possession, the Internet can supplement marketing strategies in several ways. The first and the most obvious way is in communicating with existing and potential customers. Marketing communication contributes to the creation of all the utilities, depending on how it is used. Advertising on the Internet has been increasing despite the many unknowns about it. E-mail is riding on a fine line between spam and legitimate advertising. Corporate sites try to communicate with the visitors to build corporate or product image. In all these communication efforts, the Internet has proven to be an adept tool that will solidify its position as its technology matures. This section contains articles dealing with these issues from different perspectives.

As the earlier sections mentioned, the Internet has unique communication capabilities that marketers can use. For successful use of the Internet for this purpose, marketers must understand the nature of its communication capabilities.

- It is a demand-driven process, in which the receiver initiates the process.
- It is asynchronous communication.
- It allows both sides to send information.
- The protocol, or "netiquette," of communication is significantly different from that of other modes of communication.
- Both sides value information.

The second popular way of using the Internet for marketing purposes is in selling by offering wares online, where consumers can shop from the comfort of their rooms. As Nick Wreden indicates in his article "Web Wares" later in this section, online shopping is expected to reach $6.6 billion in 2000. This represents a very significant increase from an estimated $518 million in 1996. A recent *Time* magazine article projects a six-fold increase in the number of users from 1997 to 2002, while the projected revenues from online shopping is estimated to have a twenty-fold increase in the same period.[1] Both numbers represent extraordinary developments. More people will use the Internet to buy more things and will spend more money doing it.

The current use of the Internet for selling purposes, which creates time, place, and possession utilities, mimics direct marketing by offering electronic catalogs from which the customers can choose and buy items. For most of the products sold this way, the rest of the transaction is very similar to placing an order via mail or telephone. It involves using a credit card for the payment and delivery of the products in the mail. Some products are sold in new ways that also cover the delivery, or the logistics, on the Internet. This form of selling will also create form utility directly on or through the Internet. Software and other pure information products, such as news and online entertainment, lend themselves to this kind of selling. After giving the necessary payment information, the consumer is allowed to "download" the purchased software in a given time period. Companies also sell financial transactions, specialized information services, and online entertainment in similar ways on the Internet.

The Internet can also be used to provide customer support, which is mostly a matter of information transfer from the support person to the user. Because of the nature of the process, customer service is one of the important uses of the Internet for marketers. Since customer satisfaction and support enhances the level of satisfaction, it can significantly contribute to the creation of possession utility. Using new technologies, companies can and do offer customer service and support on the Web and via e-mail. As the enabling technology in artificial intelligence improves, more and higher quality customer service may arrive on the Internet.

[1]Michael Krantz, "Click Till You Drop," *Time*, July 20, 1998, p. 40.

Questions

1. Although there are similarities between selling on the Internet and catalog or direct marketing, there are also significant differences between them. What are the major differences between these seemingly similar marketing models? What are the advantages, disadvantages, and challenges of each?

2. What are "information-rich" products? Find several examples that have not been mentioned in the section introduction and locate Web sites that market them. Are the marketers taking advantage of the strengths of the Internet in marketing these products?

3. How can products be placed in "information envelopes," thus creating "information-enriched" products? Think of several products and how they can benefit from this kind of treatment.

4. What products are deliverable on the Internet? What products will be deliverable in the same fashion in the future? Is there a need for enabling technologies to make this possible?

5. Media buying on radio and television is strongly influenced by media measurements by companies such as A.C. Nielsen and Arbitron. Are there companies offering similar services on the Internet? What do they measure? Should they use a different measurement method and measure different variables? Which ones?

6. As globalization of markets increases, strong brands will become more important. Try to argue for and against this point. Which side would you like to be on? Why?

Ten Commandments for Success on the Net

Larry Keeley

Larry Keeley lkeeley@doblin.com is president of Chicago-based Doblin Group, a leading design-strategy firm, and an adjunct professor at the Illinois Institute of Technology's Institute of Design.

A friend of mine from Microsoft recently explained how the world's most powerful software company had missed the biggest transformation in computing since the PC. His colleagues were thinking like rational engineers, he said. They assumed computer users would prefer the faster response, better sound, and crisper graphics of CD-ROM over the barely controlled chaos of the Internet. The company, he vowed, would not make the same mistake twice. Or would it? Today nearly 1,400 software engineers are expected to report each week on how they're helping Microsoft win on the Net—about the most un-Net-like approach imaginable. When another friend, this one a Microsoft rival, heard about the plan he breathed a sign of relief: "Thank goodness it's 1,400 engineers. If it were just 20 we'd be in trouble."

Welcome to the mind-bending logic of business on the Net.

The Internet is the most dramatic economic phenomenon of the decade, but many other Nets touch our lives. When I discuss "the Net" I mean any reasonably large, decentralized, interdependent system that affects how people work and live. That definition includes telephone networks; trading systems for stocks, bonds, and commodities; fax systems; travel networks. Nets don't just affect the fortunes of individual companies; they also overturn many cherished assumptions about how to compete, innovate, and manage.

In short, Nets change the guiding logic of business. Here are ten principles that explain the new logic.

1. Nets route around greed.

Forget Gordon Gekko. Nets detect and subvert excess at every turn. In theory, all markets work this way; companies that overreach or underperform create openings for new entrants. But "free markets" have never been all that free. Big companies deployed an arsenal of weapons—distribution clout, saturation advertising—to create entry barriers and limit competition. Nets obliterate those barriers.

Here too Microsoft is a case in point. Within months, its attempt to create a proprietary online service, the Microsoft Network (MSN), went from a feared juggernaut to a strategic failure. Why the retreat? Because the me-first logic of operating systems doesn't conform to the logic of the Net. Now Microsoft is scrambling to "open" MSN by forging alliances with America Online, Sun Microsystems, and other partners.

2. Generosity begets prosperity.

More than 70 years ago, Gillette turned marketing upside down when it gave away razors to sell more Blue Blades. The Gillette model has become standard operating procedure on the Net.

Netscape is the most famous example of strategic generosity. By allowing users to download its Navigator software for free, Netscape created a new technical standard. And because it established a standard, Netscape was able to sell so much server software and related products that it became the fastest-growing software startup in history.

3. **Open systems win over time.**

Nets punish ruthlessly any attempt to control how they want to evolve—a lesson Apple has learned all too painfully. Companies that follow Apple's proprietary model are doomed to suffer the same consequences. The smarter course is to embrace emerging standards and innovate within them.

Consider the market for notebook computers. The leading products are all perfectly compatible with one another and with the broader environment in which they operate. Yet each offers distinct benefits and features. Compaq's notebooks are light, rugged, and fast; Toshiba's have best-in-class displays; Dell has unsurpassed direct marketing and delivers its products overnight; IBM's notebooks have internal bays for many different modular subsystems.

Nets reward this approach to competition.

4. **You can't predict the future.**

The history of Nets is one of surprise innovations from unseen directions. That's because Nets respond to new ideas at blazing speed. It's simply not possible to predict in advance the "killer app" for a new technology or the next big use of an existing technology.

Think about the multibillion-dollar market for pagers. No market research could have predicted all the exotic new uses for pagers: investment management, news distribution, sports information, whale-migration tracking. "Researching" your way to success virtually guarantees failure. The right approach is to design products for rapid adaptation and to observe carefully as new uses emerge.

5. **More is different.**

There are no stand-alone products on the Net—and that changes the nature of products themselves. As more devices interconnect and depend on one another, they develop interactions that no one can anticipate—and that become the basis for entirely new applications.

The lowly telephone is a classic example. One telephone is an invention. Two telephones enable a conversation. Millions of telephones become the basis for a vast array of services that revolutionize how people communicate. So it is with all Nets: more of something inevitably turns it into something different.

6. **There's safety in speed.**

Nets obey the laws of increasing returns: as more people sample and select a product, they generate interest, excitement, and an installed base that attracts still more people—unleashing positive-feedback loops that increase momentum. And when products for the Net get distributed over the Net, these feedback loops operate with remarkable speed. Think of it as the "whoosh effect."

The whoosh effect explains how Netscape's engineers could begin writing code in April 1994, introduce their first product in December, and hold a 75% market share by April 1995. Distributing the Web browser didn't require Netscape to hire a fleet of trucks, conduct long negotiations over retail shelf space, design elaborate ad campaigns. Netscape posted its software on the Web and allowed users to click and download; the whoosh effect was under way.

Warning: The "best" products don't automatically achieve the greatest momentum. Companies like Netscape understand that the whoosh effect is 25% engineering and 75% imagineering—using the Net to dramatize, promote, and popularize innovations.

7. **Win-win beats win-lose.**

Too many companies associate winning with control—using an innovation to acquire a dominant position in technology, distribution, or cost. On the Net, companies seldom win unless they find ways to help others share in the wealth their innovations create.

The "value chain" is giving way to value webs— market structures in which customers have multiple pathways to the products or services they need. Value webs explain why the Net spawns so many alliances between rivals and joint ventures between companies in different industries. More than ever, winning big requires giving up a piece of the action.

8. **Familiarity overcomes inertia.**

People everywhere are prone to inertia: they do what is familiar even in the face of superior alternatives. And familiarity comes in various forms. Interface familiarity is what allows us to rent cars we've never driven before without having to learn new ways to steer or accelerate; cars are designed to maximize familiarity. Behavioral familiarity helps people accept new products because they resemble old products. Much of Intuit's success with Quicken can be explained by the fact that the software makes electronic bill-paying feel similar, visually and procedurally, to writing checks.

What works for cars and Quicken works across Nets: breakthrough innovations must evoke a sense of the familiar if they are to successfully overcome inertia.

9. **There is no central control of anything.**

Fish swim in schools without any single fish being in charge. Monarch butterflies don't need a Monday morning staff meeting to decide when to migrate south. Birds flock without voting on their destination.

Nets operate more like nature than man-made assembly lines. Indeed, the defining companies of the Net era—Netscape, Sun, Yahoo!— apply the power of distributed intelligence to how they function. They are obsessed with meeting performance goals and winning—but they are also thoroughly decentralized. They're organized around small teams that work when they want, how they want, and (often) where they want. On the Net, even the most hard-charging leaders don't fool themselves into believing that they are "in charge."

10. **No one is as smart as everyone.**

Nets enable greater participation among larger and larger groups of people. That's why millions of people are getting into the habit of visiting the World Wide Web every day. The Web changes like a newspaper, but the changes are co-constructed by the users. No one is in charge and almost anyone can find something of value. That's why intranets (knowledge-sharing systems designed for use within companies) have become the fastest growing market for Web servers and software.

In short, Nets allow individuals to shape and share information and ideas more quickly than ever before—a principle that winning organizations embrace rather than resist.

 Article Review Form at end of book.

Let Your Modem Do the Walking

Will the Internet revolutionize shopping? Look, it already has.

Thomas Easton

Investment banker Robert Broadwater, 39, spends his days shopping companies. He spends his evenings shopping for expensive or hard-to-find goods on the Web. His successes to date suggest how the Web will change retailing.

For this die-hard comparison shopper, the Internet does little more than speed up the old-fashioned game of calling several stores for price quotes. But that's no mean advantage, since it's a lot easier to cruise from Web site to Web site than to dial a half-dozen stores trying to get the right person to give the information you want. Broadwater's shopping list began to grow soon after he bought a five-bedroom Bronxville, N.Y. home in need of updating. He wanted the best of everything for it; for example, a Viking VGRC605 range, the last word in kitchen chic, with six burners, two ovens, a griddle, a grill and a ventilation hood.

A *Forbes* reporter volunteered to help Broadwater the old-fashioned way—telephone shopping, calling a half-dozen Manhattan retailers listed in the Yellow Pages that Broadwater could reasonably be expected to reach from his office. Several retailers made us feel like dirt for even mentioning price over the phone for such a luxury item as the range, suggesting in so many words that if you have to ask the price, you can't afford it. We persevered and reached an outlet disdainfully described by one of the information nonproviders as a no-service discounter. There we got a price quote of $9,600.

Then Broadwater did a Web search. He first tapped into the Web site maintained by Viking Range Corp. and got every distributor in the country. Clicking on the New York section of the site's U.S. map, he found all the regional distributors, some outside the range of his local phone book. One was willing to deliver the stove to Bronxville for $8,600. Done.

Happy with his buy, Broadwater bought from the same distant retailer a Miele GH7OSC dishwasher ($1,300) and a KitchenAid clothes dryer ($475).

The April snowstorm strewed tree branches all over Broadwater's lawn. He wanted an ax. At the Home Depot in New Rochelle, N.Y., he found good prices but an unsatisfying selection.

Back at his computer, Broadwater typed in "ax" and came up with numerous choices. Recalling the name of a tool he'd seen decades before, he ended up at the colorful Web catalog of Snow & Nealley, in Bangor, Me., where the 133-year-old firm still forges every one of its hand tools. Broadwater liked the photo of a 3 1/2-pound woodsman's ax. He followed up with a phone call, and with his credit card paid $37 plus $6 for UPS delivery.

Note that this isn't a radically new kind of retailing. There was no involvement with any intelligent agent—the sort of Web shopping assistant offered by Netbot, the software firm just acquired by Web search service Excite, Inc. Nor was there any E-cash, which is supposed to revolutionize Web commerce someday. Nor any interactivity—Snow & Nealley doesn't take orders over the Internet.

> **Why use a middleman? I need a product, not a salesperson.**

One Do-It-Yourselfer Created This Custom Department Store. Get a Search Engine and Create Your Own.

Web Source	Address	Comment
Colormagic Paint & Wallpaper	gemini.tntech.edu/~bab0898/color.html	Unusually helpful outlet from Cookeville, Tenn.
Faucet Outlet	www.faucet.com	Where to go for the kitchen sink
Home Depot	www.homedepot.com	Map to the depot, not for the depot
CarPoint	carpoint.msn.com	Microsoft's database on car prices
Porter-Cable	www.porter-cable.com	Everything you want to know about sanders— and where to get them
Snow & Nealley	www.sntools.com	Froes, weeders, trowels, broadaxes and bark spuds—all handmade
Toyota	www.toyota.com	Hub site for Toyota dealers
Toyota dealer	www.toyotadealer.com/fox-toyota	Where our man found the best deal
Viking	www.viking-range.com	Home for the range

All the Internet did here was put a customer in touch with a firm that hasn't had much success getting in touch with customers directly. But that was plenty.

Snow & Nealley's boss, David Nealley (a great-great grandson of a founder), says the business barely survived into the 1990s and started the Web site as a minor component of a promotional effort to the trade. To Nealley's amazement, orders like Broadwater's have been streaming in.

Time to find a car for Broadwater's new driveway. Before touching his keypad, Broadwater knew exactly what he wanted: a Toyota 4-Runner SR5, 4-wheel drive, in "stellar blue" or "radiant red," with a V-6, manual transmission and a particular option package.

At Microsoft's CarPoint service, he paid $4.24 with his credit card on-line for data on sticker prices for the car and the options, then went to Toyota's Web page, got the addresses of 100-plus dealers coast to coast and mass-mailed an E-note to each, conducting in essence an on-line auction. Consumer spam, you could call it. Time elapsed: two hours. The best price he got back, $30,300, came from an East Providence, R.I. dealership. Broadwater flew up one morning, drove back in the afternoon and saved $5,000 off the price quoted over the phone by a local dealer.

Broadwater considered using Auto-By-Tel, but why use an intermediary if you don't have to? He preferred skipping the middleman and getting a broader range of potential bidders without another tier of costs. Same story for CUC, the big on-line retailer that will merge with HFS this fall.

Next came sinks from up-state New York, an unusual floor sealant from New Jersey and Michael Graves wall sconces from yet another store he could never hope to visit from his office in Manhattan. Each time the winner either offered an unusual product or service or prevailed in a mini-auction conducted from Broadwater's desk.

"The key is a branded product," he explains. "I know Porter Paint, I know Toyota, I know the meaning of a comprehensive warranty. I don't need a salesperson standing across the counter to give me reasons to buy."

Sometimes Broadwater gets nothing out of his Web searches except a reassurance that the local store price is a good one. That was the case for three Porter-Cable electric sanders he bought to refinish the baby's bedroom closet. After wading through some leads he got by using Digital's AltaVista searcher, he ended up at the power tool corral at Home Depot.

The future? Dammit, the future's here. Right now.

 **Article Review Form at end of book.**

The Future of Marketing

Internet marketing pioneer Seth Godin says he wants to "change the way almost everything is marketed to almost everybody." Will you give him permission to come in and show you the future?

William C. Taylor

William C. Taylor wtaylor@fastcompany.com is a founding editor of Fast Company. Contact Seth Godin by email sethg@yoyo.com or visit Yoyodyne on the Web http://www.yoyobiz.com

Seth Godin's company, Yoyodyne Entertainment, is all about fun and games. But its mission is serious business. Godin and his colleagues are working to persuade some of the most powerful companies in the world to reinvent how they relate to their customers. His argument is as stark as it is radical: Advertising just doesn't work as well as it used to—in part because there's so much of it, in part because people have learned to ignore it, in part because the rise of the Net means that companies can go beyond it. "We are entering an era," Godin declares, "that's going to change the way almost everything is marketed to almost everybody."

The biggest problem with mass-market advertising, Godin says, is that it fights for people's attention by interrupting them. A 30-second spot interrupts a "Seinfeld" episode. A telemarketing call interrupts a family dinner. A print ad interrupts this article. "The interruption model is extremely effective when there's not an overflow of interruptions," Godin says. "But there's too much going on in our lives for us to enjoy being interrupted anymore." The new model, he argues, is built around permission. The challenge for marketers is to persuade consumers to volunteer attention—to "raise their hands" (one of Godin's favorite phrases)—to agree to learn more about a company and its products. "Permission marketing turns strangers into friends and friends into loyal customers," he says. "It's not just about entertainment—it's about education."

Yoyodyne, headquartered outside New York City, works with clients—which include AT&T, H&R Block, MCI, and Volvo—to create these new relationships. All of its campaigns use the Web, email, and other online media. All of them are built around game shows, contests, or sweepstakes. What do game shows have to do with permission marketing? Consumers give a company permission to send them messages in return for the chance to win prizes they care about. "The first rule of permission marketing is that it's based on selfishness," Godin says. "Consumers will grant a company permission to communicate only if they know what's in it for them."

Yoyodyne's techniques are catching on. The company has about 1 million active participants in its games database. It has sent more than 110 million email messages to influence consumer behavior. And it receives more email than any other company in the world. (Online services such as AOL handle more traffic, but those messages are destined for subscribers, not for the company itself.) More important, Yoyodyne's ideas are catching on. In an interview with Fast Company, Seth Godin described the future of marketing—and how your company can get there.

You've got a radical critique of conventional marketing. Why should companies listen?

We are entering an era that's going to change the way almost everything is marketed to almost everybody. Don't get me wrong. Advertising will remain a competitive weapon. Companies that advertise better will do better than companies that advertise worse. But advertising simply doesn't work as well as it used to. Do me a favor and finish this sentence: "Winston tastes good . . ."

". . . like a cigarette should."

Do you realize that the last time that commercial was aired was almost 30 years ago? If you want to build a slogan like that today, if you want to burn a message into people's brains, it costs huge amounts of money. Companies spent $175 billion on "advertising" in 1996. But 42% of that money went into things like direct mail, not into what we traditionally mean by advertising. That's because marketers are desperate for better results in a world where the old tools are becoming more expensive and less effective.

What's different today from 30 years ago?

Marketing is a contest for people's attention. Thirty years ago, people gave you their attention if you simply asked for it. You'd interrupt their TV program, and they'd listen to what you had to say. You'd put a billboard on the highway, and they'd look at it. That's not true anymore. This year, the average consumer will see or hear 1 million marketing messages—that's almost 3,000 per day. No human being can pay attention to 3,000 messages every day. The interruption model is extremely effective when there's not an overflow of interruptions. If you tap someone on the shoulder at church, you're going to get that person's attention. But there's too much going on in our lives for us to enjoy being interrupted anymore.

So our natural response is to ignore the interruptions. Television is unbelievably cluttered.

Can you recall one TV commercial you saw last night? The Web is even worse! There are more than 250 million people in the United States, and almost all of them watch TV. And maybe 10 channels really matter. That's 25 million people per channel. There are 45 million people with Web access and 1.5 million commercial sites that are vying for their attention. That's only 30 people per site. The economics just don't work.

What's the alternative?

Interruption marketing is giving way to a new model that I call permission marketing. The challenge for companies is to persuade consumers to raise their hands—to volunteer their attention. You tell consumers a little something about your company and its products, they tell you a little something about themselves, you tell them a little more, they tell you a little more—and over time, you create a mutually beneficial learning relationship. Permission marketing is marketing without interruptions.

You still have to get people's attention in the first place, of course, and that still costs lots of money. But that's the beginning of the story, not the end. You have to turn attention into permission, permission into learning, and learning into trust. Then you can get consumers to change their behavior.

Does that mean big-budget TV ads go away?

Not at all. Mass-market advertising helps companies talk to strangers. Companies will always need to talk to strangers—to persuade people to pay attention for one brief moment. But after you do the very expensive job of getting people to pay attention, then

what? That's where permission marketing comes in. People who've agreed to pay attention don't want you to waste their time with more handheld camera shots or snazzy animation. They want to get to know you. They want you to solve their problems. Permission marketing turns strangers into friends and friends into loyal customers. It's not just about entertainment—it's about education. Permission marketing is curriculum marketing.

Why would people be willing to give companies permission to talk to them?

Permission marketing is built around rational calculations by both parties. Look at it from the customer's perspective: People have money to spend on products. What people lack are the time to evaluate products and the trust in the companies that make them. The first rule of permission marketing is that it's based on selfishness: Consumers will grant a company permission to communicate only if they know what's in it for them. A company has to reward consumers, explicitly or implicitly, for paying attention to its messages. That's why the Net is such a powerful medium. It changes everything. You can use email to communicate with people frequently, quickly, and unobtrusively—so long as they've given you permission to do that.

Now look at it from the company's perspective: One of the problems with interruption-based marketing is that you have to assume that "no" means "no" —when, in fact, it usually means "maybe." If people see a TV commercial and don't buy your product, or get a piece of direct mail and don't respond, you assume that they've rejected your offer.

It's simple economics. If you send 100 people a letter and only 2 of them become customers, the cost of asking the other 98 why they didn't is exactly the same as the cost of contacting them in the first place. So you move on to the next batch of prospects.

What's so magical about the Net is that the cost of talking to the "no's" more than once is zero. With email, frequency is free. You can keep communicating with people, keep teaching them, keep trying to turn them into customers. And it doesn't cost you anything. That's so important. If you want to change behavior, you have to talk to people over and over again.

Is that why Web ads are taking off? Last year, for the first time, advertisers spent more than $1 billion on the Web.

No. Up to now, for most advertisers, the Web has been a phenomenal waste of money. Here are four oxymorons for you: "soft rock," "military intelligence," "taped live," and "Internet advertising." I guarantee you that by the year 2000, Internet banner ads will be gone. They don't work. Why? Because most companies are trying to reach consumers in this new medium by using the same model they used in the old media. Most companies use the Web to talk to strangers. They try to dazzle people with Web sites in the same way they try to dazzle people with TV ads. It's very expensive—and not very effective.

The Net is not television. It is the finest direct-marketing mechanism in the history of mankind. It is direct mail with free stamps, and it allows you to create richer and deeper relationships than you've ever been able to create before. The real killer for marketers isn't the Web—it's

email. Ordinary people understand this, by the way, which is why they get so nervous about spam. The first time they get an unsolicited email, they say to themselves, "This message didn't cost the sender anything. If I let him get away with this, there will be thousands more just like him. Then my email box won't work, and the Web won't be fun anymore." But if you get permission to use email to deliver marketing messages, and if people agree to pay attention to those messages— well, you've changed the game.

What's an example?

H&R Block wanted to introduce a new service aimed at upper-income customers. It's called Premium Tax. None of those customers knew what this was before we started. First we had to get people's attention—and we had to get the right people's attention. So we used banners on various Web sites that said, "H&R Block: We'll pay your taxes sweepstakes." The only people who clicked on those banners were people who paid taxes and knew what H&R Block was. More than 50,000 people responded. In effect, they said, "Here's my email address—tell me more about this promotion."

Then these people became players in a contest. In return for the chance to have their taxes paid by H&R Block, they gave the company permission to teach them about its new service. Every week, they had to answer trivia questions about taxes, H&R Block, and other relevant stuff. They got three emails per week for 10 weeks. We gave them fun facts about the history of taxes or sent them to H&R Block's Web site to find answers to questions. Each email also included a promotional message about

Premium Tax. The average response rate per message was 40%—meaning that, on average, every time 100 people got a specific email, 40 wrote back or took action. Over the life of the promotion, 97% of the people who entered the game stayed in it.

We did a survey at the end of the 10 weeks. We divided people into three groups: those who didn't participate in the game, those who participated but not actively, and those who participated actively. Within the first group, learning about Premium Tax was essentially zero—no surprise there. Among people who participated but not actively, 34% understood Premium Tax. For active participants, the figure was 54%. I think that's pretty cool.

We did something similar for Carter-Wallace, the consumer-products company. We created an online game around its Arrid XX "Get a Little Closer" campaign. We offered players a chance to win an all-expense-paid trip to the Caribbean. People found out about it through traditional print ads as well as through Web banners. We got more than 30,000 players. The average player received 24 emails over the course of the game. People had to read these messages to stay in the game. At the end of the game— 700,000 emails later—we did some research. The likelihood of purchase had doubled, from 24% to 49%. An astonishing 25% of players had already gone out and purchased Arrid XX during the game.

Those are two small examples. One of our first sweepstakes, the Million Dollar WebCrawl, was designed to persuade people to use AOL's search engine. We offered a prize of $1 million. Players had to visit specific Web sites and to register their email addresses at each one. This one sweepstakes attracted more than 350,000 players, and they made 2.7 million unique Web visits. Overall, we've created more than 100 online promotions—and the number of participants just keeps getting bigger.

Why contests and sweepstakes?

You can use lots of techniques to make it worthwhile for people to give you permission to talk to them. We use games because they work. Sweepstakes have been around for 700 years. Game shows were among the first programs on radio and television. Back in 1990, Prodigy asked us to create a game for it. The game's first run ended late last year, and we've started it up again. It's called Guts. Players get seven trivia questions a week. Each question is worth more points than the one before, and each is harder than the one before. You can stop at any time and keep your current score, and then come back the next week for another round. But if you miss one question, you not only lose the points from that week—you lose all your points for the whole game. So it takes guts to stay in. So far, more than 3 million people have played Guts. It's the most popular online game in history.

People love games. They're fun, exciting, engaging. We not only entertain people but also educate them—and we get paid for it! We create promotions in which the game itself involves information about products. People search for ads and read them because they have to find missing pieces of information to get the prizes they want. When's the last time you searched for a TV commercial?

How well is the concept of permission marketing catching on?

Just look at Yoyodyne's growth curve. Over the last seven years, we have sent out more than 100 million email messages—all to consumers who have given us permission to send them. Our "Get Rich Click" database, which is our core inventory of players, has 1 million active email addresses—of people who have given us overt permission to send them information we think they might want to know. Recently, during one five-day period, we processed 2.3 million email messages. In fact, we now receive more email than any other company in the world. So the idea is catching on.

That said, lots of agencies and companies resist such ideas. Permission marketing challenges some of the most cherished assumptions on Madison Avenue. People in this country are born thinking they have two inalienable rights. One is to become President of the United States; the other is to direct a major motion picture. Making a flashy TV ad is a bit like making a movie. That's what an ad agency is good at. That's why people want to work there. But an ad agency isn't equipped to figure out how to persuade customers to grant a company permission to communicate with them. People there don't want to do it. Permission marketing also changes how companies evaluate their marketing campaigns. In this model, you don't care about cheap impressions. You care about deep relationships. Forget Nielsen ratings, clicks, hits, page views—that's all rubbish. How many consumers have given you permission to talk

to them? How far does that permission go? Does every marketing piece you create invite consumers to "raise their hands," to volunteer to hear more?

There's one last barrier to overcome. If you get permission to talk to customers, you'd better have something to say. You need a marketing curriculum. The point of permission marketing is not just to entertain people (although it does need to be entertaining) but also to teach them about your products. And deep down, lots of companies don't really believe they can make a rational case for what they sell. They think they have to rely on style rather than substance.

Is the Net the only place where these ideas can work?

The Net is the ultimate tool for permission marketing. But the idea itself is more about mind-set than about medium. Many of the best-known Web companies don't get this. Yahoo! is a wonderfully successful operation. But every month, 25 million unique users show up at this site, and Yahoo! flushes those people down the toilet. Yahoo! doesn't know who they are, where they live, what they like—it's all anonymous. That strikes me as foolish. Why doesn't Yahoo! get permission to find out who they are, to learn more about their preferences, to lock in an overt learning relationship?

On the other hand, some companies with mundane products understand these ideas very well. I'm a baker. And I never use any flour but King Arthur flour. That's because every three months, the company sends me a catalog loaded with baking tools, recipes, and flours. King Arthur educates me. It talks to me in a language I understand. It has permission to send this catalog to me. It has permission to follow up with other mailings. In return, I learn a lot about its products. So I bake more often, I eat more flour—and the company makes a lot more money off of me than Pillsbury ever will.

Let's go beyond permission marketing and talk about marketing in general: What other changes are on the horizon?

I see three huge shifts. First, we're going to move from a world where companies sell products to one where they sell subscriptions. Do you know how much it costs America Online to attract one new customer? Something like $98. That's how expensive it is now to talk to strangers. But AOL can afford to spend that much because it's selling subscriptions, not a one-time service. So companies will focus more on creating deep relationships with existing customers than on attracting new customers. Marketing will become less visible—a private affair between consumers and the com-

panies they buy from. The business model I love most is the Book-of-the-Month Club. You give the company permission to make buying choices for you. Why can't lots of other companies operate this way? If I were advising Amazon.com, I would tell [CEO] Jeff Bezos to stop engaging in price wars with Barnes & Noble and to start his own version of the Book-of-the-Month Club. Instead of creating just one club, he could create thousands of clubs, each one tailored to the preferences of certain customers. I love business books. Once a month, in my email box, I should find a message about the four business books that Amazon.com thinks I should read. I'm willing to give Jeff and his people permission to make choices for me. In that sense, I am willing to subscribe to Amazon.com.

At the same time, Jeff's competitors will have to try to convince me to switch to them—as expensive as that may be. And this is the second big shift: Forget interruption marketing as we know it today. Tomorrow I'll have

someone or something that negotiates on my behalf. Every time a company wants me to pay attention, it will have to offer some tangible benefits. Essentially, companies will have to pay me to listen to their ads.

The flip side of this change—and this is the third big shift in marketing—is that less and less content will be free. You will pay for things you don't have to pay for today, because interruption-based advertising will not be able to subsidize them anymore. And if you're not willing to pay for content, you'll have to put up with a world filled with even more interruptions. We're living with this shift already. You can pay $4 to see a movie without interruption, either on video or through pay-per-view. Or you can wait a year, see it for free on network television, and endure constant interruptions. More and more entertainment will end up working this way.

 Article Review Form at end of book.

Web Wares

Why are so many companies starting to sell products and services on the Internet? They are attracted by the growing number of Net surfers, the promise of lower sales costs and the feedback from new target markets.

Nick Wreden

Nick Wreden works for Aspen Communications, a Norcross, Ga., agency that provides editorial services to high-tech companies.

In 1989, Petals helped pioneer electronic commerce by being among the first companies to sell products via an online network. After the manufacturer of silk flowers and other home accessories grossed about $250,000 during its only year of online sales, it decided to give up that channel in favor of more traditional—and more profitable—marketing relationships with catalog retailers.

Now, Petals is back in the world of electronic commerce, attracted by the rapidly expanding number of global Internet surfers, the promise of lower sales costs and the ability to enjoy immediate feedback from new target markets. The White Plains, N.Y.-based firm joins tens of thousands of other companies that have rushed to the Web hoping to tap into a lucrative, fast-growing market.

Revenue from online shopping is expected to increase dramatically over the next few years.

Forrester Research, a Cambridge, Mass.-based research organization, forecasts that annual online sales in 2000 will approach $6.6 billion, up from an estimated $518 million in 1996.

Despite these imposing numbers, E-commerce represents just a few drops in the ocean of global commerce. The Mountain View, Calif.-based research firm INPUT estimates that only 2 percent of business-to-business sales worldwide in 2000 will be generated over the Web. Still, companies should start positioning themselves to tap into the rapidly growing world of electronic commerce.

"Early experience indicates that the most successful electronic commerce entrepreneurs are those that start from the ground up," reports Jack Shaw, president of Electronic Commerce Strategies, a Marietta, Ga.-based consultancy. "This permits them to tailor their approach to the unique demands of the Internet, instead of carrying over industrial-age business models to the electronic age."

Some enterprises, like Petals, are establishing independent Internet sites that supplement traditional catalogs or other sales efforts. Others are linking up to so-called Internet malls, which include a collection of online storefronts that are accessible through a single site.

Staking Claim to Piece of Web

Like prospectors during a gold rush, companies are finding that the path to riches is strewn with obstacles as well as opportunities. Transforming surfers into customers dictates continual cross-promotion to drive traffic to the site, a willingness to modify the site as frequently as Macy's changes its window displays, and the use of incentives such as lower pricing or try-before-you-buy offers.

Every company dipping its toe into the electronic commerce waters is moving through the same three stages. First, organizations rush to stake a claim in cyberspace with something— anything—that can be called a home page. Later, they expand their offerings, add graphics and interactivity, and work to incorporate continual customer input. Eventually, enterprises use their site to take one-to-one marketing to the next level, tailoring their efforts to specific customers.

Petals decided to return to electronic commerce with an online catalog last spring, to take advantage of a market that seemed to come out of nowhere, recalls John Shannon, director of electronic media. In the first six months, the site generated more than 12,000 sales leads. The company recently expanded its online offerings from 14 items to 125, which represents about 30 percent of its traditional paper catalog.

Petals had hoped to produce an expanded online catalog much faster, but its debut was delayed by infrastructure problems and an internal debate over the site's strategic goals. "We asked whether the purpose of the site was sales or lead generation," Shannon recalls. "We concluded that we wanted sales, and worked to expand our capabilities to close sales online."

Prospects who access the Petals site can retrieve an online catalog. Subsequent online orders are tracked individually using a key code. Two percent of these online catalog requests result in orders, a number that the company expects to rise by one percent a year as the number of online items rises.

Electronic commerce also opens new target markets. "Our typical customer has been a woman who is more than 50 years old, but we're now selling to more customers between the ages of 35 and 45," Shannon says, noting that women comprise 90 percent of Petals' online patrons.

Today, revenue from online sales is an inconsequential part of Petals' $50 million in revenue. Shannon has set a 1997 goal for the site of $1 million in revenue, as its visibility and number of offerings increase. Still, Petals' electronic commerce budget totaled less than $50,000 for 1996—about the cost of a one-time ad in a major national magazine. That's not bad for an investment in a long-term distribution channel.

Second-Generation Sites

In the rush to get onto the Web, many enterprises took the quick, easy step of digitizing existing brochures and placing them online. But that approach became as dated as the reading material in a dentist's office. Consequently, many firms are revisiting their E-commerce efforts and are incorporating better graphics, more interactivity and more targeted material.

David Van Kalsbeek, senior vice president and director of marketing and strategic planning for ITT Sheraton, admits that the Boston-based hotel chain's early electronic commerce effort—a listing of hotels internationally—"wasn't terribly creative or effective."

After surveying its customers, ITT Sheraton redesigned its site last November to offer one that is more interactive, with more complete information on the company and its programs and the ability to make reservations online. Key among these is the new ITT Sheraton Club International section, the company's frequent guest program. Members can access information on at least their last five transactions, obtain an up-to-date Club Mile balance and receive customized information on redeeming those Club Miles based on their individual stay history and current Club Mile balance.

"The Internet is rapidly becoming a tool that is used by more and more of our business customers," says Van Kalsbeek. As a result, the hotel improved its website with enhanced animation, graphics and service.

For instance, the addition of Apple Computer's QuickTime VR virtual reality technology for many of the company's hotels enables site visitors to "walk" through a hotel room and see the difference, say, between a partial ocean view and a full ocean view, or check out a 360-degree panorama of the banquet facilities.

However, the appeal of E-commerce goes deeper than its ability to attract new customers. It can also bypass the constraints of paper-based promotional efforts. Take the case of New York-based McGraw-Hill's Professional Book Group, a division of the publishing conglomerate. The group has its catalog of more than 9,000 business and technical books online, and is receiving more than 200,000 hits a month at its site, a rate that is increasing at 25 to 30 percent a month.

As impressive as that number is, business publisher Philip Ruppel notes: "Today, at least, more people walk into bookstores every day than visit our catalog on the Internet."

But what makes the Internet attractive to McGraw-Hill is its ability to segment audiences and target interests while eliminating many of the costs of promotion. "We are able to precisely segment our target audiences on the Web," says Ruppel.

"We highlight specific sites in our books and catalogs, and we also link to complementary sites, so prospects are encouraged to visit and find information that is tailored to their interests. This gives us the ability to market far more effectively without the high costs of printing, mailing or telemarketing."

Nevertheless, persuading consumers to buy online may take more than pretty pictures and scintillating descriptions, because consumers are used to flipping through books to scan their contents. For that reason, McGraw-Hill is experimenting with a try-before-you-buy technology that allows readers to download chapters or other material from books. This capability is based on IBM-developed Cryptolope technology, which provides a secure methodology to deliver copyrighted materials over the Internet.

Heading to the Mall

While companies such as Petals and ITT Sheraton provide stand-alone websites, other organizations are banding together in electronic malls, which host a synergistic collection of online retailers. Online malls offer stores a quick-to-market way to tap into the large number of prospects who want to shop at a single convenient site.

The Cleveland Institute of Electronics (CIE), which offers programs of independent computer study, uses Online Interactive's FreeShop Online website to attract students. CIE sends out a free course catalog and a handbook of electronic symbols to those requesting them. Ted Sheroke, the school's advertising manager, reports that the quality of leads is better than those received from other marketing efforts because the people viewing its online site already have some computer knowledge.

Robert Waxman Camera, a Denver-based camera chain, has set up its virtual shop on IBM's World Avenue. "In retailing, the three most important criteria for success are location, location and

location," says Chris Midyet, director of interactive product marketing for RWI Interactive Information Services, a Robert Waxman Camera spin-off. "The IBM home page is consistently ranked among the top 10 most-visited sites, so we thought that World Avenue would be an ideal place for us to open a new store in cyberspace."

World Avenue offers Robert Waxman Camera the opportunity for add-on selling of camera and video products tailored to an online audience. It can guide consumers to the most appropriate purchases based on their responses to questions concerning desired features and capabilities. If a consumer buys a camera, the site can automatically suggest accessories such as a tripod.

Midyet points out that World Avenue and the camera chain's existing online retail catalog, which features more than 7,300 products, are not meant as substitutes for its eight retail outlets. "Instead, we see this as a way to extend our reach and become a global retailer," he explains. "We're now selling in places like South America and Russia, and we expect that business to expand significantly in the near future."

One of the obstacles slowing the expansion of E-commerce is consumer concern over security. That's one reason the Security Store, a San Diego-based supplier of residential and commercial security hardware, is using IBM's World Distributor to market residential and light commercial security products such as entry locks and deadbolts. Since most purchases are made using a credit card, the Security Store felt that World Distributor's method of encrypting E-mail would give prospects the reassurance they

seek. The company's headquarters decrypts the information and sends the order to the one of its 11 distribution centers that is nearest to the customer. The branch then ships the product.

"We believe the security provided by World Distributor boosts consumer confidence and, ultimately, sales," states Gina Gombar, vice president of sales and marketing. She also notes that electronic commerce provides customer service 24 hours a day, seven days a week. And, since customers handle the order selection and billing processes, the sales force can spend more time on market expansion and development.

World Distributor affords the Security Store a way of testing demand for new products without the expense and time-lag of printing catalogs. Plus, products can be hot-linked to complementary accessories to generate additional sales.

Product Samples

Despite the advantages of global reach, targeted marketing and a generally lower cost of sales, it's not easy to strike the mother lode of electronic commerce. At this stage, it requires giving customers an incentive to try this new medium beyond round-the-clock purchasing.

In some cases, that can mean using a try-before-you-buy strategy like McGraw-Hill does, or lowering prices like the Security Store, which prices its online products about 10 percent below retail. Petals provides free shipping and handling to online buyers and is looking at a 20 percent discount to attract more non-traditional purchasers.

It's also important to pay close attention to the unique issues surrounding information distribution over the Internet. While it's desirable for companies to remain current with technological offerings, they shouldn't incorporate the latest-and-greatest because that may exclude some prospective customers. "Stay away from the eye-candy offerings and avoid showing off technically," Robert Waxman's Midyet advises. "Extensive graphics that take a long time to download will test the patience of your prospects, while consumers coming in from online services will not be able to download certain features."

Many companies underestimate the need to promote the site. "Avoid being the world's best online secret by registering with online search directories, placing listings in yellow page directories, and promoting the site in collateral and other marketing activities," urges Petals' Shannon. "The number of visitors to our site quadruples when we pay for a banner on another appropriate page."

It's also important to maintain close, interactive communications with customers. Petals created an E-mail club, which generated more than 5,000 requests in 12 weeks. Subscribers to

Taking It to the Bank

With a growing number of consumers buying goods and services online, it won't be long before these individuals will be conducting other financial transactions over the Internet.

That's why First Chicago NBD, the nation's ninth-largest bank holding company, is joining 14 other banks and IBM in creating the Integrion Financial Network. Beginning early this year, Integrion will help ensure that member banks can deliver secure and convenient electronic banking services to their customers over the Internet and other electronic channels.

"We want to be involved in creating the railroad tracks that will transport financial information in the future," reports Thomas Kelly, vice president of media relations of the Chicago-based bank. "Online banking provides a competitive advantage. It enables us to offer our customers a wide range of choices and let them decide what's best for them."

Standard Security

Representing more than half of the retail banking population in North America, Integrion provides a standards-based way to help member banks overcome security and other infrastructure concerns. Consumers will benefit by being able to bank directly with an Integrion financial institution via the access method of their choice, using such electronic banking services as balance inquiries, fund transfers, bill payments and check reconciliation.

In addition to First Chicago NBD and IBM, the initial owners of Integrion include ABN AMRO, BANC ONE, Bank of America, Barnett Bank, Comerica, First Bank Systems, Fleet Financial Group, KeyCorp, Mellon Bank, Michigan National Bank, NationsBank, PNC Bank, Royal Bank of Canada and Washington Mutual.

—N.W.

the club receive an online newsletter that contains decorating tips, photos of customers' silk flower arrangements and new products, among other offerings. After receiving customer input, Petals added the capability to intelligently search its offerings for requested features.

An investment in electronic commerce may not pay off for years, but it is one that no business with its eye on the 21st century can afford to miss.

 **Article Review Form at end of book.**

Web Sites That Sell

There's no confusing Marshall Industries with some ultracool Web startup in Seattle or Silicon Alley. For one thing, it is an Industrial Era company that's just making the transition to the Internet Era. For another, it has built a Web site that generates real sales and profits—a claim that precious few Web startups can make.

Indeed, Marshall's online presence is a model for companies that are serious about selling on the Web. Marshall on the Internet (http://www.marshall.com), the company's umbrella site, was launched in July 1994. It now averages more than 1 million hits a week and visits from 60 countries. The site contains 170,000 part numbers, more than 100,000 pages of data sheets, and up-to-date inventory and pricing information from 150 major suppliers.

"We tell the world about new products faster than anybody else in the industry," says Kerry Young, Marshall's director of distributed computing. "We've taken everything that we do physically and converted it to the Net."

Marshall's Net conversion is making converts in the market. "Marshall's Internet site is a major weapon in our strategy for our most important product," says Kevin McGarity, senior vice president of worldwide marketing for Texas Instruments. McGarity is referring to digital signal processors (DSPs), chips that improve the performance of high-tech hardware from headphones to computer hard disks to power steering in cars. TI estimates that it will ship more than $1 billion worth of DSPs in 1997.

Why is Marshall's Web presence so critical to TI's market presence? Because it provides direct access to thousands of engineers around the world who might use the company's DSPs in their new products. The actual sales transaction, it turns out, is the least important part of what Marshall's Web site does for TI. What really matters is what happens before and after the sale.

Let's say you're an engineer designing a new piece of multimedia hardware. Could a digital signal processor from TI enhance its performance? A few years ago, you would have called Marshall,

requested technical literature, reviewed it, and ordered a developer's kit. The interaction might have taken weeks.

Today you visit Marshall's Electronic Design Center (http://www.electronicdesign.com). Not only will you find the technical specs you need, but you can also simulate designs using TI chips. You download sample code, modify the code to suit the product you're building, test it on a virtual chip that's "attached" to the Net, and analyze its performance. If you like the results, Marshall can download your code, burn it into physical chips, and send you samples for designing prototypes. The interaction takes minutes.

Then it's time for volume testing. You can order shipments via MarshallNet (http://partner-net.marshall.com), the company's secure extranet connection with suppliers and customers—1,250 of whom use it daily. Each customer sees a Web site modified to its specific needs. If you build multimedia entertainment products, you see prices and quantities for parts that are relevant to your business. After you order the chips, MarshallNet connects you to the company's proprietary database. Customers see the same shipment data that's available to Marshall salespeople over the Lotus Notes database.

Of course, new technologies require extensive after-sale training. But who wants to send yet another team of engineers to yet another meeting room in a hotel? NetSeminar (www.netseminar. com), a Web site connected to Marshall's digital studio, allows suppliers to train customers with video, audio, and real-time chat capabilities. NetSeminar organizes sessions for groups ranging from a handful of engineers to thousands of conference attendees.

The result of all these technologies is a Web presence that demonstrates the change-the-rules promise of electronic commerce.

 Article Review Form at end of book.

The Virtual Mall Gets Real

Online buying is expected to hit $4.8 billion in '98, and the Net may now be the place retailers have to be.

Heather Green in New York, Gail DeGeorge in Miami, and Amy Barrett in Philadelphia

For the past two months, Office Depot Inc. has been using the image of Dilbert, the cartoon character, in its advertising to help sell everything from staples to personal computers. But now, the wisecracking Dilbert is going interactive. On Jan. 16, when Office Depot launches its online store, the cartoon character will double as a sales clerk who helps cybershoppers find what they're looking for and walks them through their first online purchase. Office Depot figures Dilbert may make the experience easier as a new crop of shoppers flocks to the Net this year. "People have voted with their mouse clicks that if you make it more convenient, they will come," says Paul Gaffney, Office Depot's vice-president for systems development. "There is a huge opportunity here."

Indeed, online sales have never been better. In the quarter just ended, cybernauts snapped up everything from airline tickets to tennis rackets, to the tune of

nearly $1 billion—twice the volume for the same period a year ago and higher than any previous quarter, according to Forrester Research Inc. Experts now say that 1998 is the year when electronic commerce could finally begin to fulfill its promise as a vast new marketplace. Online sales are projected to reach $4.8 billion this year, double that of 1997. "We're moving people from being window-shoppers to buyers," says Robert W. Pittman, president of America Online Networks, the division that runs the No. 1 online service.

So whose virtual cash registers are ringing in the New Year? The early winners are those hawking computers and other high-tech gear—$863 million worth in 1997, a total that's expected to grow 85% this year, to some $1.6 billion. Dell Computer Corp. is the PC king on the Net, selling an average of $3 million a day. But even lesser-knowns are making hay. Computer reseller NECX, based in Peabody, Mass., sold $60 million on the Web in 1997, a fivefold jump over the previous year.

The computer crowd won't hold sway forever. Sales of everything from music CDs to shoes

are on the upswing. But the biggest corner of cyberspace activity could be in travel. Web merchants selling airline tickets and booking hotel and car reservations accounted for $654 million in sales last year. Travelocity, Preview Travel, and Microsoft's Expedia, for example, are booking more than $2 million a week, on average. And Travelocity says it has topped $3 million several times in recent months. It could get better yet. By 1999, travel is expected to be the No. 1 electronic commerce category, with some $2.8 billion in total sales, according to Forrester.

Open Window

Why are online sales taking off? For one, the number of U.S. households dialing into the Web is on an upward path: from 20 million in 1997 to an expected 26 million by the end of 1998, says market researcher Yankee Group Inc. That has prompted a slew of brand-name companies to open shop, including Bloomingdale's, the Gap, Sears, and Clinique—which, in turn, draws more shoppers. "This is a great way to get to a large number of people," says Angela Kapp, vice-president for

How Internet Shopping Is Shaping Up

Key Categories:	1997*	2000*
	(millions of dollars)	
PC hardware and sales	$863	$2,901
Travel	654	4,741
Entertainment	298	1,921
Books and music	156	761
Gifts, flowers, and greetings	149	591
Apparel and footwear	92	361
Food and beverages	90	354
Jewelry	38	107
Sporting goods	20	63
Consumer electronics	19	93
Other (toys, home, etc.)	65	197

* Estimates
Data: Forrester Research Inc.

Total Spending on the Net

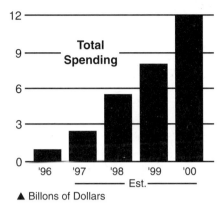

▲ Billons of Dollars

Data: Forrester Research Inc. ©BW

special markets and new media for Estee Lauder Inc., which owns Clinique. "There is a window of opportunity here now."

Just so. Merchants hopping on the Net say that some of the impetus is seeing the success of early pioneers, such as Amazon.com. The Seattle-based startup was the first to open a mega-bookstore online, offering 2.5 million titles—more than any bricks-and-mortar counterpart. Amazon's huge selection, easy-to-use site, and hacker-free track record helped propel 1997 sales to an expected $131.7 million, up from $15.8 million a year ago, estimates Hambrecht & Quist Inc. Now, Barnes & Noble Inc. is fighting back, investing in its own Internet site, and bookseller Borders Inc. has plans for the Web, too.

The lesson: Getting on the Net early can be a huge advantage, especially for tiny startups. Even big-name retailers can't afford to wait. "I'm constantly pounding the tables, telling the companies whose boards I sit on, "Don't get Amazoned," says James F. McCann, president of 1-800-FLOWERS, which has been selling online for three years. Clearly, cybershoppers have signaled they won't wait for the brand names if Net startups can offer a good selection, discounts, convenience, and security. Danielle Battle, a housewife in Bedford, Mass., is a point in case. She has spent about $1,500 over the past couple of years at fledgling online stores, including Amazon. "With the modem and the PC, you have the world before you," she says. "It is a bit of fun and a big convenience."

Wish List

It's also getting more customer-friendly by the day. In recent months, many Web-site operators have gotten smarter about how to appeal to buyers. Walt Disney Co.'s site, for example, has made it easy to find shopping online by putting links to its virtual store on the opening page of its site—no more plowing through Web page after Web page. And this week, iQVC, the online division of QVC Inc., launched a separate section on its site called Gemsandjewels.com that offers general information about gold and stone cuttings. QVC also features a new service that lets visitors set up a wish list of items friends or family can look through when searching for a gift.

At the same time, merchants are streamlining the online shopping experience with better technology. They have improved so-called cybershopping carts that let consumers put the products they want in a virtual basket. That way, shoppers can continue browsing the site rather than having to pay for each product before selecting the next one on that site. And merchants, such as Amazon and L.L. Bean, are using passwords to preserve billing and credit-card information so that once shoppers register at a site, they don't have to fill in that data again.

E-merchants also are making headway in figuring out how to grab Web surfers' attention. Many online merchants have begun using the heavily trafficked Net search engine sites as a springboard to their sites. Consumers using No. 1 search engine Yahoo!, for example, can click on an icon that links directly to Hallmark Cards Inc.'s Web site, where the greeting-card company offers 17,000 graphics and messages—some for free and others for a fee. And Yahoo!, AOL, Lycos, Infoseek, and Excite! have all introduced or redesigned shopping areas to highlight specific online shops, such as Eddie Bauer, Barnes & Noble, or J.C. Penney. Merchants can pay millions of dollars for top billing on these popular sites. "From a retailer's perspective, you can build a great store, but if the traffic isn't there, it's like a phone number in the white pages," says AOL's Pittman. "You've got to be where the people are."

Security Fears

Even with the improvements, shopping online isn't always a breeze. Consumers still have to type in order forms at each sepa-

rate site. And the Web has a ways to go before it delivers on the promise of easy-to-find goods for every taste and price range. In November, Yahoo! and Excite introduced shopping tools that are designed to search according to price or product. Still, they include only a few hundred merchants. Technology that can scour the entire Web and the thousands of shops out there isn't available yet. And it's still hard to judge colors and sizes on Web pages. "I'm waiting for the online avatar that can make suggestions and show me how things look on me," says Harold Wolhandler, director of research at ActivMedia Inc., a technology consultant based in Peterborough, N.H.

Concerns also linger about security, especially among those consumers who are new to the Web. Technology developed by

Visa USA Inc. and MasterCard International Inc. that outlines how credit-card transactions are handled by merchants and banks is still in the testing phase. That means that the marketing machines of two of the most trusted credit-card companies haven't begun pushing consumers to buy online—yet.

Still, some experts say the grassroots growth of cybershoppers is almost making the endorsement by credit-card companies a non-issue, especially when giants such as AT&T and IBM are pushing electronic commerce in TV and print ads. That could help put the Internet on any savvy shopper's list of places to shop till they drop.

 Article Review Form at end of book.

Web Ads Start to Click

As Web marketing starts to show significant results, mainstream advertisers are jumping in.

Linda Himelssein, Ellen Neuborne, and Paul M. Eng

It began as an experiment. Bristol-Myers Squibb Co. wanted to see if the Internet was all it was cracked up to be when it came to plugging products and services. So during the 1997 tax season, the giant drug company teamed up with financial software maker Intuit Inc. and launched an online advertising campaign extolling Excedrin as "the tax headache medicine." For 30 days, Bristol-Myers ran ads on financial Web sites offering a free sample of Excedrin to Net surfers who clicked on the ad and typed in their name and address.

The response was as good as any elixir. In just one month, Bristol-Myers added 30,000 new names to its customer list—some 1,000 per day—and tripled the company's best-case scenario. What's more, the cost of obtaining those names was only half that of traditional marketing methods. "I don't think anyone can deny the long-term potential of the Web as a marketing tool,"

concludes Margaret Kelly, Bristol-Myers' vice-president for advertising services. Adds Seth Goldstein, president of CKS Site Specific in New York, which produced the campaign: "We turned a packaged-goods company into QVC."

Ah, the power of advertising—on the Net, that is, and at long last. In the past nine months, swarms of new ad banners, buttons, sponsorships, even TV-like commercials in which a car explodes onto your computer screen and speeds away, are now splashing their way across the World Wide Web. In the first quarter of 1997, Internet ad spending hit $133 million—still just a fraction of the billions spent on TV advertising, but a remarkable fivefold increase over the same period last year. What's more, analysts now say that Web advertising will approach the $1 billion milestone by yearend. "Net advertising, " says Andrew S. Grove, CEO of computer chip powerhouse Intel Corp., "is becoming a big deal."

Not surprisingly, tech giants, already the biggest online ad spenders, are planning to pump up the volume even louder. In

August, Intel announced that it will extend its cooperative-advertising program, which subsidizes ad dollars spent by its industry partners, to include Web promotions—a move that analysts say will boost all online ad spending some 40% in 1998. IBM says it's placing ads on 500 Web sites this year, a tactic that will balloon its Web advertising budget 300% above its 1996 level. And software giant Microsoft Corp. is upping its Net outlay by as much as 70% in fiscal year 1998, on top of the $24 million it spent in fiscal 1997, which ended in June. "This year, Web advertising is a permanent part of our marketing constellation," says Microsoft's John Zagula, director of marketing for desktop applications.

But the biggest change yet in this surge of cyber ads is that it's not all coming from computerdom. Today, makers of everything from Toyota Corollas to Kellogg's Corn Pops are hawking their wares over the Web. Yahoo! Inc., the first Net startup to turn a profit just from ad sales, says its mix of advertisers has gone from 85% tech in 1995 to almost 80% consumer brands today. Excite Inc., the No. 2 search company,

How Web Ads Work

has seen its proportion of nontech advertisers grow from 38% to 59% in just the past six months.

Proof is in the list of top-20 advertisers in the first three months of this year. According to New York-based researcher Jupiter Communications Inc., online high rollers now include General Motors, American Express, Walt Disney, Procter & Gamble, and publishers such as Dow Jones. "The Internet is no longer in the realm of experiment," says Farris Khan, Internet advertising coordinator for Saturn Corp. "It's part of our mainstream advertising, like television or print."

In ad parlance, the Net has come a long way, baby. Just a year ago, Web site operators were wringing their hands over disappointing ad sales—$301 million for the full year, hardly a flyspeck amid the $175 billion pumped into all U.S. advertising in 1996. This was even more distressing since ad sales had been expected to be the Internet's cash machine—a rich and ready supply of revenues that could support all the jazzy Web 'zines, flashy entertainment guides, elaborate sports sites, even Internet E-mail.

So what changed? Why is advertising on the Net starting to

click? For starters, the sheer number of Netizens prowling the Web, some 24 million today, is becoming too large for companies to ignore. Forrester Research Inc. expects that number to double to 52 million by 2000, putting the Web on a fast track to coveted mass-media status. What's more, in the past two years, the Net has gone from being a haven for nerds and academics to a hangout for professionals, teenagers, and grandmothers alike. This rich demographic shift, coupled with technology that promises to make Net ads almost as much of a "must see" as those on TV, have finally turned the Web into a hip place to pitch.

Tight Focus

At the same time, the buzz about how the Net's technology makes it possible to target specific customers is becoming a reality. Unlike a TV ad on say, *Seinfeld*, which is aimed broadly at the cool, thirtysomething crowd, a cyber-promo can zero in on Netizens who live in a specific part of town, are female, and who have shown an interest in certain topics or products.

Toothpaste maker Mentadent got a taste of that when it re-

cently launched a two-week test on the Net with PointCast Inc., an information network based in Sunnyvale, Calif. But first, PointCast sent E-mails to random visitors to its site asking about their dental-hygiene habits: 72% said they brushed twice a day, and 33% brushed at the office. Mentadent was then convinced the PointCast audience was ripe for its pitch. The result: Double the average number of people clicked on the ad for more info. "The Internet is a marketer's dream," says analyst Peter Storck of Jupiter Communications.

And a nightmare for some Netizens. While advertisers drool over the ability to target specific customers, Web surfers who preciously guard their privacy may find it unnerving and start to talk, throwing a monkey wrench into this newfound ad machine. A new BUSINESS WEEK/Harris Poll, for example, found that 65% of those surveyed say they are not willing to share personal information about themselves so online ads can be targeted to their tastes. "If I think someone is tracking me, it bothers me," says Matthew Hart, a 23-year-old Los Angeles Web surfer who is willing to give out information when he chooses.

Buzz Words

Click Through

How often a viewer will respond to an ad by clicking on it. Also known as the Click Rate.

Cookies

Information from a site that gets stored on a viewer's Web browser to help identify that particular person—or at least that particular browser—the next time it visits. Cookies can help determine traffic to Web sites by keeping track of how often a particular surfer returns—into that advertisers covet.

Cost Per Click (CPC)

The ad rate charged only if the surfer responds to a displayed ad.

Cost Per Lead/Sale

The rate charged to advertisers only if the viewer responds with personal info such as E-mail address or hobbies. The info must provide either a sales lead or product sale to obtain the fee.

Cost Per Thousand (CPM)

The ad rate Web sites charge for displaying a particular ad one thousand times, or "impressions."

Impressions

The total number of times an ad is displayed on a Web page. Impressions are not the same as "hits," which count the number of times each page or element in a page is retrieved. Since a single complicated page on a Web site could consist of five or more individual elements, including graphics and text, one viewer calling up that page would register multiple hits but just a single impression.

Interstitials, or In-Your-Face Ads

Akin to TV ads, these use video and sound. When users click on the "nutrition" site at Phys.com, a health site produced by Conde Nast, a separate window pops up to display an animated ad for Procter & Gamble's Sunny Delight drink. These ads are controversial, however, because they can be intrusive—sometimes appearing before the Web page that was called up.

Keyword Ads

Featured primarily on Web search-engine sites, such as Yahoo!, advertisers can link a specific ad to text or subject matter that an information seeker may enter. Miller Brewing, for example, bought the word "beer" on Yahoo! so that every time someone conducts a search using that term, an ad for "Miller Genuine Draft Beer" pops up.

Secret Stash

Many Netizens may not even know their Web habits are being monitored. Much of this is done through a technology called "cookies," which is like an electronic footprint that chronicles your movements on a particular Web site—what ads you saw or what you clicked on for more info. That data is stored in a "cookie file" in your browser. The next time you drop by the same Web site, the server picks up your footprint and gathers more info that can then be shared with advertisers.

Privacy advocates fret about cookies, but Web site operators insist they're not a problem since surfers can disable them by clicking on a browser option to reject cookies. Indeed, as cybernauts become more familiar with the Net, they will either get accustomed to handing out personal data or slam the door. "If you're under the impression you're anonymous when surfing the Internet, you're wrong," says Dennis L. Wilson, a 31-year-old intellectual-property lawyer in Los Angeles who cruises the Net regularly. "I don't have a problem with that. It's how you get advertisers to pay."

That's the attitude admeisters are banking on. Netizens are opening their arms to ads in cyberspace, though sometimes grudgingly. The *Business Week/ Harris* poll showed that 67% of those surveyed were not willing to pay users' fees to avoid online commercials. What's more, 57% said they "somewhat agree" that Net ads are useful sources for product data and information. On the flip side, 46% also said they "somewhat agree" that it's easy to ignore Web ads.

And that's the rub. While there is more ad activity on the Web than ever before, much of it is still crude and far from the standard-setting slickness of TV commercials. But that doesn't mean Net advertising isn't headed in that direction. To be sure, Web advertising is borrowing pages from its broadcast counterpart with the gradual addition of sound and animation and the growing use of sponsorship ads, such as Visa's backing of Restaurant Row on the GeoCities Web site, where Netizens swap recipes and chat with guest chefs.

The next step: Netmercials. The biggest attempt yet to mirror TV can be found in a new genre called "interstitials." These are full-screen, in-your-face ads that pop up either in the lag time between requesting a Web page and its appearance on the screen or, much like TV commercials, between segments of shows produced exclusively for the Web.

Take the Web site for You Don't Know Jack. This irreverent quiz show, a favorite among CD-ROM game players, now offers its game online, where companies

Leading the Cyber-Ad Charge

Big advertisers are hiking their spending.

Technology-Based Company	QI 1996	QI 1997
	Millions of Dollars	
Microsoft	$0.90	$7.2
Excite	0.41	3.2
IBM	1.32	3.0
Netscape	0.86	1.8
Ziff-Davis	0.11	1.7
Sportsline USA	0.18	1.6
Nynex	0.55	1.6
AT&T	0.56	1.5
Infoseek	0.32	1.5
Lycos	0.02	1.3

Non-Technology-Based Company	QI 1996	QI 1997
	Millions of Dollars	
Toyota	$0.32	$0.95
GMC	0.25	0.75
Disney	N/A	0.60
Charles Schwab	0.06	0.56
Visa	0.05	0.55
P&G	N/A	0.54
Dow Jones	0.03	0.54
American Express	0.12	0.47
Chase	N/A	0.47
Hearst	0.17	0.46

Data: Jupiter Communications

such as Seven Up, Hugo Boss, and 20th Century Fox Film reach out to the site's 150,000 players each month. There, they show 15-second ads that run the gamut from previews of movies such as Speed 2 to an insect riding a motorcycle across your screen hawking Cuervo Gold. The cost: $14,000 for every 100,000 games played—still a fraction of what companies pay for a slot on TV. "Advertisers see this and say: 'Now I see what the Internet can do for me,'" says Chris Deyo of Berkeley Systems Inc., which produces the game show.

So far, reaction from Web surfers is mixed. While interstitials have more pizzazz than banners, some Netizens think more animation can be downright irritating. AT&T found that out the hard way. In mid-September, the telecommunications giant silenced an ad showing a young, sassy girl knocking on a door and asking to be let in. Again and again, she knocked until the Web surfer clicked on the door. She then walked through the doorway and said she was off to college, and users then got info about AT&T's communications services. But many found her voice annoying. "In a word, it backfired," says an AT&T spokesman.

Today, in-your-face ads account for just 5% of the pitches made online. Instead, the ads of choice are banners, which amount to 80% of all electronic plugs. Typically, banners are plastered across the top or bottom of a Web page, much like a billboard on the Info Highway. A click on one of these ads usually whisks the Netizen off to the Web site of that company, where more info can be found.

Burning Rubber

No company knows the power of banner ads better than Toyota. The auto maker slaps these road signs all over the Net. For the 12 months ended in May, Toyota says 152,000 Web users typed in their name and address and requested a brochure or video about a car. Toyota later matched those names with buyers at its dealerships. It turned out the Web ads led to the sale of 7,329 cars—a remarkable 5% conversion rate. "The Internet," says Jon Bucci, national interactive communications manager for Toyota Motor Sales USA Inc., "is the No. 1 lead generator for Toyota."

But the static, wallpaper-like approach of banners also draws criticism as a cyber-snore. "There's a certain coldness to the Web. It's quiet and flat," says Stephen Block, AT&T's director of brand and interactive advertising. Adds Jupiter's Storck: "I have yet to see a banner that can make me cry the way an AT&T television ad can."

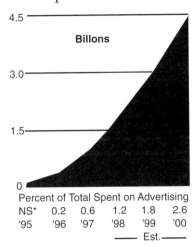

Total Ad Dollars Spent on the Net

Billions

4.5

3.0

1.5

0

Percent of Total Spent on Advertising

NS*	0.2	0.6	1.2	1.8	2.6
'95	'96	'97	'98	'99	'00

—— Est. ——

*Not significant

Data: Jupiter Communications ©BW

Net advertisers are working on that. Today banner ads are getting a makeover with animation, music, even games that help advertisers build brand awareness. Cereal powerhouse Kellogg Co., for example, is running a series of interactive games about Corn Pops and Pop Tarts inside banners. One, called "Mean Granny," is aimed at kids on the Sony PlayStation site where players try to keep grandma from getting to the Corn Pops.

No matter what form they take, online ads are being targeted to more precise audiences than in any other medium. Using keywords is one effective way. These are words surfers type into a search engine to generate a list of sites about a particular topic. These days, companies are paying for the rights to easy-to-remember words such as "beer," which instantly triggers an ad from Miller Brewing on Yahoo!'s site. IBM pays for some 200 words, including laptop, notebook, and Nagano, site of the 1998 Winter Olympics. In an especially aggressive move, Big

Blue once bought the word of its major rival, "Microsoft."

An even more pointed route to the ideal consumer is through an approach by Infoseek Corp., a Sunnyvale (Calif.) Internet search service. Infoseek is using artificial intelligence software developed by Aptex Software Inc., a San Diego company, to create a program called Ultramatch. This automatically takes cookie data and sorts them into 20 categories of users, such as those interested in entertainment or sports.

Customer PC Financial Network, an online brokerage, was so intrigued by the idea that it did an experiment. It ran banner ads in Infoseek's finance area and on the keyword "finance." It also directed the same ads to Ultramatch's business users—those seeking company news, stock quotes, or investment info. The result: PCFN got an 8% to 12% response rate from the Ultramatch ads, vs. less than 1.5% for banners. "It's not how many people you reach," says Keith Halloran, the company's vice-president for marketing. "It's how many of the right people you reach."

That's the secret of E*Trade Group Inc.'s success on the Net. The Palo Alto (Calif.) online brokerage integrates its print and TV campaigns with its efforts on the Web. E*Trade is spending about 7% of its media budget on the Net, but it plans to increase that to 15% next year after the results it has had so far. In May, E*Trade began an ad campaign on Yahoo!'s finance site. In the first ten days, the ads generated some 3,118 leads for new accounts. Today, 17% of all E*Trade's leads come from online advertising. "A media strategy without the Internet is suicidal," says CEO Christos M. Cotsakos.

Scrambling

No wonder, then, that marketers from Silicon Valley to Madison Avenue are now scrambling to take advantage of the Net. "I'd say 75% of our clients are asking us how they can use the Internet as an ad vehicle," says Greg Smith, director of strategic services at Darwin Digital, a dedicated Web-advertising unit of Saatchi & Saatchi.

Indeed, in contrast with the ho-hum approach Madison Avenue once took toward the online world, it is now going all out to make it a core part of the business. Early this year, Ogilvy & Mather established an electronic arm, OglivyOne Interactive, that caters to clients such as IBM. Not to be outdone, giants such as Young & Rubicam and Leo Burnett are joining Saatchi in setting up their own shops to focus on the Net (page 138). Says OgilvyOne's J. Sandom: "We need to be on the stick."

Huge billings are the incentive. According to Jupiter, online advertising revenues will soar in 1997, to $940 million, more than triple last year, but still less than 1% of all ad spending this year. Jupiter predicts that by 2002, Net ad revenues will approach $8 billion—some 4.1% of total ad budgets.

Some online operators are already watching the ad dollars roll in. Netscape Communications Corp. nabbed $24.1 million from ads in its most recent quarter, triple the same period a year ago. And Yahoo!'s revenues of $23 million in the past two quarters have surpassed its take for all of last year. So have its advertisers, which totaled 900 in its most recent quarter—nearly nine times the number it had in early 1996. "Whatever the growth is this year, it'll be twice or three times that next year," says Marc L. Andreessen, Netscape's cofounder.

Revenues are jumping in part because the most popular Web sites are starting to command more money per ad. In general, advertisers pay a fee for every 1,000 times their ads are displayed, known as "cost per thousand," or CPM. The average rate for banner ads is $17, says Forrester Research, but search-engine company Lycos charges $20 to $22 to gain access to its 15 million visitors a month. That compares sharply with ad rates for TV, for example, which are $5 to $6 per thousand, while consumer magazines such as Cosmopolitan can command $35. Net ads carry higher fees than TV because they are able to target preferred customers. "The technology has matured so much that if you just put your zip code in once, we can tag you," says Halsey Minor, CEO of CNET Inc., a San Francisco interactive-media company.

CNET is doing its part to hurry along the process. On Sept. 22, it launched Snap! Online, a consumer-information service that is going head-to-head with America Online Inc. Minor says Snap!'s charter advertisers, such as American Express Financial Services and Visa USA, will receive a first-of-its-kind monthly statement about the ages of the people who clicked on their ads, what part of the country they came from, and a slew of other demographic statistics they are willing to hand over. Yahoo!, Excite, AOL, and others are working up similar user profiles.

Key to the Net's arrival as a hot ad spot, however, is the establishment of independent measurement tools to gauge the effectiveness of ads. Accounting giants Ernst & Young, Coopers & Lybrand, and Price Waterhouse have recently begun auditing claims made by Web sites about their audiences and the number of impressions an advertiser gets. This month, Microsoft will begin sending its advertisers quarterly reports of all its Web sites, audited by Coopers & Lybrand. And on Sept. 9, the New York-based Internet Advertising Bureau issued guidelines to create standards for Internet advertising.

If advertisers still aren't satisfied, they can follow the path carved out by marketing heavyweight Procter & Gamble. It was one of the first companies to pay a Web site operator for ads only when someone clicked on them. "[Advertisers] like to tie somebody else's feet to the fire, saying: 'You're my partner, you're going to deliver the ads, and you're going to have a vested interest in increasing the performance of them, just like I do,'" says Yahoo! CEO Tim Koogle.

That ability of advertisers to hold Web sites accountable is just what experts say will ultimately make the Internet as easy an ad sell as a spot on *Seinfeld*. Indeed, Web site operators are out to prove to advertisers that, like Visa, the Net "is everywhere you want to be."

BW/Harris Poll: A Lot of Looking, Not Much Buying—Yet

Advertising on the Internet has been slow to evolve, but it's picking up speed. Some 80% of the Web surfers who responded to a recent Baruch College-Harris Poll commissioned by *Business Week* say they've seen ads online. More significantly, 49% say they have clicked on an ad for more information. Yet, only 19% say they've purchased a product after viewing a cyber ad.

In this survey of computer users examining Internet usage, some 48% say they cruise the Net, and they are spending so much time there that it's beginning to affect other parts of their lives. While basics such as sleeping, eating, and working have remained pretty much untouched, fully 48% of surfers say they now spend less time watching television, and 26% say they're reading less.

On or Off?

	Use	Do Not Use
Do you personally use a computer, or not?	59%	41%

Surf's Not That Up

(If you use a computer) Do you personally use the computer to . . .

	Use	Do Not Use
Access an online service such as American Online or CompuServe?	20%	80%
Access the Internet or the World Wide Web?	48%	52%

Buyer or Window-Shopper?

(If you have gone online) Have you ever used the Internet, World Wide Web, or an online service to purchase anything, or not?

Have purchased	19%	Have not	81%

Been There, Saw That

(If you have gone online) Have you seen or noticed any advertising for products or services, or not?

Have seen ads	80%	Have not seen ads	20%

Mouse Tracks

(If you have seen ads) Have you ever clicked on any online advertising, or not?

Clicked on advertising	49%	Have not clicked	51%

What Grabs You?

(If you clicked on ads) In general, what draws your attention to online ads most often? Is it interesting graphics, offers of information, promises of a free product or service, or something else?

Interesting graphics	22%
Offers of information	41%
Promises of a free product or service	12%
Something else	25%

Seen Any Good Ones Lately?

(If you clicked on ads) How often do you click on them—often, sometimes, or rarely?

Often	5%	Sometimes	45%	Rarely	50%

Mixed Signals

(If you have seen ads) In general, would you agree or disagree with each of the following:

	Strongly agree	Somewhat agree	Somewhat disagree	Strongly disagree	Don't know
Advertisements located on Web sites are useful sources of products and information	19%	52%	18%	9%	2%
	Strongly agree	Somewhat agree	Somewhat disagree	Strongly disagree	Don't know
Advertisements located on Web sites are easy to ignore	29%	46%	18%	7%	0%

Just Looking

(If you have seen ads) Have you purchased a product or service for which you saw online advertising, or not?

Have purchased	19%	Have not purchased	81%

[BW/Harris Poll continued on next page]

Point of Sale

(If you have purchased anything) Did you purchase the product or service on the Internet, over the phone, in a retail store, or by mail?

Internet	37%
Phone	22%
Retail store	31%
Mail	10%

In the Shopping Cart

(If you have purchased anything) What did you buy?*

Airline tickets	3%
Cars	7%
Computer hardware	26%
Music or books	17%
Services	4%
Software	14%
Other (specify)	27%
Don't know	3%

Thanks But No Thanks

(If you have seen ads) Compared with ads on television, in print, or in other mediums, are you more or less likely to purchase something advertised on the Internet, the World Wide Web, or online services?

More likely	18%	About as likely	8%	Less likely	74%

Keep It Free

(If you have gone online) Would you be willing to pay user fees to support the Internet, World Wide Web, or online services if it meant avoiding online commercials, or not?

Willing to pay user fees	29%
Not willing to pay user fees	67%
Don't know	4%

The 27-Hour Day?

(If you have gone online) Does the time you spend on the Internet, World Wide Web, or online mean you spend less time . . . .

	Yes	No
Eating	7%	93%
Watching television	48%	52%
Exercising	19%	81%
Reading	26%	74%
Working	10%	90%
Sleeping	11%	89%

Here's the Rub

(If you have gone online) How willing are you to share personal and financial information about yourself so that online ads can be targeted to your tastes and interests?

Very willing	1%	Not very willing	23%
Somewhat willing	11%	Not willing at all	65%

*Multiple answers allowed; figures add up to more than 100%

Survey of 1,002 adults, including 345 Internet/World Wide Web users and 280 who have seen online advertising, conducted Sept. 17–21, 1997, for *Business Week* Louis Harris & Associates Inc. and Baruch College of the City University of New York.

Edited by Keith H. Hammonds

Article Review Form at end of book.

Customer Service 'Gets Real'

Christy Walker
PC Week

Business Evolution Inc. last week unveiled a real-time customer service application for electronic commerce to expedite Internet-based sales.

The Princeton, N.J., company's Interact.Express enables businesses to receive and respond to customer inquiries in real time via the Web.

Users who visit an Interact.Express-supported Web site can click on the "Instant Response" button and type a short message or inquiry in the pop-up screen. The message is forwarded immediately to the Interact.Express agent and sits in a queue until a customer service representative reads it.

Users are free to browse and navigate within the Web site while waiting for the answer, which will appear in the pop-up screen, according to Business Evolution officials.

Interact.Express is designed to increase online sales, officials said.

SkyMall Inc. is testing the application as an extension to e-mail, with hopes of increasing its customer service response rate and cutting its telephone costs.

"It's important not just to be on the Web for revenue but also for additional customer service," said Annette Marino, general manager of electronic commerce at Phoenix-based SkyMall, which produces the multimerchant publications found on airplanes.

"One focus is to have customers use the Web as a cost saving for SkyMall with no 800-number costs," Marino added. "We are looking at [Interact.Express] not just for traditional customer service but also [for] helping customers on the Web, through their purchasing experience with a real-time response."

Such instant customer service applications hold great potential, according to one analyst.

"If it works well, it's fantastic; it's getting an online answer as close to live communication in a consumer-to-business way as we've seen so far," said Kate Doyle, an analyst with Jupiter Communications Inc., in New York.

"However, if a company doesn't scale up the number of reps in time, it could turn people off," Doyle added.

The Interact.Express server-based Java applet runs on Windows NT and goes through proxy firewalls via the HTTP transport, officials said.

The application also supports Secure Sockets Layer and can be tied to any relational database, so that when a recurring question is sent to a customer service representative, the integrated search engine will pick it up with the corresponding questions and answers, company officials said.

Interact.Express supports Netscape Communications Corp.'s Navigator 3.0 and higher and Microsoft Corp.'s Internet Explorer 3.0 and higher.

The Interact.Express Starter Pack, which includes the server applet and one customer service license, is priced at $2,995. Additional licenses cost $1,000 apiece. A free 30-day trial download of Interact.Express is available now.

Business Evolution can be reached at (800) 984-8341 or www.businessevolution.com

 Article Review Form at end of book.

ISP Customers
Reliability wins

Rebecca Wetzel

Last fall, Inter@ctive Week and PC Week published preliminary results of the first annual TeleChoice Inc. Internet service provider survey, in which business users were asked to rate their ISP. Since the October 1997 publication, additional responses have come in, enabling the expansion of the survey's results to include more ISPs.

This update reflects another 200 completed questionnaires that arrived after the initial publication. The overall response rate was 33 percent, which is high for mail service. Late replies often better approximate the opinions of people who don't reply, so changes to the ratings that are the result of the late respondences have special significance.

The point of this study is that an ISP's ability to provide reliable service is the single most important criterion for businesses selecting an ISP. Reliability also is tops when businesses select a Web outsourcing vendor. Ninety percent of respondents rated reliable operations as the top Web outsourcing selection criterion.

The premium placed on reliability should come as no surprise to ISPs. Internet connectivity is, after all, the core service they sell, and customers rely on the service to work. With many ISPs focusing resources on increasing market share through massive marketing and merger and acquisition efforts, however, operations and infrastructure have been severely strained at most service providers, and their ability to keep up with customers' needs has wavered in some cases. Here is our updated report on how the ISPs are keeping up, and even moving ahead of the pack in the eyes of customers.

In the final analysis, the five most important criteria continue to be service reliability, service performance, speed of repair, competence of the technical staff and price. But the order of importance has changed. In the preliminary findings, service reliability was rated most important, followed closely by service performance and then by speed of repair. In the end, however, competence of customer service and technical support edged out price

for fourth place. When push came to shove, competence won by a nose over price.

Who's on Top

UUnet Technologies Inc. (www.uu.net) held fast to its first-place ranking—with its overall score actually increasing by 3 percent. AT&T WorldNet (www.att.net) continued in second place and GTE Internetworking (www.bbn.com) placed third without notable changes in scores.

The most interesting development occurred in the fourth and fifth positions. MindSpring Enterprises Inc. (www.mindspring.com) was previously not in the pool because it did not receive a sufficient number of responses. That changed with the additional responses. MindSpring not only joined the ranks, but was rated fourth overall. No single local phone company received enough rankings to be included by name, but the category of all local phone companies combined did reach critical mass and, as a group, did well, rating fifth in the pack of 13. MindSpring and the local phone company ISPs edged out MCI Communications Corp. (www.mci.com), though MCI's rating was basically unchanged.

Since reliability is the most important ISP selection criterion, a good showing in this category carries considerable weight. Previously, GTE Internetworking was tied with UUnet for first place, but additional responses broke the tie, and GTE Internetworking took the lead. The phone companies, as a group, came in third, then AT&T and MindSpring. This top tier of providers had much better scores than the rest of the pack, with a full 12 percentage point spread between the fifth- and sixth-rated ISPs.

For the second most important criterion—performance—UUnet tied with the local phone company pack for first place; GTE Internetworking remained in second place and AT&T in third. Again, there is a clear tier of top-quality providers, with 9 percentage points separating the third- and fourth-rated providers.

In the speed of repair category, UUnet held onto first place, with the previously unrated phone companies in second. MindSpring popped up in third place, closely followed by previous second-place holder, AT&T.

UUnet walked away with top honors in competence and knowledge of its customer service and technical support staff. New addition MindSpring came in second, and the phone companies, AT&T and GTE Internetworking tied three ways for third.

In the price category, MindSpring led the pack, with 70 percent satisfied with pricing for the level of service required. The next-best competitor, the phone companies, had only a 51 percent satisfaction rating. The number of respondents satisfied with UUnet's pricing actually rose in the final analysis, but that brought it only to third place. MindSpring seems to have found a formula for offering excellent service at very competitive prices, which puts it in a strong position with price-sensitive small businesses.

So, who really provides businesses with Internet access? Hundreds of different ISPs were listed by respondents as their primary access providers. Small ISPs made up almost half of responses. AT&T boasts the largest single share of survey respondents, at 8.1 percent. MCI holds 6.1 percent of respondents' primary access business. Despite low quality ratings, America Online Inc. (www.aol.com) matched MCI's

share with 6.1 percent. Netcom On-Line Communication Services Inc. (www.netcom.com) took a 5.9 percent share, and the overall quality leader, UUnet, came in fifth with 4.8 percent of respondents.

Businesses have identified differences in the quality of service, but, as of fall 1997, there were many customers that remained with their primary ISP despite high dissatisfaction ratings.

Several factors cause such inertia. Foremost is that the market continues to change very rapidly. ISPs are merging, joining alliances or being acquired at a fast clip. Quality of service increases and decreases with technology change on the network and with popularity of the ISP. Once a business decides to switch service providers, there may be contractual issues, employee training or—a real thorn—Internet Protocol addressing, which make it difficult to actually make the switch. Nevertheless, TeleChoice (www.telechoice.com) expects to see businesses migrate toward the ISPs offering high service quality in the 1998 study.

 Article Review Form at end of book.

Businesses Buy Into E-Commerce

Mel Duvall

In some corners, 1997 will go down as a disappointing year in the electronic commerce arena. Early analyst forecasts have proven to be far too rosy, as consumers in particular waited until as late as Christmas before taking their first tentative steps toward buying online.

International Data Corp., for one, reduced its e-commerce revenue forecast for 1997 from $50 billion to a much more modest $10.6 billion.

One area that has proven to live up to expectations, however, is the business-to-business sector. It may not have the sex appeal of buying clothes or books online, but the daily humdrum task of ordering supplies and trading goods and services with business partners has gained a significant foothold in the digital world.

"This market doesn't have the hype or the spikes of the other Web areas," says Greg Martin, director of product marketing for Sterling Commerce Inc.'s Gentran division (www.sterlingcommerce.com). "But what it does have is the strongest long-term

potential. It's pretty easy to show companies the savings and productivity gains that can be achieved by implementing these systems."

A case in point is Trade Compass (www.tradecompass.com), a Washington, D.C.-based firm that allows importers and exporters to file hundreds of trade-related documents electronically.

Browning Rockwell, Trade Compass' president, owned and operated an international shipping company for 18 years and knows the delays and headaches that can be created by pushing papers around. He devised a system, using Sterling's software, that allows companies to fill out such forms as purchase orders, invoices, customs declarations and manifests, and ship those forms electronically over the Net.

"Any company can link into our application with a simple browser, so there isn't really a barrier to entry," Browning says. "In return, they've been able to achieve significant time and costs savings and improve their trading links."

Martin expects sales of Web-based solutions like this will grow at a rate of 40 percent for

Sterling in 1998. From basically no revenue two years ago, they will account for about $35 million in annual sales.

Forecasts on the size of the business-to-business electronic commerce market vary, but Erica Rugullies, an analyst with Giga Information Group Inc., says while growth was strong last year, 1998 will be the year in which Internet Protocol-based trading systems catch on "like wildfire."

The reasons, she says, are simple. The market has moved beyond the pilot stage, and there are now a number of solid products to choose from such heavyweights as General Electric Information Services (www.geis.com), Harbinger Corp. (www.harbinger.com), IBM Corp. (www.ibm.com) and Open Market Inc. (www.openmarket.com).

Open Market is looking to grab a piece of that action with its LiveCommerce offering. The software allows companies to create highly personalized catalogs for viewing and ordering over the Internet, intranets or extranets, and when combined with its trademark Transact software, it acts as an end-to-end transaction processing system.

Bob Weinberger, vice president of marketing, says the toughest challenge was breaking into a few key accounts. Now that Open Market counts AT&T Corp., BankOne, and the Disney Store among its clients, momentum is taking over.

"It's like any new innovation," he says. "Once the early adopters get involved, it turns up the heat a thousand degrees on every other customer to respond."

Indeed, some early adopters report returns on investment in the range of 20 percent at the low end to as high as 1,000 percent.

Of course, moving a company's critical business applications onto a Web server is not without its risks and complications. Unlike a paper-based process, when a company's server or network goes down, so goes the business. Companies must factor in what would happen if suppliers and partners were suddenly unable to access a system

for hours or possibly more than a day as a problem is sorted out.

Despite the fact that applications are moving into more reliable second and third generations, companies joining the electronic commerce club now are still very much in the leading wave and must be prepared to deal with bugs and glitches.

But those drawbacks don't seem to be slowing the market.

 Article Review Form at end of book.

Spam King

I'll pay to spam

Coming from the man who used to relish his "King of Spam" title, it's a pretty startling statement.

Maria Seminerio

"We realize that the spam business model has run into a lot of roadblocks," said Sanford Wallace, CEO of bulk e-mail marketer Cyber Promotions Inc., in an interview following the news that the company had reached a settlement in a lawsuit against it by EarthLink Networks Inc.

The once-defiant Wallace, saying he's moving his company in a different direction while still trying to deliver on the opportunity some see in consumers' e-mail in-boxes, said next week Cyber Promotions will roll out its long-rumored "spam backbone" along with a service for Internet service providers to get paid to accept bulk e-mail.

"This way, the onus is on the ISP" if consumers feel they're being bombarded with too much promotional mail, Wallace said. ISPs can then ask their customers to opt in or out of the program—and those that sign up can get price breaks on their monthly bill, he said.

Involving the ISPs

Asking how much ISPs will be offered to join the program, he said: "We're asking them to name their price." The amount of savings to the individual subscriber would be up to the ISP, he said.

Wallace said Cyber Promotions has inked a deal with a company to provide the backbone, but would not reveal its name, saying that, "In the past, when we've said who we had agreements with, those agreements were derailed" by anti-spam activists.

> **'We're asking them to name their price.'—Sanford Wallace**

The difference between such an advertising model and that of America Online Inc., "which sues everybody it can get its hands on but then spams its members with its own ads," is that this system would give subscribers more control over the ads they receive, Wallace said.

The outcry from Internet users wanting to stamp out spam has been Wallace's biggest challenge. His company has been hit with lawsuits from all sides, and he's been forced into numerous settlements such as the EarthLink deal that calls for Cyber Promotions to pay $2 million to the ISP. The settlement also makes Wallace personally liable, up to a $1 million fine, if he or any company he is associated with sends spam to EarthLink members.

Kicked Off Many ISPs

In the past four years, Cyber Promotions has also been kicked off at least five Internet services.

He bristles at the suggestion that the company has lost the lawsuits, however. "We haven't lost a single case, in spite of what's been reported," Wallace said. Rumors that the company is in bankruptcy are also unfounded, he said.

"If we are, that's news to me," Wallace said.

 Article Review Form at end of book.

The Evolving World of Bulk E-Mail

Jeri Clausing

The Internet's notorious king of spam last month stunned a Philadelphia audience by apologizing for what he admitted has become an obnoxious business, and by saying he will try to get spammers to mend their ways.

Could it mean the end of those annoying unsolicited messages touting everything from get-rich schemes to adult Web sites? Not quite. But the seemingly remarkable shift in the attitude of the man blamed for starting the business of unsolicited, mass commercial e-mail, coupled with the emergence of consumer friendly e-mail advertising signals an evolution, or maturation, of sorts in Internet marketing.

The most noticeable change is the entrance of bulk mailers who send targeted ads only to people who ask for them.

Leading that movement is Steve Markowitz, a 27-year-old San Francisco entrepreneur who came up with the novel idea of "paying" people to read e-mail advertisements. His company, Intellipost doesn't pay actual cash, but it has developed some reputable partnerships that allow consumers to earn airline miles and bonuses like gift certificates for nationally known businesses.

"What we're doing is rewarding the consumer to read relevant offers," he explained. "The system is called BonusMail. The consumer comes to the Web site, reads our proposal, which is that you can get rewarded to read ads that are relevant to you. If the consumers decide this is something they want to participate in, they fill out a profile. And based on that, the consumer gets targeted, relevant ads. And the consumer gets rewarded to read those ads."

To get credit, each ad has a so-called magic word. After reading the ad, all the reader has to do is hit reply, then type the magic word in the message subject line and they will get points for reading the ad. Although no purchase is ever necessary to accumulate bonus points, Markowitz said the system is designed for people who will occasionally take advantage of some of the offers. That's where the bulk of the points are earned.

Among the advertisers: credit card companies, magazine and book publishers and direct-marketing companies like Omaha Steaks and Lands End.

Launched last June, the BonusMail program now has quarter of a million consumers enrolled, Markowitz said in an interview last week. He estimates the company will have a million participants by mid-year and roughly 2 million by year's end.

Markowitz has some reputable rewards partners— American and United Airlines, the Chilis restaurant chain, MCI and the Gap. He also has some big name Wall Street backers. So he is quite proud to talk about the booming business.

Just make sure you don't compare him to Sanford Wallace, the young Philadelphia entrepreneur largely blamed with developing the widespread practice of spamming. Though Wallace's business boomed for a few years, he recently has been unable to find any Internet service providers to host his business because backlash from angry spam recipients kept crashing their networks.

At a forum in Philadelphia last month, Wallace acknowledged that there was "too much obnoxious e-mail advertising out there on the Web." He even said he was leading a movement to encourage other spam companies to clean up their acts.

"We are in a very different boat from Sanford Wallace," said Markowitz, who is active in groups pushing legislation in Congress and the State of California to outlaw spam. "We do not send spam. We send targeted bulk mailings to consumers who have asked to participate in the program. . . . I hope that the combination of what we're doing and legislation will push out spam."

Indeed, the BonusMail program and other opt-in services such as NetCreations' Postmaster Direct and Cybergold that send just targeted mail to consumers who sign up to receive ads for specific hobbies or topics are changing the landscape of e-mail marketing and further widening the gap between the legitimate and fraudulent mass marketers on the Internet.

And it's a change that may eventually help those trying to outlaw spam.

Just last week, the Federal Trade Commission issued notices to more than 1,000 junk e-mailers that they were being monitored for possible fraud. In announcing the crackdown, Jodie Bernstein, who heads the agency's Bureau of Consumer Protection, said her agency's review of unsolicited commercial email indicates the vast majority of it is fraudulent.

Deirdre Mulligan, a lawyer with the Center for Democracy and Technology, which has worked with the FTC and other interest groups in trying to develop an industry-led solution to the problems of spam, said businesses like Markowitz's help further delineate between the reputable and the scammers.

"I think that there's probably an evolution going on because I think large companies or companies that have a reputation at stake, or a brand image, probably have been reluctant to use unsolicited email as a marketing tool," she said. "So I think that you see them trying to figure out how to establish a responsible relationship with the consumer so they can have a productive relationship and the message can be received."

There are three different proposals to regulate spam pending in Congress, including one that would create an outright ban on unsolicited commercial e-mail just like Congress several years ago banned the sending of unsolicited junk faxes. Others would place differing levels of regulation on the businesses. A hearing is tentatively scheduled this summer.

Though unsolicited junk e-mail can be annoying as well as costly to Internet service providers and people who download their e-mail long distance, many fear banning spam would set a precedent for regulating Internet communications.

Mulligan said the Center for Democracy and Technology has neither supported nor opposed any of the measures. But that doesn't mean it won't.

"We want to make sure wherever we end up is the right place. At this point I'm not going to tell you I'm opposed to a complete ban, but it's not a place I was comfortable starting," Mulligan said.

She said the growth of legitimate companies like Markowitz's and findings like those by the FTC are creating a much-needed record for lawmakers to make a final decision on how to deal with spam.

"If you have findings that a majority of people using mass unsolicited e-mail are engaged in fraud, that's probably another nail in the coffin," Mulligan said.

 **Article Review Form at end of book.**

Keeping the Junk Out of E-Mailboxes

Paul M. Eng

So-called "push" technologies that deliver personalized information from the Internet and corporate intranets may be all the buzz now, but such tricks aren't limited just to those who want to experiment with the latest Webcasting software. In fact, everyone connected to the Net today already has access to the most personal form of "pushed" content: electronic mail. And with an estimated 90 million E-mail addresses worldwide—almost four electronic in-boxes per Net surfer—it's an avenue that some Net companies have been quick to exploit.

If the experience of E-mail is any guide, however, the world of push delivery could alienate customers faster than it attracts them. Just ask any of the millions of subscribers to America Online (AOL) or CompuServe. For the past year, privately held Cyber Promotions in Philadelphia was bombarding members of those online services with "spam," the electronic equivalent of junk mail. Hawking everything from easy-money opportunities to cheap computer modems, Cyber Promotions and other marketers claimed to be offering readers and advertisers a valuable service and argued that they shouldn't be barred.

A Ban on Spam

But the protest of outraged AOL and CompuServe members prompted the online services to block unsolicited E-mail. On Feb. 3, the U.S. District Court in Columbus, Ohio, upheld CompuServe's spam ban, saying that the mass E-mail was equivalent to trespassing on that service's "private property."

The new generation of direct E-mailers is treading carefully. One such company is Denver-based Mercury Mail Inc., which delivers news briefs, stock quotes, weather reports, and ads based on an individual subscriber's specific profile. This could be a good business, says Mercury's Chairman John Funk. "When you start to measure the amount of time a Net surfer spends online and what they do," he says, "E-mail dominates more than the Web."

Since its rollout last year, Mercury claims to have over 375,000 subscribers and generates over 1.1 million E-mail messages per day—a number that will quintuple by yearend as Mercury adds new features such as digital photos. What's more, since Mercury's revenues are dependent on the number of subscribers who view the ads embedded in its messages, the growth could portend a revenue windfall. With ad rates of $30 to $70 per thousand viewers, Funk says Mercury will be profitable as early as the end of 1997.

As long as those messages don't become nuisances. "To some extent, there's an industry awareness against [unsolicited E-mail]," says Funk. "You don't want to annoy your subscribers and kill the golden goose." So Mercury takes great pains to distance itself from the spammers. Through its Web site, subscribers can very easily customize what and how much E-mail is delivered and, more important, unsubscribe from Mercury.

Message Filters

Other Internet companies are trying to keep electronic mailboxes from bursting. Web sites such as www.getlost.com and www.junk-busters.com will attempt to remove your E-mail address from spam lists. And in addition to blocking E-mail from spammers, AOL is looking at so-called collaborative filtering technologies. Such software, also called "agent technology," resides on your PC and watches where you go and what you choose to view. The agent "learns" from that and will filter material that is pushed by content providers, keeping only the items that match materials you have seen before.

Net powerhouses Netscape Communications Corp. and Microsoft Corp. are trying their best, too, not to leave their users deluged with information. Future versions of Netscape's and Microsoft's Net-accessing software will come with filters that will sort E-mail—last night's football scores in a "sports" folder, say—automatically. And tidbits that are gleaned from the Net might come with "expiration dates" so that news clippings more than three months old, for example, could be automatically deleted. How thoughtful. Software that cleans up after itself.

 **Article Review Form at end of book.**

Business Secrets of the Billion-Dollar Website

Yes, the Web is already big business—just ask netMarket.com, where over $1.2 billion of goods were sold in 1997. This Website may be the future of retailing.

Mary J. Cronin

Mary J. Cronin is a professor of management at Boston College and strategic adviser to Mainspring Communications. An expanded version of her column is available online at www.mainspring.com. Cronin can be reached at cronin@mainspring.com

Even though fewer than one in five of the largest retailers in the U.S. sell their wares on the Internet, consumers managed to spend more than $10 billion shopping on the Web in 1997. Over 10% of that was spent at a single Website—netMarket, an online discount service created for its dues-paying members by CUC International. NetMarket handled over $1.2 billion in sales last year.

The site now offers more than one million items for sale. CUC founder Walter Forbes says that he learned early on that most consumers don't want to bother searching the Internet for bargains. Instead, they want to buy everything—from automobiles to books to camping equipment—in one place, as long as they are dealing with a trusted vendor that guarantees them a low price. CUC has been making money by selling convenience to consumers for years. More than 73 million consumers pay annual fees to subscribe to CUC's traditional discount-shopping programs. To date, the bulk of CUC's annual revenues ($2.3 billion in fiscal 1997) come from membership fees. That may change now that CUC and franchising giant HFS have agreed to merge. The new combined company, called Cendant, will have a $29 billion market cap and control brand names like Avis, Days Inn, Ramada, and Century 21. So future revenues will be a mix of sales of products made by companies it owns, franchising fees, and subscriptions.

Forbes believes the combination will produce an online powerhouse. He may be right. Web shopping sites have a built-in pricing advantage over brick-and-mortar stores because they don't have the expense of a physical storefront and labor-intensive staffing. But competing on price can be dangerous strategy for startups because they can't sustain a prolonged price war with a well-established retailer. So many online sites need other sources of revenue besides direct sales to generate profits. Partnering with other Websites and relying on banner advertising are the most common sources of additional revenue, but neither has proved itself a reliable income stream yet. Forbes, on the other hand, simply does what he does in the real world—charge people subscription fees, in this case for membership in netMarket. "In traditional retail," says Forbes, "it takes about $10 billion in sales to make $150 million in profits. Cendant will make much more money selling memberships to consumers interested in discount Web shopping than just selling retail goods."

So far, netMarket has signed up about 700,000 members, many at an introductory rate of $1 for three months. Over 100,000 new members join each month; according to Forbes, a "significant" percentage of them stay on, paying the full annual fee of $69. Forbes expects over two million members by the end of 1998.

Forbes' formula for retail success on the Web—provide guaranteed low prices, all-in-one convenience, and an incentive to pay for membership-based shopping—is hard to replicate. But traditional retailers need to check out netMarket—it may be a glimpse of the future of retailing. Forbes envisions an international migration of consumers to the Web over the next five years. By then, netMarket will be customized so that people who log on from different countries will be able to get products tailored to regional tastes. If traditional retailers can't master the economics of Web shopping soon, they'll discover that a lot of the world's consumers have found a whole new way to shop.

 Article Review Form at end of book.

A River Runs Through It

Three floors above an art gallery on a slightly seedy street in Seattle, the world's biggest bookstore, Amazon.com, hums inside a refrigerator-sized box in the corner of a jumbled storeroom. "It's not much to look at," says Jeff Bezos, Amazon's boss, with some understatement. Where the virtual world meets the physical, disappointments like this are common. But there is a lot more to Amazon than a humming box of computer hardware running its Web site. Companies around the world are studying it as perhaps the best model for tomorrow's successes in electronic commerce.

Amazon demonstrates two particular virtues of Internet commerce. The first is the more obvious: Amazon's virtual shelves claim to hold 2.5 million books, ten times as many as even the biggest bookshops in the physical world. But Amazon itself keeps only the top-selling 400 or so titles in stock. Most of the others it orders from the nearby warehouse of Ingram Book, one of America's largest book distributors, whose proximity was the main reason for Amazon's setting up in Seattle. More obscure books it orders direct from the publish-

ers, routing them through its own warehouse. For best-sellers, Amazon charges 40% below list price; for nearly everything else, at least 10% below. Without the costs of maintaining physical shops, Amazon finds it easy to match or beat the discounts of most conventional booksellers, sometimes even when shipping costs are included. Result: sales of $16 million last year, almost three times the figure for its nearest on-line competitor, with revenues that have been doubling each quarter.

But once someone has shown the way, competitors find it easy to set up their own databases and deal with distributors. To fend them off, Amazon relies on customer loyalty that goes deeper than looking for the lowest price in the market. This is where the second virtue of its electronic-commerce model comes in. Amazon does not just sell books, but offers a service: information about books. Best of all, it gets others to do most of the work. It offers reviews from various media. Authors submit their own "interviews," robotically queried by Amazon's software. Readers are invited to add their

own reviews, and many do. The site also includes excerpts from books, and links to related material, as well as to other books by the same author.

Add Ingredients and Stir

This is a cyberspace equivalent of the fairytale about stone soup, in which two men set up a big pot full of water over a fire in a town square, drop in a stone, and start stirring. The first curious passer-by asks what it is, and is told it will be a delicious stone soup; all it lacks is a few carrots. The passer-by fetches some carrots and drops them in. Other passers-by add potatoes, onions and so on until the soup really is delicious, and is served to all. Amazon has set up the pot and dropped in the stone; the Internet's townsfolk are contributing most of what makes it perfect.

This has several advantages. The first is the community of book-buyers Amazon has built, which provides an enviable amount of positive feedback. People come to the site because it has the most reviews written by readers, and they often stop to write some of their own, attracting even more people. The more books you buy and the more information you give Amazon about your tastes, the better it will become at finding things you might like. It will send you an e-mail message when a book you are looking for (or might just be interested in) is coming out, hooking you ever more firmly.

Another form of community is Amazon's "associates program," which offers other Web sites up to an 8% share of each sale they direct to the bookshop. Amazon knows that it will probably never be the very best site for rock-climbing information or quantum-physics discussions, but that the sites specializing in such subjects could be great places to sell books. A link to Amazon is an easy, and potentially lucrative, way for such specialist sites to do that at one remove; a click on the link takes a viewer to Amazon's relevant page. It is also a cheap way for Amazon to advertise. However, it carries some risks. Customers may be loyal to the referring site rather than to Amazon, and if some other bookseller offers a better deal, the site may transfer its allegiance.

Given all that outsourcing, it is no wonder that Amazon's own operation is the lean-and-hungry kind. A physical bookstore of its size would have a huge sales staff, a vast distribution network and legions of stock clerks. Teams of experts would be scouting for prime retail locations and redesigning store interiors to spur sales. Amazon has just two floors of offices and cubicles. On one floor, about two dozen editorial staff write book reviews, while down a hall perhaps as many programmers keep the software running.

But turn the corner, and you experience another of those jarring moments when the Internet meets the real world. What you see is a room full of computers, and next to it a classroom stuffed with people being trained to man them. This is the one area where Amazon has to spend just as much on staff and overheads as its physical counterparts: customer service. When customers cannot remember any more about a book than its red cover with a jumping dog, or think they may have typed in their address wrongly, the humming box in the storeroom will be no help. And because of the Internet's word-of-mouth amplification powers, Mr. Bezos cannot risk sending customers away grumbling. The limits of the robotic online superstore are drawn by old-fashioned human fallibility.

Getting to Know All About You

Despite the expense, all this feedback from customers has its rewards. Amazon now has a vast database of customers' preferences and buying patterns, tied to their e-mail and postal addresses.

Publishers would kill for this stuff: they know practically nothing about their readers, and have no way of contacting them directly. That relationship has traditionally been monopolized by the bookshops, and even they rarely keep track of what individual customers like. Amazon offers publishers a more immediate link. "Ultimately, we're an information broker," says Mr. Bezos. "On the left side we have lots of products, on the right side we have lots of customers. We're in the middle making the connections. The consequence is that we have two sets of customers: consumers looking for books and publishers looking for consumers. Readers find books or books find readers."

This is a generic model that could work in plenty of industries: anywhere with enough different products—and consumer tastes—to call for a big catalogue and a lot of advice. When Mr. Bezos started Amazon, he knew nothing about the book trade; he simply understood the power of electronic commerce. As a former financial analyst, he picked books because existing margins and distribution patterns seemed most favourable to an online business. In future, Amazon may expand into music and videos. Once you understand the model, the applications seem almost limitless.

 **Article Review Form at end of book.**

Brands Bite Back

New names have been created on the Internet, but the grand old brands are making ground against them. Will there be any more new, Internet-based brands?

For two years, Barnes & Noble, one of America's biggest book-sellers, sat back and watched Amazon.com, an Internet start-up, run off with the online book-retailing business. Now it is pouring money into the race to catch up. Last week, it announced that it had lost $9 million on a $15 million turnover on its online operations. The company has a way to go: its online sales were only a tenth of Amazon's in 1997, though its losses were about the same. Now, though, Barnes & Noble has signed exclusive deals to sell books on a number of popular websites, including Disney's, and is creeping up the list of the world's most visited sites.

To those whose businesses grew up in the real world, the Internet looks like a strange planet populated by new, unfamiliar brands—AOL, Netscape, Yahoo, Amazon. Other than Microsoft, the real world's big brands do not seem to have made much headway there. That, however, is changing.

Look at the list of "most visited sites" and it is dominated by the new Internet-based brands. But almost all of those are concerned with giving people access to the Internet, or helping them find their way around it. Some, like AOL, are commercial services that put people online; some, like Netscape, are browsers; some, like Yahoo, are search engines. Those inevitably get a lot of traffic, as the pavement in front of a real-life row of shops gets a lot of traffic.

Strip out the sites belonging to companies that help people find places on the Internet, and you find that the places people are going to are a more familiar bunch. Aside from the burgeoning "communities" (see box on next page), most of the "content" sites that are biggest on the Net belong to companies whose brands are big in the rest of the world—companies such as Sony, Disney, Time Warner, ESPN and CNN.

While the big names are establishing themselves on the Internet, the content sites that have grown organically out of the new medium are suffering. *Word*, one of the first and hippest of the online magazines, closed earlier this month, along with its sister publication, *Charged*. Wired Ventures, whose print magazine has been the bible of the Internet generation, recently shed 20% of the staff of Wired Digital, its on-line arm.

So what happened to the Internet's promise? Once upon a time, some hoped and others feared, it seemed to be turning the world upside down by providing a new generation with the means of distributing output at a fraction of the cost of television or print. But distribution costs seem to matter less to the businesses concerned than marketing and maintaining a site.

Here, the old brands have the cash. Despite the Internet's rapid growth, it is still producing more hype than money, and establishing and maintaining a site is not as cheap as was once thought. According to Forrester Research, a technology consultancy, a high-profile content site costs an average of $3.1 million a year to run. Many Internet start-ups have run through their venture capital and out of money.

The big challenge for content sites is to be noticed. While the low barriers to entry on the Internet are part of its attraction, they also create a problem. Because anybody can create a site on the Internet, everybody is hard to find. So brands that are already big have an enormous advantage, particularly among people coming online for the first time who will tend to turn to names familiar from the real world.

But perhaps most important, the big media companies can promote their Internet sites on other media. Disney, CNN, Time Warner, ESPN, MSNBC and others can all plug their Internet site on their television channels. That was the main reason why SportsLine USA, a sports news site, sold 22% of itself to CBS last year: the investment guaranteed that CBS would provide it with the television advertising necessary to distinguish a content site from the crowd.

CNET, a computer information site, is the nearest thing to a new, Internet-based publishing brand; but, as its founder, Halsey Minor, points out, his popular television programmes and Internet operations help to promote each other. Its main competitor, ZDNet, is owned by a large computer-magazine publisher, whose print products promote its website.

The fact that the big media companies have an advantage on the Internet does not mean that all their properties are working well. Time Warner, for instance, has chosen the curious strategy of creating a new brand— "Pathfinder"—to group together such familiar names as *Time*, *People* and *Fortune*. It is a slow, badly designed site. Nevertheless, the power of its brands attracts customers.

Disney's site works better. Its designers have thought hard about adapting the product to the new medium. They have, for instance, created a cartoon detective who is a brain in a jar—a small, grey, immobile hero who does not

The American Dream, Virtually

The most visited place on the Internet is not just a new brand—it is a new sort of thing altogether. GeoCities is an Internet "community", a collection of web pages created by individuals. Some 1.5 million people have displayed pages at GeoCities; 8,000 more do so every day.

"I really got into this", says its CEO, David Bohnett, "to make people count, to make them feel empowered." The imagery of GeoCities is of the American frontier. The customers are "homesteaders," giving each other a helping hand with the tough tasks of site design and maintenance. And the pioneers are coming, in their bizarre variety: the Rev and Mrs Whatley ("if you have a prayer request, click on Prayer button"), just a "neighbourhood" away from a bilingual Peruvian page on housetraining dogs.

GeoCities is a stunningly simple business idea. To attract the customers who will attract the advertisers and retailers who pay the money, website owners have to provide some interesting content. That can be expensive. GeoCities, by offering free pages and a

buzzing environment in which people are likely to visit each other's sites, persuades the customers to put up the content themselves. And by defining them according to their interests (home improvements, pets, gay) it packages them for the advertisers and retailers who want to sell them things (new kitchens, dog food, sex).

Others have also spotted the potential of "communities". There is Tripod (for 18–30s) and Third Age (for the over-50s) and more are springing up. But GeoCities was biggest first, and on the Internet, just as in real life, the size of a city is part of its attraction.

Advertisers and retailers are still unsure about the Internet, so GeoCities is not yet profitable, but some serious money thinks it will be. Softbank, a Japanese computer company which is the biggest investor in Yahoo, put $51 million in the company last year. This year Mr Bohnett is hoping to go for an initial public offering, the sunset into which all Internet entrepreneurs hope to walk, hand in hand with a great deal of money.

much tax the graphic limitations of the Internet.

The smartest big-brand site is that of ESPN. It is put together by Starwave, a company whose head of technology is Patrick Naughton, one of the designers of the Java software language. Starwave specialises in applying its Internet expertise to other big names. The site is a happy marriage of technology and brand. It has a large free area as well as a premium service which is sports-nerd heaven: it can manipulate a massive database of sports statistics, plotting, for instance, the annual variation in the position and direction of any baseball player's hits on any particular ground.

Does growing colonisation by the old brands mean that the Internet will generate no more new ones? Not quite; but the next

lot of Internet brands are unlikely to come from content. Most probably, like the last lot, they will spring from developments in technology. David Weir, who was head of content at Wired Digital until the cutbacks, and now teaches at the University of California at Berkeley, reckons that "new brand opportunities will follow the technological corridors that open up." One brand that is already on its way is Real Networks, a company that produces audio and video software for the Internet. Sound and moving pictures are still clumsy on the Internet, but they are improving. And when they are everywhere, so will Real be.

 **Article Review Form at end of book.**

Branding the Globe

Carol Hildebrand

Senior Editor Carol Hildebrand can be reached at cjh@cio.com

Paging through *Gourmet* magazine the other day, I happened upon an attention-grabbing advertisement sandwiched between worshipful photos of plates of food and exotic locales. It wasn't the content that gave me pause—although the ad featured a vanful of people clad in what looked like pastel tinfoil spacesuits—so much as it was the company. Why was Intel pushing computer chips in a magazine devoted to mouth-watering foods and high living?

The short answer, says Dennis Carter, vice president and director of the sales and marketing group at Intel Corp., is that, "We think people who read Gourmet are prime candidates to buy PCs." There's more to the spacesuit ad than consumer demographics, however. The Santa Clara, Calif.-based Intel, after all, doesn't sell PCs; it sells computer chips. Since 1991, when the company launched its "Intel Inside" campaign, it has steadily built a powerful brand awareness of its products, to the point where the

most memorable thing about a television commercial for a PC is the four-note "bong" that sounds when the "Intel Inside" icon appears. "Basically, they made it more important to buy the chip than to buy the box," notes Martyn Straw, president of Interbrand Corp., a branding consultancy based in New York City. Intel's ability to promote its own brand name in another company's advertisements is a marketing department's dream. And Intel's brand acumen isn't restricted to U.S. borders—the company is building a powerful global message as well.

Many companies are no longer content with being a well-recognized name in one country. Instead, companies are seeking to build brand awareness from customers in both Kutztown and Kuala Lumpur. Straw says global branding campaigns have accelerated in the past several years, as different geographic regions gradually blend into one world-wide market. "It may be a cliché, but we're a global village now," he says. And technology, such as the Internet, has helped global branding considerably. After all, a Web site essentially gives a com-

pany a global presence, and a global direct marketing campaign via e-mail is a lot simpler than dealing with the postal regulations of dozens of countries.

Building name recognition worldwide requires an advertising and marketing game plan that stresses consistency. Compaq Computer Corp., based in Houston, for example, recently dumped its European advertising agency, Bates Worldwide Inc., and consolidated its $200 million worldwide account to Ammirati Puris Lintas in New York City. Why? Because Compaq wanted to send a consistent message worldwide and felt it could do that best with one agency at the helm.

"There's a big difference between local and global branding," says Scott Nelson, research director of the marketing knowledge and technology service at Gartner Group Inc. in Stamford, Conn. "Trying to go global can open a whole can of worms of different pressures, legal issues and cultures. Companies have to decide, 'Is it worth it to try to leverage a brand on a broader setting?' and if it is, 'Can you spend the money to do it effectively?'"

Nelson says global brand building means more than attaching an attractive logo to every piece of marketing and advertising material. Brand builders must make their names resonate with the same sense of trust and security that their customers find at the local mom-and-pop shop on the corner. The best brands are global symbols that evoke visceral, emotional responses from consumers. When people think of Nike, they don't necessarily think of sneakers. Instead, they think of "Just Do It," or an image of Michael Jordan's spectacular grace and athleticism flashes in their minds. Straw uses the example of Coke. "It almost doesn't matter that the product is brown, fizzy water," he says. "They're selling an internationally valuable idea based on traditional values and Americana." Think of it as branding as gestalt rather than as product. And, says Nelson, although technology is vital to conveying a particular global brand message, it also has drawbacks. While the Internet has opened a global line of communication to companies of every size, it also has removed an element of control that companies once held over their brands. For example, there's nothing stopping any person or organization from linking to a company's Web site. Links from less-desirable sites may send the wrong message, brandwise, about the company a particular brand keeps.

Technology, it seems, pulls off the neat trick of removing some branding problems while simultaneously creating others. But smart brand builders, like the three profiled below, use technology selectively to focus on what Nelson calls the top three priorities of global branding: consistency, community and customer service. KFC (formerly Kentucky Fried Chicken), for example, depends on a CD-ROM toolkit to send a consistent brand message to its franchises worldwide. Owens Corning has built an online community that enhances its image as a brand that helps its customers. And AMD's Net Seminars help it convey information to its smaller customers, who might otherwise fall through the cracks. These strategies are just a part of an overall global brand strategy at each company. AMD, for example, has an extensive print ad campaign that it uses to reinforce consistency. But by using technology to push their messages, all three companies hope their global brand campaigns will be that much stronger.

Consistency: The Colonel Across Cultures

Your typical KFC franchisee in Bombay, India, probably wasn't brought up on a media diet of the Colonel and finger-lickin' good, so it's easy to see why he or she might not realize the importance of that brand heritage. But, "Colonel Sanders was and always will be the core of our concept," says Kip Knight, vice president of marketing for KFC International in Dallas, whose parent company is Tricon Global Restaurants Inc. in Louisville, Ky. Knight calls Sanders "a little piece of Americana. We've done studies, and he's far and away one of the most recognized people on the planet." While people might recognize the Colonel's trademark white Vandyke beard and black string tie, it's a little more difficult to convey in a consistent manner KFC's specific marketing tactics to franchisees across 5,000 restaurants in 83 countries and 24 different time zones. And experts agree that good global branding means sending a consistent message across all aspects of a product, from quality and service, to pricing, image and looks.

"Consistency is one of the key drivers of brand strength," says Straw. "Companies used to be able to position their products one way in one country and very differently in another. But you can't do that anymore in this era of world travel. Products need to be presented [in the] same way 'round the world." Knight agrees. "We want everybody to sing out of the same hymn book," he says. "Otherwise we'll end up with a brand that's morphed into something very different." But the international marketing division lacked both the manpower and the technology to easily handle the needs of all those franchisees and regional marketers. "We could never have a big enough staff to meet the needs of 5,000 restaurants scattered around the planet," says Knight. So Knight and KFC Brand Manager Elana A. Gold turned to a brand-management tool from DNA Visual Business Solutions Inc. to help standardize the message.

"When you walk into a KFC, whether it's in Shanghai or in Cleveland, you want the same look, service and food," says David Wallinga, president and CEO of DNA in Chicago. "It's the branding that draws you in the door." The brand toolkit DNA and Tricon developed helps regional marketing folks and franchisees foster a consistent perception. The toolkit comes on CD-ROM, which users can browse by nine different categories, including brand history, advertising, promotions, menu management and pricing. "People can sit down and review an interview with the Colonel or old advertising," says Knight. "These are all things people couldn't do unless they got on a plane to Louisville, Ky., to visit our museum."

Knight says the toolkit, which is currently in use at about 1,000 restaurants, also helps improve the quality of local advertisements in smaller countries. "It helps set the bar at a certain height," he says. "If left to local devices and budgets, you can end up with food photography that's not very appetizing." But the toolkit shows pictures and ads that are up to corporate KFC standards, so viewers get a better idea of what's appetizing in advertising.

Gold says she hasn't yet crunched the ROI numbers for the toolkit, but she hears a lot of anecdotal praise. "I get a lot of comments," she says. For example, she says, the KFCs in Asia used it to develop a kids' program, and South American franchises are following suit. "If you're a franchisee in a small country, you might be the only person there building a brand," says Knight. "This gives a certain comfort level. They get access to world-class materials with the click of a button."

Community: Chatting with the Panther

The Pink Panther has come a long way since his early days starring in the credits of Peter Sellars movies. Today you can spot his paw prints all over the Web site of Owens Corning, the Toledo, Ohio-based manufacturer of building materials, most notably pink (what else?) insulation. The company is attempting to buttress its brand image by building a strong Web community through its Web site (www.owenscorning.com).

"Branding is all about a relationship with the consumer," says Karen L. Strauss, director of marketing and marketing communications at Owens Corning. For Owens Corning, which is separated from the consumer by a network of distributors and retailers, technologies such as the Web establish a direct line of interactive communication with the end user, which can sharpen a company's brand image. She points out that selling through a distributor or retailer increases the chances that customers might misinterpret the brand image. "The Web is an opportunity to create a relationship with users," she says.

Gartner's Nelson agrees. "It lets you know a customer a lot better," he says. One way to do that, he points out, is "to create a community of common interest, where users with an affinity for something can use the Internet to share ideas." That is precisely the intent behind Owens Corning's "Let's Talk" section of its Web site, which has been humming along since July 1996. Built using Proxicom Inc.'s interactive discussion software, the site lets contractors exchange ideas and tips on projects, whether it's installing a new roof or insulating a cellar. There's also an area that allows visitors to pose questions directly to Owens Corning experts. This discussion forum has had hits from more than 137 countries, although, like much Internet traffic, the preponderance of the hits come from the United States, says Craig Landwehr, the Internet process leader at Owens Corning. (See "So Many Ideas, So Little Site," *Webmaster*, July 1997).

For example, Artie from Michigan is finishing a basement room and wants to know if he can install an insulating layer between the carpet and the concrete

floor without losing significant room height. He gets three replies: Syddad recommends installing two inches of blue foam and a vapor barrier. Rocky tells of a new kind of insulating pad called the Enviro Cushion, and Brian says that Artie will have to put down floor joists with insulation between them and then nail the subfloor to the joists. Community achieved: Artie's happy and so is Owens Corning.

Strauss says that the company's Web site also serves as a global community by offering a number of different country pages. Most countries have unique building codes, and Owens Corning sells products that comply with those codes.

The Web offers the perfect medium for community building, says Landwehr. "If you look at other media, you really don't know if the customer is paying attention," he points out. "Here, you know they're involved, and it's interactive." Strauss agrees. "The Web is a natural vehicle for us," she says. "It really helps us educate and get straight to the people."

Customer Service: Live on the Web

As AMD's presentation on its new K6 chip winds down, the questions start flying from hundreds of value-added resellers (VARs) that make a living building and installing computers and networks for small businesses. Ivan wants to know the price difference between two chips, and whether the speed difference between the two is worth the increased price tag. Another VAR wants to know whether a production delay on one AMD chip will also affect availability on a couple of other products.

And the best part is, neither of them had to leave their chairs to attend the session. Advanced Micro Devices Inc. or AMD, a computer chip maker based in Sunnyvale, Calif., hosts quarterly NetSeminars, which are put on by Education, News & Entertainment Network (ENEN), a Web production company in San Diego. The program is for small VARs, a segment of AMD's customer base that is geographically scattered and hard to reach. With NetSeminars, these customers receive "e-vites" from ENEN that explain the event and assign passwords and logons to each person.

Invitees can log on to the ENEN Web site (www.enen.com), watch a live slide presentation with audio and lob questions to AMD reps through a chat feature built into the site. For AMD, it's a great way to offer service to an estimated 30,000 VAR customers who are scattered all over the world and who may not have the time or ability to travel to a central location. "Everything we do has to be focused on making our customers successful," says Bob Kennedy, manager of corporate advertising at AMD. "That's how we convey our brand and values."

Programs such as the NetSeminar represent a unique method of branding through customer service, and Gartner's Nelson says that "improving customer service is becoming an important part of branding. Companies are realizing that a large part of what goes into a brand is how the customer is treated."

Peter Holmes, the ENEN program manager at AMD, says his group put together the seminars, which run about 90 minutes or so, as a way to reach a customer base that doesn't get quite as much attention from, say, Compaq or Dell. "If they don't hear from us, the easy route is for them to recommend Intel," he says. This way, AMD increases brand awareness while simultaneously offering customer support. "We've had tremendous response," says Holmes. "It's nice for the customer to find that they can spend an hour or so, get all the information they need and discuss pertinent issues without having to leave their businesses."

 **Article Review Form at end of book.**

Getting Down to E-Business

Dan Ruby

If the business of the Internet is indeed business, it certainly didn't start out that way. Commerce was specifically excluded from the Net in the early days, and for a long time after that it was barely tolerated. The slightest whiff of commercial speech generated nasty flames. Dot-com was a second-class address. That we've come a long way is evident from the feature articles in *NewMedia* over the past few months. Our editorial interest has spanned **intranets** (May 5), **digital branding** (June 2), micropayment transactions (this issue) and online advertising (next issue). These topics cover a broad range, but perhaps lack a comprehensive framework. Let's try to connect the dots.

The mainstream business community paid no attention to the Internet until the first graphical Web browsers arrived in 1993. Then companies seized the Web as a medium to convey information about products and services, initiating the Web's first wave of commercial use—for marketing communications.

Problem was, early brochure-wares site were less than compelling. Companies tried to make their Web pages interesting by packaging editorial content around product messages. Businesses whose primary function was to sell soap, software or whatever were running around trying to produce media. Little surprise that most of them did it badly.

Companies typically responded to this dilemma by having their marketing departments call in an ad agency. The end result was elaborate Web presentations and million-dollar budgets, but still relatively little impact. No matter how glitzy the production values, consumers are not drawn to sites for commodity products.

Hand in hand with expensive business-to-consumer Web sites came experimentation with other forms of Web marketing, including banner advertising and sponsorship programs. Here, finally, was a pure form of marketing—without any pesky editorial content. Marketers, however, had trouble justifying substantial budgets, given the questionable effectiveness of ad-

vertising in an underdeveloped medium.

Meanwhile, as marketing departments everywhere were going hyperactive, IS departments were beginning to see the Web as a platform for serious applications. The basic elements of the Web, HTML and HTTP servers, were flimsier than the tools IS managers were used to, but the possibilities were obvious. So along came the intranet, linking departments within companies, and (even better) the extranet, which seemed to provide businesses with a long-sought method of tying customers and suppliers into corporate systems.

Such collaborative information systems represent the second important commercial use of the Net. All well and good—but intranets, it turns out, are also content-driven, and IS workers are even more clueless about producing media than their marketing colleagues are.

The third important commercial use of the Net entails nothing less than reinventing the basic business proposition. In the digital age, smart companies are supplementing existing pricing and channels with new systems for electronic ordering and delivery. Representing the ultimate step in this direction are businesses created explicitly for conducting commerce electronically. The most successful—companies like Amazon.com, E-Trade and Auto-By-Tel—produce information-rich sites featuring plenty of expensive content.

The Future Is Now

So what have we learned from this accelerated history? First, that content is integral to doing business on the Web. Companies need to think about developing in-house expertise. At minimum, they must budget for serious content creation. And they must understand that this is not just a matter of initial site design, but of ongoing, perhaps daily, media production.

Businesses must also realize that having a great promotional site does not replace media spending. While the Web provides a way to bypass expensive advertising and take messages directly to the market, most of the time that market isn't listening. Media sites are still necessary to aggregate audiences.

Every business can benefit from putting its communication and business systems on an intranet. Extranet applications that connect business partners to information systems also can provide a competitive advantage.

Truly robust Web applications grow out of a merger of marketing and MIS strategies. A company's Web service may be its most critical business system and should be treated as such. Substantial tools from trusted technology suppliers can form the foundation for reliable systems.

There is vast potential for businesses to reinvent traditional commerce for the information age. There are also untold risks for companies that need to protect their existing revenue streams. Companies living in endangered analog niches should anticipate the radical shifts ahead and determine how to transform their business models for the digital future.

Business on the Internet started out as an oxymoron, became a curiosity and is now mission-critical. For any company that hasn't done so already, it's time to roll up your sleeves and get down to e-business.

 **Article Review Form at end of book.**

E-Shop Till You Drop (int'l edition)

Consumers are the big gainers as retailers brace for a Net onslaught.

David Woodruff in Frankfurt

With William Echikson in Brussels, Julia Flynn in London, and bureau reports

Pekka Nurmiranta wanted to buy several hard-to-find tomes on marketing. Rather than scour the bookshops near his Brussels home, the 39-year-old manager at Siemens-Nixdorf Software hit the Internet. Several mouse clicks landed him at Amazon.com Inc., the online bookstore based in Seattle. He dropped three titles into his virtual shopping basket and paid with a credit card. The books arrived on his doorstep two weeks later. "Amazon was very convenient," he says.

Like Nurmiranta, European consumers increasingly are discovering the joy of shopping for everything from computers to groceries online. By 2001, nearly 7% of households will make cyberpurchases totaling $3.5 billion, up from less than 1% and $96 million last year, figures Datamonitor, a market researcher in London (chart). Experienced online merchants from the U.S., such as Dell Computer Corp. and Music Boulevard, are setting up multilingual Web sites to take advantage of the boom. A few European retailers, such as Germany's Otto Versand mail-order house, also are ready to cash in. But many more are scrambling belatedly to set up online stores.

For European retailers, the online surge will only sharpen an already brutal rivalry. E-commerce makes comparison shopping a whiz. It will unleash fierce price wars that may shake to their foundations retailers that have never faced unfettered competition before. The low cost of launching a cyberstore—as little as $1,500—reduces the financial hurdles for small specialty retailers intent on nabbing customers from bigger players.

Crossing Borders

The arrival of a single currency in less than a year will make it that much easier for online retailers to sell across borders. And although online sellers don't save European consumers from the notoriously stiff value-added tax, they can eliminate duties if a company sets up shop on the Continent, as Dell has. Online sellers "have started to challenge local operators," says Jonathan Reynolds, a professor at the Oxford Institute of Retail Management.

So far, the most popular online purchases are of computer hardware and software, books, music, and travel packages. Sales of those items should grow fastest as more consumers shop on the Internet. Less than a year after launching cybersales in Europe, for instance, Dell brings in $1 million a day online. Some catalog merchants are showing good results as well. Otto Versand, which launched a Web catalog in 1995 selling everything from clothing to vacation packages, now garners 6% of its sales online.

Although some items clearly lend themselves more readily than others to cybersales, European consumers can already buy just about anything online. In Britain, a company called Eagle Star Direct offers auto insurance at attractive prices. Tesco PLC, Britain's No.1 supermarket chain, sells cases of wine via the Internet. An experimental home shopping service allows consumers in some parts of London to order groceries by computer. They are delivered for a small fee. Although the service is not yet available to general Internet users, demand has been so strong that Tesco may broaden the program.

European companies can find it tough going head-to-head with U.S. competitors. For example, because wholesale book prices in Britain are higher than in the U.S., online shoppers often get a better deal from Amazon than from the Internet Bookshop (iBS) in Cambridge, Europe's biggest online bookstore. Stephen King's novel *Wizard and Glass* costs only $14.30, including shipping to Britain. That's 32% lower than iBS's price.

Music Boulevard, a two-year-old, New York-based online seller of recorded music, is expanding aggressively in Europe and Japan, where CD prices average 30% more than in the U.S. The company, which carries 200,000 titles, already has a French-language Web site as part of a joint venture with publisher Hachette. Similar alliances are in the works for all major countries, and a European distribution center is planned for later this year, says Lawrence L. Rosen, CEO of Music Boulevard's parent, N2K Inc. That should push overseas revenues from 30% of sales, which totaled $11.2 million in 1997, to about 70% in the next several years.

Such aggressive growth has European companies hustling to respond. Bertelsmann, the German media giant, has a team preparing the technical framework for large-scale online sales in Europe. The company's book division, with annual sales of $4 billion, now has limited online ordering available only to members of its book club. Company officials acknowledge they're under pressure to respond to the threat from Amazon, Barnes & Noble

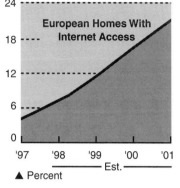

More Europeans Will Jump Online . . .

European Homes With Internet Access

▲ Percent

Data: Datamonitor ©BW

. . . and Go Cyber Shopping

European Homes Shopping Online

▲ Percent

Inc., and similar online competitors in bookselling.

Small specialty retailers are finding the Internet a cheap way to broaden their geographic reach. Spinnrad, a $100 million German retailer of environmentally friendly drugstore products, is spending $1 million to set up an online catalog that will be available later this year. The company, which currently sells only in Germany, will use the Internet to target ecology-minded customers as far away as Japan.

Card Worries

There's still some resistance to electronic commerce in Europe. Europeans don't use credit cards as much as Americans do. Partly for that reason, they are more anxious about revealing card numbers on a public medium like the Internet, say analysts. The higher cost of going online remains a deterrent as well. Bertelsmann figures that 20 hours of online use in Germany costs $74—$54 for phone charges alone—vs. an average of $29 in the U.S. Moreover, consumers in southern Europe have been slow to join the computer age. Only about 10% of homes in Spain and Italy will be online in 2002, vs. 35% in technology-

friendly Sweden, according to Datamonitor. And fewer than one-fifth of them actually will buy anything through the computer.

Europe's two biggest markets, Germany and France, will develop more quickly. In France, credit goes to Minitel, the text-based online service that France Telecom has offered for more than a decade. There are 6.3 million Minitel terminals in use, and consumers have become quite comfortable using them to shop. General merchandise mail-order house La Redoute, for instance, receives $333 million in orders annually that way, 17% of its total. Minitel is shifting its services to the Internet.

The biggest gainers from the move to E-commerce, of course, are consumers. Suddenly, they can bypass strict shop-closing rules in places like Germany and Austria. Comparison shopping is increasingly simple. And obscure products can be tracked down from the comfort of a desk chair. Is it any wonder that shoppers like Nurmiranta are ordering everything from shirts to software online?

Article Review Form at end of book.

Behind the "Top Sites" Lists

Andrew Marlatt

According to the "leader in measuring the World Wide Web," the phone-directory site Switchboard was the 10th most popular Web site accessed from home in January, while Hotmail was 24th. But according to the suppliers of the "accepted standard in Web measurement," Switchboard was 22nd, Hotmail was No. 11. So who is right? For many sites, the more important question is, "Which list are we on?"

Each month, Media Metrix, The PC Meter Company, the self-professed "leader," and RelevantKnowledge, the self-professed "standard," release their oft-quoted rankings of Top 25 Web sites, basing their results on "reach," or the number of individuals who have accessed a site in the past month. Both companies make profit through custom research for clients, but it's their Top Sites rankings that put them in the spotlight. Though placement differs, the lists often present the usual suspects: Yahoo, Netscape, Microsoft,

GeoCities. Further down, however, the rankings diverge, giving more sites a highly sought-after place in the sun.

A Top 25 ranking is "incredibly valuable, a tremendous marketing tool," says analyst Chris Charron with Forrester Research. "It's important to attracting advertisers and investment, to increasing brand awareness among users, and in forming partnerships with content and commerce sites. These online services are doing a deal a day and content providers don't want to be shut out, and if they look at the landscape and who it is they want to partner with, obviously they look at traffic and reach."

But whose traffic and reach numbers should they rely on? According to Charron, neither service has a monopoly on accuracy. "Right now, advertisers and content sites we speak with are buying information from all of these providers because nobody has it right yet," he says. "These people-meters are in the embryonic stage. Methodologies vary, sample sizes are very small, so they are, at best, rough approximations of traffic on the Web."

Charron questions the rankings' sample size most. RelevantKnowledge has a base of 8,000 users, 3,500 of whom were tracked for the January ratings, which he says is not a projectable sample. Media Metrix has the larger pool of 45,000 panelists, of which nearly 10,000 are used in its monthly ratings; but here, too, size is a problem. Media Metrix breaks its Top 25 lists into two categories: Internet access from home and work. Of those 10,000 panelists, more than 90 percent were used to generate the at-home ratings. The at-work rankings were based on a panel of only 700 users. RelevantKnowledge's January ratings relied on even fewer at-work users: 490.

Charron's discomfort about the companies' calculations, however, pales in comparison to each company's "concern" about the other. In their efforts to attract business, Media Metrix and RelevantKnowledge have developed an aggressive, antagonistic rivalry worthy of the browser wars, and taking sides is often a subjective decision.

Each month, Atlanta-based RelevantKnowledge brags that its Top 25 site ratings come out first. New York-based Media Metrix counters that its delayed ratings are more detailed. Media Metrix touts the fact that its research is based on the full calendar month, while RelevantKnowledge's January rankings, for instance, tracked usage Dec. 29 through Jan. 25. RelevantKnowledge CEO Jeff Levy counters that they use four-week periods because calendar months are unequal; a January with five weekends is not equal to a February with four. "If some Web site gets a lot of traffic on weekends," Levy told IW Daily, "they'd get 20 percent more traffic in the January ratings than with February."

While both companies load software onto users' machines to track Web movement, Relevant-Knowledge tracks users age 12 and above recruited via phone surveys using random-digit dialing. This statistically validated method for contacting prospective respondents is better than the Media Metrix approach, asserts Levy, in which users age 2 (yes, 2) and above are primarily enlisted through targeted direct-mail inquiries. Mary Ann Packo, Media Metrix's president, concedes that random-digit dialing is considered more desirable, but insists responses from direct-mail recruits are similar.

Levy is not shy in blasting, and arguably miscalculating, his competition's reliance on commercial online services. RelevantKnowledge ranked aol.com sixth in January, while Media Metrix had it first among at-home users. Levy contends that 70 percent of Media Metrix's panel is comprised of online-ser-

vice users, including more than 50 percent from AOL. Packo responds that only 47 percent of its panelists access the Web through online services, including 39 percent from AOL. Meanwhile, Packo says, 75 percent of its sample audience gets online through ISPs. (Users often have more than one access point, accounting for the greater than 100 percent total.) And as for Levy's challenge, Packo adds, "They have to take that position because they're getting so beat up by AOL for under-representing them."

Oddly enough, one of the few things Packo and Levy do agree on is the bottom-line impact of their Top 25 lists. They both want to relieve their lists of the responsibility for driving ad dollars. "Everybody likes to see their name in lights, but I don't know that ad dollars are traded off the lists," says Packo.

"Certainly some of the public companies' stock jumps when they show up on these lists," says Levy. "[But] that's just a PR list we put out. That's not the information people are using to sell [ads]."

Those who appear in those lists, however, tell another story. "It's becoming more important as advertisers begin to rely more on the measurement services," says Dick LaMonica, sales manager at Switchboard. "Certainly the sites in the top 10 or 20 are those getting the most Requests for Proposal. As we see our own ranking increase, we see a noticeable increase in number of unsolicited RFPs."

Not surprisingly, LaMonica is partial to the purveyors of his site's higher ranking, though it seems that stance depends on Switchboard's position. "At this

time," LaMonica says, "we believe Media Metrix does a more random and projectable study than RelevantKnowledge."

Would he say that if Switchboard were also in RelevantKnowledge's Top 10? "No comment."

Meanwhile, off most radar screens is tiny Web21, which inherited Marimba's old Palo Alto offices but not the push vendor's public-relations magnetism. Web21 is home to 100hot.com, a weekly list of the top "metasites," or Web properties, such as Yahoo!/Four11. Its research is based on proxy-server logs sent daily via FTP from "anyone who will send them," says 100hot president Bert Fornaciari. These include ISPs, companies, and universities who trade server logs for data. AOL, Prodigy, and CompuServe are not in the samplings.

The 100hot rankings are based on home-page views, which produces sometimes significantly different results from the reach-measurement services. Unlike the Media Metrix or RelevantKnowledge top-property lists for January, Web21's Top 10 included the chat site Mirabilis; its Top 25 includes WorldCom, FilePile, and Go2Net.

And at No. 18 is AltaVista Technology—not the Digital search-engine site, but the software company that occupies the altavista.com domain and gets untold numbers of accidental tourist hits. While AltaVista Technology's high rank is based on user confusion, that doesn't negate the importance of its appearance on the list. Fornaciari insists, "Hey, if I'm an advertiser, I might try to advertise with them," he says. "Mistake or not, they're getting hits."

Fornaciari doesn't claim to have a monopoly on measurement, instead suggesting his rankings could be used in conjunction with Media Metrix or RelevantKnowledge's. But Charron counters that it all comes down to the quality of the users.

"Advertisers are becoming less concerned with traffic and more concerned with people: Who is going to a Web site, what content areas interest them, what are their demographics, what are their purchasing patterns?" he says. "Methods that are user-focused have an advantage over those that are proxy-server focused, because you don't know who those users are."

 Article Review Form at end of book.

E-Muscle

Industrial buyers are getting more mileage out of on-line comparison shopping than individuals are. Why?

Scott Woolley

Glen Meakem paced nervously last June 24 as bids from Caterpillar Inc.'s suppliers started dribbling in over the Internet. At stake was a $2.4 million order for hydraulic fittings. Small potatoes for the $19 billion bulldozer company, but a big deal to Meakem, 34, and his then two-year-old FreeMarkets Online, which had designed the Internet-based auction. Meakem had told Caterpillar's purchasing chief that the company could save hundreds of thousands on just this one small trial run of Internet shopping.

All this is new to Caterpillar's purchasing department. It had always requested a few suppliers of low-tech goods to fax in bids. This time FreeMarkets Online rounded up 23 potential suppliers for the metal parts for hydraulic lines. The parts are simple but important. If one blows, it can hobble a $2 million earthmover.

Meakem fretted as the first bids came in high. But by auction's end nine suppliers were furiously undercutting each

other. For one straight stainless steel hydraulic connector, the low bid came in at 22 cents. That compares with the 30 cents that Cat had paid in the past. By the time the electronic gavel fell, Caterpillar saved an average of 6%.

Internet seers have long predicted that "electronic agents" would give consumers the same power to comparison shop cheaply and easily. It works for business, why not for consumers? The agents were to function like FreeMarket's auction, efficiently getting bids from dozens of suppliers. Power to the consumer.

But retailers have fought back. On-line music stores crippled an effort to make comparison shopping for records simpler. The offending Web site let users enter what compact disc they wanted; then the site's "shopping agent" would quickly visit all the other Internet sites that sell CDs, checking for price and availability. Big CD vendors blocked the effort by programming their Web sites to recognize the agent and keep it out. Requests to the site now turn up options from only a fraction of the 50-plus on-line music stores.

The problem for retail customers is simple: They don't have the clout to structure transactions on their own terms. Businesses do. General Electric Information Services led the way into business-to-business electronic commerce largely by dint of GE's $30 billion a year in purchasing power. FreeMarkets Online has succeeded by recruiting big buyers such as Caterpillar, GM and United Technologies. Purchase Pro, a system hotels use to buy everything from steaks to alarm clocks on-line, got started with the help of gambling magnate Stephen Wynn, who provided venture capital and steered his purchasing agents to the service.

Consumers are doing a lot of buying on the Web, but more often on the supplier's terms, not theirs. Dell Computer, Amazon.com and other high-volume sites offer good deals, but users must still do their own comparison shopping with other on-line retailers. Auto-By-Tel, a Web site for car buyers, solicits one bid electronically from one of its 2,700 dealerships, but other dealers don't get to undercut the price on-line. Internet auctions directed at consumers have recently caught on, but this simply brings in more bidders, which potentially, at least, helps the seller more than the buyer.

It is easy to see why retailers don't want to see their customers get more bargaining power: They see what that has done to suppliers of industrial goods. One industrial goods vendor entered a recent auction in an attempt to retain the business of a longtime customer. This supplier won the bid, for machine parts, but at a price 20% below what he used to charge. Says Charles Johnson Jr., founder of Purchase Pro: "Some suppliers hate us."

But then Meakem and partner Sam E. Kinney—both former McKinsey & Co. consultants who founded FreeMarkets Online in 1995—are not bent on making suppliers happy. Their Pittsburgh-based startup brokered $103 million in goods last year. Average buyer savings: 15%. With savings like this, the business is growing fast. This January it did more than half as much business as it did in all of 1997. "This can't be stopped," Meakem says. "Industrial buyers will have their way." How long will it be before ordinary consumers do, too?

 Article Review Form at end of book.

Special Reports — Technology

Supply chain

Arthur Andersen

Retailers face great unknowns right now. How soon will shoppers prefer to buy your products on line? Will they ever? When will you be ready to sell on line? Will you tailor your products to each customer? Before your competition does?

What seems certain is that on-line shopping is on its way. At the Internet Society's last count, the number of commercial Web sites had jumped from 1,000 in April 1994 to over 110,000 in October 1995. The Society says the figure is now doubling every month.

The bad news for retailers—and the good news for manufacturers—is that the Net may help manufacturers bypass retailers altogether. Why not buy that sports coat directly from Polo instead of paying a department store's mark-up? Levi's already sells its jeans directly to consumers over the Internet. Manufacturers will begin thinking like retailers and rethinking who their customers are. Retailers, some victims of disintermediation, will begin pondering why people should buy from them, how to add value.

But the emergence of the Net does not herald open season on retailers. As with stores, vendors in the electronic marketplace must have a name or make a name. This is why brand names and established retailers will have an advantage.

Established retailers also have the means to ally with electronic-commerce experts before opening virtual stores. Why make mistakes trying to invent your own wheel when someone else can supply you with a car? Some consulting firms and technology companies already know what technology is here and what's coming, what works on line and what doesn't, how to turn technology into cash.

When developing its Web site, for example, **Wal-Mart** asked **Microsoft** to help develop standard Web-retailing procedures—procedures many merchants could adopt—so that customers need not learn a new site layout and shopping system every time they visit a different on-line retailer. Wal-Mart then created its Web site in-house.

Categories of goods include automotive, entertainment, gift ideas, hardware, small office/home office, sporting goods and toys. Select country music, and a list of about 85 titles and prices appears. Click on Travis Tritt's "The Restless Kind" CD, and the site shows the CD's cover art, song list and shipping weight. After registering on the site, returning shoppers need only enter an ID and password. They can encrypt their transactions to protect their credit card numbers.

Merchandising and Marketing Strategies on the Internet

Cyberspace shopping has no shelves, no aisles, no retail space whatsoever. To create product awareness and brand loyalty in cyberspace, both retailers and manufacturers must learn to exploit the unusual nature of the World Wide Web. As you consider about where the Internet will fall in your supply chain, remember the following:

The Internet is a tool for direct marketing, not mass marketing. Any

Web retailer can hold a dialogue with any Web user, so develop a relationship with your customers.

Try accepting e-mail from those who hit your site to find out who they are and what interests them. **Lands' End**, which already received 39,000 letters a year and launched its Web site in July 1996, invites e-mail from customers. Customers suggest products, ask about their orders and describe trips to distant places. The company usually responds within 24 hours.

Target your promotions. **The Sharper Image's** site lets each visitor tailor the site to only contain products he or she cares about.

Any changes you make to your site's contents and message can reach the Web's global audience immediately. How often are you updating your site? Customers may return more often if they know they'll find something new.

The Web has advertising possibilities not available in print, radio or television. Visitors to the **Walt Disney Co.'s** Web site can listen to songs from "The Hunchback of Notre Dame" and "101 Dalmations," view animation stills or read an on-line "Pocahontas" storybook.

The Web also helps businesses interconnect far more than malls ever have. Does your Web site contain hyperlinks to other sites that might interest your target market? Do sites related to your products contain links to your site? On the Internet, traffic means business. How will people find you?

In October 1996 the Giga Information Group reported that it costs $700 to $20,000 per month to have a link to your site on another site, depending on how popular the other site is. If your site is a popular one, you can charge other companies for a spot on your site. Two sites of like popularity could even agree to promote each other's sites for free.

The Internet spans the globe. If you intend to market to the globe, does your Web page convey a message relevant to consumers around the world? Have you accommodated their unique needs and concerns? For example, is your page multilingual? Does it offer better deals to local consumers than to those overseas?

You may charge less to deliver to local customers, or, to be viewed as truly global, you may cross-subsidize delivery rates to make them equal for everyone.

On-line goods are only virtual. Cybershoppers cannot touch them. Are you showing your products as clearly and thoroughly as possible? Are you giving customers enough information? Remember that Web shoppers cannot read product labels, feel fabrics, taste sauces or read nutrition labels.

Customer service still matters. In cyberspace, consumers have control—they can visit you and leave you in two clicks, never having seen your wares. Again, get them to look at what's there and to come back again and again. Are you making their virtual shopping experience pleasant, simple and exciting? Will they receive their purchase quickly? Can they get answers to all their questions?

Visitors to the **Lands' End** Web site can get tips on tying Windsor and half-Windsor knots, read an explanation of how the tie became standard business attire, or order a specialty catalog of men's tailored clothing.

Your customers can visit any other cyberstore just as easily as yours. They can compare every price out there. They have the bargaining power. You've got to come to them.

Customers won't wait for images that download slowly. Complicated visuals usually don't mix with speed and efficiency, at least with current technology. Does your Web page balance excitement and practicality? It can be visually exciting, but keep it simple, logical.

The **Lands' End** site uses text instead of images wherever possible. Mike Atkin, vp of marketing, says his company found that on-line shoppers want easy navigation and "content that doesn't waste their precious time."

Fulfilling On-Line Orders

Goods with high value for their size make sense to deliver, goods such as apparel. But low-value, low-margin, high-mass goods are too costly to deliver; there is no profit in delivering a few bags of rice and cans of beans. Bundle them with higher-margin goods, however, and deliver them often to regular customers, and the numbers begin to work. Sears has made delivery work for decades.

Whether virtual supermarkets will be able to offer cheaper groceries is uncertain. Delivery costs money, but retailers will need fewer locations and less space to stock food—perhaps only a single, centralized warehouse—and may be able to do high-volume business with restaurants, hotels and universities.

If delivering your goods costs too much, meet the customer halfway. In the pick-and-pack system, the customer orders goods on line; employees in a store, warehouse or distribution center shop for and pack the goods; then the customer picks them up.

Some have proposed that large retailers assign franchise territories to delivery firms such as UPS. Will increased home deliveries cause intolerable automobile traffic? With consumers shopping on line instead of driving to stores, traffic may actually drop below current levels.

Processing Payment

Security concerns and small, single-item purchases have made consumers wary of using credit cards for Internet transactions. The rapid growth of the World Wide Web, and the number of small-ticket items in cyberspace, have created the need for a better currency.

Hence Ecash, offered by St. Louis' **Mark Twain Bank**, developed by Amsterdam's **DigiCash**.

As America's Community Banker reported in June 1996, Ecash gives on-line shoppers access to a "virtual ATM." When a shopper decides to buy a product on line—no matter how small— she can simply link up to the "Ecash Mint" on the Internet, prove she has an account and withdraw the money she needs.

But she gets no hard cash. Instead, her software stores the digital cash onto her PC's hard disk. She then confirms what she is buying, whom she is paying and how much she is paying. The Ecash software transfers the correct value in digital cash from her PC to the merchant. The merchant banks the digital cash electronically.

Once federal regulators and the private sector resolve legal questions of regulation and consumer protection, both consumers and retailers in cyberspace will profit.

 Article Review Form at end of book.

WiseGuide Wrap-Up

The technologies that have been developing in the past two decades will change the way we live, work, earn a living, and educate and entertain ourselves. What still remains a mystery is how these changes will occur. Ironically, if we can imagine these changes, we probably have the technology to make them happen. There lies the challenge to our imagination, as the words of Einstein echo one more time: "Imagination is more important than knowledge."

R.E.A.L. Sites

This list provides a print preview of typical **coursewise** R.E.A.L. sites. There are over 100 such sites at the **courselinks**™ site. The danger in printing URLs is that web sites can change overnight. As we went to press, these sites were functional using the URLs provided. If you come across one that isn't, please let us know via email to: webmaster@coursewise.com. Use your Passport to access the most current list of R.E.A.L. sites at the **courselinks**™ site.

Site name: United States Government Electronic Commerce Policy

URL: http://www.ecommerce.gov/

Why is it R.E.A.L.? That such a document exists, and it exists on the Internet is highly significant. It also details, in a lengthy report titled *The Emerging Digital Economy*, economic analyses and case studies to emphasize the importance of electronic commerce.

Key topics: Electronic commerce, marketing on the Internet, advertising, technology, consumers, digital economy, digital age

section 5

Legal and Ethical Issues of the Internet

The prominence of the Internet brought forth a new set of legal and ethical issues and heightened our awareness of them. These include, but are not limited to, the issues of civil liberties, privacy, security, encryption, intellectual property, copyrights, computer crime, and obscenity and pornography. By themselves, each of these issues represents immense challenges to the legal minds, since most seem to have ambiguous frameworks, perhaps by design. Their already fuzzy standards may become totally out of focus when taken in the context of virtual worlds. Compounding the complexity of the legal and ethical problems on the Internet is its unique structure, without national borders. This introduces multinational and international dimensions, with varying legal and ethical frames of reference to an already complex set of issues.

Fraud, breaking the law, unethical behavior, and their derivatives are not limited to the Internet and electronic world. Societies have experienced all of the issues mentioned and have found their own ways to deal with them. There is precedent. Because of this cumulative experience and knowledge, laws dealing with these issues use the real world as their reference point. Obscenity, for instance, has geographical boundaries in the real world. However, in a borderless virtual world, the same concept may need a new standard. Applying the laws of the real world becomes, to put it mildly, very difficult in cyberspace.

The infrastructure that makes all these possible is also enormously complex. This complexity sometimes hides unethical or fraudulent activities behind a shroud of mystery. How else can anyone create a "virtual nation" to help in an international con job? The implementation of some of these scams usually requires technical sophistication. When completed, these scams are difficult to understand for nontechnical people, contributing to confusion.

One of the volatile issues on the Internet is pornography and other offensive sites. The possibility of children getting exposed to such material concerns many, and the prospect of censorship of the Internet scares many others. In an information-rich environment like the Internet, where publishing requires only a minimal investment, "offensive" Web sites exist. In due time, societies will find solutions to the problems posed by these sites that will satisfy their standard.

Learning Objectives

- Understand the legal dimensions of the Internet

- Explore the new concepts that push the legal envelope, requiring a review of the established legal thought.

- Explore the challenges brought by technology to the legal arena.

Questions

1. How do you think the potential of fraud may affect marketing on the Internet? Does it concern consumers more than it does marketers?

2. Articulate arguments for and against regulating the Internet.

3. What approach could be taken to evaluate the arguments you posed in the previous question? What is necessary to make such a system a reality?

Data Collection as Free Speech

Solveig Singleton

Solveig Singleton (sberns@cato.org) is Associate Director of Telecommunications & Technology Studies at the Cato Institute, Washington, D.C.

This article explains why I have a right to collect information about you—and sell it for commercial purposes to third parties. Nobody said that free speech would never make anybody nervous.

A *New Yorker* cartoon notoriously said, "On the Internet, Nobody Knows You're a Dog." But it isn't true. The operators of anonymizer.com note that "on today's Internet, people do know you're a dog." Web sites offering fun and games collect information from hapless children. Technology enables operators of web sites to collect information about the equipment and software you are using to access their site, to learn your email address, to track your visits to other sites, and to record what content you view there. This information could be supplemented with that from other sources, such as records of credit card transactions, to provide detailed profiles of customer buying patterns.

This prospect angers a lot of people. Many privacy advocates support the idea that businesses should not be permitted to compile or transfer information about a customer's buying habits without the customer's knowledge or consent. But this regime, generally known as "mandatory opt-in," would run afoul of free speech principles. This article explores this conflict between privacy and the free flow of information. It concludes that the creation of new privacy rights would do more harm than good, eroding free speech and impeding the growth of new businesses and business models.

The idea that one should have the right to give consent before information about oneself is relayed to third parties has been explored thoroughly in the area of medical ethics, where the right is incorporated by custom into our ordinary understanding of medical contracts. But what about more ordinary transactions, where a customer simply visits a web site or uses the Internet to buy aquarium supplies or sweaters on sale? Do we "own" this information? Would it be wrong for others to collect this information and sell it without our permission?

The Dubious Origins of Privacy Rights

In the nineteenth century, legal limits on the power of governments to collect information were familiar. The Fourth Amendment to the United States Constitution, which prohibits law enforcement officers from conducting searches and seizures without a proper warrant, is typical of these. But there were very few limits on the power of the private sector to collect and distribute information, other than laws protecting the sanctity of physical property.

Rights to privacy independent of physical property rights began with an 1890 article authored by Louis D. Brandeis (before he became Justice Brandeis) and Samuel D. Warren. The authors' target was the press, which was "overstepping in every direction the obvious bounds of propriety and of decency." Warren was especially irritated to discover details of his home life discussed in the Boston press. Brandeis and Warren argued that courts should create a new kind of property right in personal information. Disastrously, they never considered whether the creation of new rights to restrict information published by the press would violate principles of free speech.

The publication of the Brandeis and Warren article gave birth to a hodge-podge of privacy torts and statutes. But courts and commentators only occasionally recognized the conflict between privacy and free speech. Luckily, the new privacy rights were narrowly defined. The general rule remained that human beings could gossip and exchange information about one another as they always had.

Free Speech Versus Privacy on the Internet

The conflict between privacy rights enforced by mandatory opt-in and free speech is a straight-forward one. Suppose I visit a web site or buy goods from a web vendor. At least two parties are involved in this transaction—myself, and the web site operator. It is flatly incompatible with principles of free speech to prohibit the web site operator from communicating truthful information about this real event and the real people involved to others, including other businesses.

Clearly, I should be free to communicate information about my purchase from or visit to a web site to my friends, to participants in a newsgroup, to Consumer Reports or the Better Business Bureau. There seems to be no reason that the web site operator should not be equally free to communicate information about the transaction—even for profit. Journalists are not required to ask the subjects of a news story for permission to print the results of the journalist's research (tradi-

tionally, the story may not be defamatory . . . but defamation law itself conflicts with free speech).

One might argue in response that consumers need to be protected from business, while the converse is not true. First, though, there seems to be little or no danger here for consumers to be protected from. Businesses that collect data on customer profiles usually do so because they are trying to sell something. As human motives go, this is not an especially sinister one. Even web sites that successfully collect data from children and use that data to launch marketing pitches are likely to expose children only to the danger of accumulating somewhat more trendy junk than the children otherwise would. The "consumer protection" rationale is unconvincing.

In-so-far as there is a real danger from data collected over the Internet, this danger is not unique to Internet sites. Certainly, consumer profiling data might be used by criminals such as pedophiles to identify potential victims. But information commonly printed in newspapers and phone books could be used the same way. In one infamous case, an imprisoned pedophile used stories about children cut from small-town newspapers to compile a list of 300 children to target. But this would not justify regulation of newspapers, even though it is more likely that convicts would see newspapers than marketing lists.

Furthermore, the danger posed to children or others from data collected by commercial Internet sites is probably much less, on the whole, from data that could be collected in noncommer-

cial chat rooms, or from sites devoted to political discussions. Those who value the free flow of information usually will not submit to regulation just because regulation might possibly forestall the remote possibility of some harm.

The imposition of a mandatory opt-in regime for the Internet would therefore be the equivalent of a law banning gossip. In the course of every casual encounter, human beings exchange a good bit of detailed personal information about one another. Only in rare circumstances will anyone feel any obligation to ask another's permission before relaying this information to third parties, however embarrassing it could be to the subject of their conversation ("don't you think that Ms. Smith is spending a lot of time with Mr. Jones?"). Just like a law banning gossip, a law against consumer profiling on the Internet shrinks the traditional sphere of freely flowing information.

Gossip and customer profiling cannot be distinguished on the grounds that gossip is harmless. From the standpoint of an individual, gossip can be devastating. Anthropologist Sally Engle Merry describes life in an isolated Spanish village:

"Every event is regarded as common property and is commented upon endlessly. . . . People are virtuous for fear of what will be said."

Indeed, gossip and customer profiling serve similar and related social functions. While it seems harmful to the subject of gossip, to others, gossip is not only interesting—it can be the glue that holds communities together and informs economic decisions in preliterate societies.

Customer profiling does the same thing. Once, entrepreneurs could increase their sales through personal knowledge of their customers' buying habits and local gossip. Businesses relied heavily on such informal networks. Dun & Bradstreet, which reports on the creditworthiness of businesses, originated when Lewis Tappan, who managed credit accounts in his brother's silk business, began to exchange letters with 180 correspondents throughout the country about the creditworthiness of businesses in their communities. The increased automation of commerce over electronic networks such as the Internet will make personal contacts between businesses, and between businesses and their customers much more rare.

In the new computerized world, it would be very surprising if entrepreneurs did not try to learn about the customer from customer profiles, lists, and credit reporting services. Databases are a natural entrepreneurial adaptation to a world where we have freed ourselves of many informal social ties. Once this evolution is understood, proposals to prohibit businesses from trading information about their customers without their consent appear to be wholly unnecessary restraints on traditional freedoms, shrinking the public domain of information without making the public any safer.

Conclusion: Mandatory Voluntary Opt-In for the Internet

Once one recognizes the conflict between free speech principles and privacy rights, current proposals to regulate privacy on the Internet seem particularly alarming. In the United States, the regulatory tactic of choice is to demand "industry self-regulation." Of course, "self-regulation" approved, demanded, and supervised by regulators is not "self-regulation" at all. NTIA chief counsel Barbara Wellberry says, "we favor self-regulation, but self-regulation with teeth. But people say self-regulation, and that's the end of the conversation. We're looking at self-regulation more analytically: to see where it works, where it may not work." True self-regulation does not violate rights of free speech, because no government action is involved. But this faux "self-regulation" may substantially restrict the flow of information, without anyone clearly recognizing the free speech issues.

The United States government is also willing to consider more heavy-handed regulation, such as the creation of a federal privacy agency or office. Other governments, particularly those in Europe, have long gone far beyond self-regulation. To those who are concerned with the free flow of information, neither the abandonment of "self-regulation"

nor the insistence on false "self-regulation" provide much comfort.

Some, of course, simply do not care about the free speech rights of commercial enterprises. In my view, this is a serious intellectual error. Commerce and trade drive real improvements in standards of living worldwide. It is a mistake to subordinate commercial speech to political speech in one's scheme of values.

Some predict that a mandatory opt-in regime would effectively prohibit trade in customer profiles in marketing lists. This would have its greatest impact on newer or smaller businesses, who rely on the profiles to get started. Older, established firms will have existing customer databases to draw on. Mandatory opt-in might preclude the formation of entirely new business models. Had mandatory opt-in been in place a couple generations ago, for example, consumer credit reporting might never have developed. Consumers, especially the poor, would be unable to buy goods on credit unless they were well known by reputation to a particular business.

The current rush to impose new privacy regulations cannot be reconciled with a principled approach to individual rights. In the long run, it will only hurt the Internet community to join the ranks of those who greet any new technology with fear.

 Article Review Form at end of book.

Moldovascam. com

A complicated case of electronic and telephone fraud suggests just how vulnerable Internet users may be.

Marshall Jon Fisher

Marshall Jon Fisher is a freelance writer and the co-author with David E. Fisher of Tube: The Invention of Television *(1996).*

Moldova is a former Soviet republic, a croissant-shaped nation the size of Maryland, surrounded by Ukraine and Romania. It is not, as a friend of mine guessed, the fictitious country in the Marx Brothers movie *Duck Soup.* Yet it figured recently in a scheme as tangled and improbable as anything Prime Minister Rufus T. Firefly of Freedonia might have cooked up—a case involving pornography, the Internet, telecommunications fraud, and a Trojan horse. An examination of the case brings to light some of the perils of our nascent electronic world—a world in which everything from "sites" to telephone calls to countries themselves is sometimes only virtual.

Last December and January, Internet users might have found themselves, after caroming around cyberspace as their predilections dictated, on Web sites called sexygirls.com, Iadult.com, and beavisbutthead.com. Each of these sites promised free "adult" pictures.

First, though, would-be voyeurs needed to download a viewer application—a program that would allow them to display the photos on their personal computers. There was nothing especially suspicious about this: Internet devotees routinely download software, from new versions of Netscape's Web browser to video games such as Doom and Quake to Budweiser's Bud Ice screen saver.

This particular program, however, was different. It was what is known infamously in computer circles as a "Trojan horse"—a program that fulfills its stated function while secretly carrying out another. The most common type of Trojan horse, according to Dan Geer, the vice-president of CertCo, an electronic-commerce security firm in New York, is one that records your name and password as you log on to an electronic account and then passes them along to someone else—who might be able to read your E-mail, draw on your checking account, or gain access to some other private domain. Trojan horses are probably not very common: most people would know if

they were being stolen from, and most people's private information is not worth the trouble to steal or the risks involved. Still, no one really knows how prevalent the programs are. As Geer laments, "The computer-security arena is plagued with underreporting."

In the case involving Moldova, while the downloaded program was providing access to the pornographic photos, a hidden regiment of subcommands was ransacking the user's computer. First the program ordered the volume on the computer's speakers turned off, to prevent the usual telephonic sounds a modem makes. Then it hung up the line to which the modem was connected and dialed a number in Moldova. That call was answered by a computer that reconnected the user to the adult site. The promised photos—or at least one of them—finally appeared on the screen. The viewer had no idea that while he was looking at pictures he was paying for a transatlantic phone call.

The assault didn't end there. Even after the viewer left the site, disappointed with what was often only a single photo, the phone call continued. The Moldovan horse, as it might be called, didn't allow the modem to hang up even when the customer signed off the Internet—at which point a modem normally would. Only when the computer or the modem itself was shut off did the phone call terminate.

Who stood to make money in this scheme? To answer that question we need to look at what happens when a person calls a foreign country. International phone calls involve separate charges levied by each carrier concerned. American customers pay a single fee per call to their long-distance provider—for example, AT&T—and that provider pays the foreign company its share. Phone companies in developing nations are often in dire need of customers. Few of the nations' citizens have phones, and not many calls come in from abroad. So the companies sometimes contract with entrepreneurs in the United States and elsewhere who set up phone-sex lines or other services that require calls to the country. U.S. long-distance rates are governed by the Federal Communications Commission, but for many foreign companies the sky's the limit: they can charge enough to cover sizable fees to their partners—the providers of the phone sex or other "audiotext" product—and still make a profit themselves. Pornography needn't be part of the arrangement, but there aren't many better ways to keep people on an expensive phone call.

The involvement of foreign phone companies in teleporn is nothing new, nor is it illegal in itself. "There's a huge business in international pay-per-call sex lines," says Eileen Harrington, a Federal Trade Commission specialist in telecommunications

fraud. One reason is that if a phone-sex service uses a 900 number, as most U.S.-based services do, inadvertent customers can go through a grievance process and are likely to have their charges waived, whereas if a foreign phone company is owed money, the victims are usually held accountable by their own long-distance carriers for the charges. In addition, many people apparently find calls to Haiti, Antigua, or Montserrat easier than 900 numbers to explain to their spouses.

Again, none of this is illegal, so long as advertising clearly discloses the cost of the phone call. There are also at the moment no laws restricting pornography on the Internet, and adult Web sites and newsgroups abound there. What is illegal is deception in commerce, as in a case last fall when people found messages on their pagers or answering machines asking them to call back to learn about job openings or free vacations. The ten-digit numbers looked just like mainland U.S. numbers but in fact were for Guyana, on the northern coast of South America, and some Caribbean islands, where the phone companies charge exorbitant rates. The person who answered would keep the victim on the phone as long as possible, generating a hefty kickback from the phone company.

International phone scams, then, are old hat; and so are Trojan-horse programs. What's novel about the Moldava case is the harnessing of a Trojan horse to hijack customers' modems and initiate phone fraud. "It combines the worst of two types of fraud," says Paul Luehr, the FTC's lead trial attorney on the case.

Of course, the scam couldn't go on for long. Members of

AT&T's Fraud Control Group and their counterparts at other U.S. long-distance companies, who regularly pore over phone-traffic data looking for unusual spikes in activity, soon found a big one: some 800,000 minutes of phone time to Moldova had accumulated in only six weeks—several orders of magnitude more than usual. And when people found mysterious charges for calls to Moldova on their bills, ranging from $50 to $3,000, naturally they complained. The FTC began an intensive investigation in January, breaking down the components of the Trojan-horse program and tracing the registrations of the Web sites involved. Within a month it had shut down the sites and brought suit against the alleged perpetrators, three people on Long Island, in New York. Criminal charges have yet to be filed, but they may well be soon.

The FTC suit specifically seeks to preclude the use of such Trojan horses by invoking Section Five of the FTC Act, which prohibits deceptive acts and practices in commerce. "This is a case that we brought in record time," Luehr told me recently. "We really knocked ourselves out putting this thing together, because we realized that it wasn't just pornography customers who could be targeted; this same sort of downloading activity could take place with Mickey Mouse pictures. We wanted to protect the Internet as a viable source of commercial activity." If a shopping mall acquires a reputation as a pickpockets' hangout, it soon becomes a ghost mall.

There is no simple way for people to protect themselves against Trojan-horse attacks. Although some experts I have talked with asserted that an Internet-savvy surfer would not be victimized by such a scheme, others disagreed. "I can easily imagine being fooled by it," says Alan Albert, a software designer and the inventor of FileMaker Pro, a popular database-management program. "I download files all the time. Some work well, and some have bugs, but in general I assume that they're going to do what they say they'll do."

If people are aware of an ongoing scam that commandeers modems, they can watch for it; they might even set up their computers to tell them if the modem disconnects. The next scam, however, might not involve the modem. It might be something like what the Chaos Computer Club, a group of defiant hackers in Hamburg, Germany, did earlier this year simply to demonstrate the susceptibility to sabotage of supposed juggernauts like Microsoft. The hackers wrote a Microsoft ActiveX control—a kind of Web program that when someone visits a Web site that uses it, can automatically download itself onto that person's computer, activate, and go to work. In this case the control made a hidden transaction in Quicken, a popular personal-finance program. The next time the person paid his bills online, he would also unknowingly make a payment to the hacker-thieves' account. Microsoft insists that its Web browser, Internet Explorer, will not run unauthorized ActiveX controls without warning the user. And yet the company had to admit that "malicious developers can create malicious executable code," though it claimed that "this problem exists for all downloaded executable code." In other words: Come on in, the water's fine—but watch out for those fins.

If the FTC or another policing body can uncover a hoax, it can be stopped. Discovery is not always easy, however, when the Internet is involved. In the Moldova case there were smoking phone calls. But in many Internet scams—for example, those in which passwords are stolen—the victims might not ever know they've been victimized. Many Trojan horses even erase themselves after the act— the perfect getaway. And the very nature of the Internet lends itself to camouflage. "There's no 'place' on the Internet," Geer says. "Nowhere to go looking for the culprit."

In the Moldova case the locus of the crime was particularly elusive, because although Moldovan phone numbers had been dialed, no telephones rang there. According to an international agreement, all calls from North America to Moldova go through Canada. These particular calls never got any farther; they were answered in Scarborough, Ontario, where the computer that reconnected the unwitting customers to the adult site was located. This made no difference to the Moldovan phone company or to the Long Island entrepreneurs to whom it gave kickbacks: people are charged for the number they dial, not for where the call is answered. Moldova in this instance was a virtual nation, no more substantial than any site in cyberspace. Only by tracing the registrations of the offending Web-site programs were the FTC and the Royal Canadian Mounted Police able to track down the actual scene of the crime.

How three people in Long Island were able to divert phone calls in Ontario remains a mystery. For obvious reasons the au-

thorities are circumspect; phone messages I left for the directors of network security at AT&T and Bell Canada were returned by media-relations spokespeople who professed ignorance. Apparently, though, there is no limit to what a few lines of clever code can accomplish. The personal computer is mightier than the phone company.

Options for consumer defense against Trojan-horse programs are limited. "The only good method," Geer says, "is to make sure you know what software you're running. For the ordinary person this is quite a difficult matter." The great majority of Internet patrons are no more knowledgeable about the architecture of the software they are using than they are about how their microwave ovens work. Therefore, as Web sites increasingly require the downloading of special programs, dependable security is becoming more critical. It's not something that computer companies like to talk about, just as airlines don't tend to advertise that their planes crash less often than the competition's; however, as in airline safety, according to Geer, "there's an implicit competition that's raising the standard."

There are two main types of security for downloaded programs. The first requires that companies mark their software with a digital "signature." For instance, as a simplified example, the publisher of this magazine could translate all of its text into digital values, total those up, divide the sum by a particular number, and "stamp" the result on the electronic version of the magazine. If you connected to the magazine's Web site, your browser would check to make sure the signature had the correct value. If a terrorist group tried to add its manifesto as though it had been accepted and published by the editors, then your browser would produce the wrong result when it performed the signature computation, showing that the text had been tampered with.

In the second, or "sandbox," approach, a company instructs its program to remain quarantined in a virtual sandbox maintained by your Web browser in the computer's "back yard." This limits the program to certain specified functions, such as writing on the screen and communicating back to the Web site. It does not permit access to other parts of the yard, where vital programs are located. The Moldovan horse, confined in this way, would have been unable to hang up the modem and redial.

Each approach has strengths and weaknesses; neither is perfect. There will always remain the possibility of a Trojan horse so brilliantly programmed that it can mathematically forge digital signatures, so devious that it can trick your computer into letting it out of the sandbox. In the end, Geer says, "all technology secu-

rity is about propagating trust." Microsoft favors the signature method, and in doing so what it's really saying is "When you download software with the Microsoft Authenticode signature, you can trust it." This is no different from trusting a car to be safe or dependable. When a person downloads a program written in Java that favors the sandbox strategy, he or she is also expressing trust—trust that the program won't be able to leave the sandbox.

Downloading a program from an unknown Web site is a little like buying a sleeping pill that hasn't been approved by the Food and Drug Administration— or, in some cases, like buying snake oil by the side of a dusty country road. The drug industry, though, relies on a governing body to give it credibility. Internet commerce is just the opposite: its success depends on the existence of millions of independent, largely unregulated vendors.

As we move toward a more fully digital world, the cost of manipulating information approaches zero, and the hazards therein multiply. Even our pri-

vacy is in peril. The "clickstream" pouring in to Web merchants— the information that you provide with clicks of your mouse, from your Social Security number to what music you listen to and where you like to eat—lets those merchants personalize their marketing, but it may be more information than you want to share widely. And some Web entrepreneurs collect this information and sell it. Supermarket scan cards may be more convenient than coupons, but, as Geer warns, they, too, "put a market price on privacy." The activities in these examples are perfectly legal, of course, but they increase the potential for electronic malfeasance.

Any new technology can be a constructive or a destructive tool. Trojan horses are simply one of the hazards of the Internet, just as telephone fraud is a hazard of Mr. Bell's invention. To some extent the snake oil will always get through.

 **Article Review Form at end of book.**

The Dark Side of the Net

Richard L. Brandt

Richard L. Brandt is editor of UPSIDE.

Jacob Milne: No matter how imperfect things are, if you've got a free press everything is correctable, and without it everything is concealable.

Ruth Carson: I'm with you on the free press. It's the newspapers I can't stand.

—Tom Stoppard,
"Night and Day," Act 1

Everybody (with the possible exception of a few totalitarian governments) understands the benefits of a free press, at least in theory. In practice, we complain about the abuses, the sensationalism, the ridiculous obsession with overlurid details that appeal to our baser instincts rather than the nobler ideals that make a free press worthwhile.

Unfortunately, it's impossible to defend and protect the publishing rights of the *New York Times* without extending those rights to the *National Inquirer* and *Hustler.*

The free press debate lately has become more intense, with higher stakes. The Internet is a new form of publishing: broader, less structured and more anarchic than paper journalism. Look at Hillary Clinton's recent talk with reporters, complaining about the lack of a "gatekeeping function" on the Internet, and the fact that even the venerable *Wall Street Journal* had to backpedal on one of its online stories.

Everybody who worships at the altar of technology loves the ideal of a free Internet. We bask in the rarefied air of libertarian values and faith in this technology. But nobody likes everything that appears on the Internet. Much of it is a waste of electrons, some of it is of questionable taste or value, and some is absolutely despicable. It's the price we pay for the freedom the Internet provides.

In any time of change, governments are prone to step in and try to control the chaos. In early February, the Senate Commerce Committee again began debating ways to censor the Internet. Sen. Dan Coats, R-Ind., has proposed a bill to make commercial Web sites ensure that they do not allow minors to view "harmful" sexually oriented material. Sen. John McCain, R-Ariz., wants to force libraries to restrict children's access to adult sites.

If we permit free speech, our children will read or see things we would rather they didn't. That means it's up to us to educate them about the dangers, not to try to make it absolutely safe. Freedom is dangerous. A police state may cut the homicide rate, but I don't want to live in one.

Yet among the digerati, there exists a disturbing trend of defense through denial. We criticize politicians and publications for overhyping the problems of porn on the Net.

Porn's ubiquity on the Web is overblown. Purely in the interest of writing this column (that's my story, and I'm sticking to it), I did a little smut-surfing. I typed "pornography" into Yahoo and got listings for many intellectual sites and publications discussing ways of avoiding porn. I also got an ad for the Amateur Hardcore Web site. I typed in "sex," got 2,008 sites and an ad shouting "Live Sorority Sluts!" Most of the sites I came across were sophomorically titillating and relatively harmless. Some were amusing, and a couple I even found cute. Of course, your tastes may vary.

But the fear is not overblown. There's some nasty stuff

on the dark side of the Net. Pornography, in all its mediums, is a big, diverse business, one that lends itself to sleaze. On the Internet, that includes password and picture theft, click-through scams and outright deception. It also includes sadomasochism, bestiality and child porn. And how will the public feel about censorship when a clear case of Internet sexual predation hits the headlines?

Of course, because of its global reach, the Internet will prove impossible to censor. But we can do a lot of harm by trying. The line of impropriety is never sharp, and when the censors get started, I will surely have to conform to someone else's idea of what's dangerous.

After a tough examination of the nobility, the dangers and the blemishes of journalism, playwright Tom Stoppard has his character George Guthrie sum up: "I've been around a lot of places. People do awful things to each other. But it's worse in places where everybody is kept in the dark. . . . Information, in itself, about anything, is light."

Now that it's here, it's important to preserve a free Internet. Despite its dark side, it's the brightest light we've ever seen.

 Article Review Form at end of book.

The Case for Electronic Commerce

The emergence of the Internet as a conduit for buying and selling goods and services raises a host of legal issues. Resolving them will require our finest legal minds.

Mark Mehler

Mark Mehler is a New York-based business and technology writer.

"The first thing we do, let's kill all the lawyers," wrote William Shakespeare 400 years ago. In today's complicated electronic world, that's not a good idea.

Aside from the obvious violation of human rights, pruning the ranks of attorneys would cause some critical problems. The emergence of the Internet as a conduit for buying and selling goods and services raises a host of legal issues. Resolving these issues will require the talents of our finest legal minds.

The most pressing of these problems include:

- taxing Internet transactions that are location-independent;
- tracking and storing digital records to satisfy federal and state tax authorities;
- sorting out the debate over trademarks and Internet domain names; and
- reaching international agreements on uniform

contract documents, digital encryption methods and bank secrecy laws.

To Benjamin Wright, a Dallas-based attorney and author of *The Law of Electronic Commerce* (Boston:Little, Brown and Co., 1995), all these issues—and more—need to be addressed to ensure the Internet's long-term future as a safe, secure commercial vehicle. But there is such a thing as being too cautious, he warns.

"One of the things I hear a lot from managers who are not technologically savvy is that they can't feel comfortable doing business on the Internet until the law has caught up with the changes in technology," he explains. "The message I try to pass on is not to let the legal problems hold you back. Although the problems need attention, none of them is a show-stopper."

Electronic commerce specialist Alan Sutin, an attorney with the New York offices of the Miami-based firm of Greenberg, Traurig, Hoffman, Lipoff, Rosen and Quentel, agrees that short-

comings in the law are no reason for timidity. "In some respects, particularly in terms of international commerce, the law does have some catching up to do," he says. "But the biggest problems of electronic commerce are not legal in nature. The legal questions are not deal-breakers and will eventually be sorted out.

"Companies should consider the fundamental business reasons for getting on the Internet. They should ask themselves if they need to be online to bring real value to their customers. These are the questions that should determine a company's electronic commerce strategy—not legal questions."

Some legal scholars advise that while the lawyers debate the fine points of jurisprudence, companies go full speed ahead with their Internet initiatives, using common sense and historical precedent to guide them. That's the strategy adopted by Express, a Columbus, Ohio-based retailer of women's apparel and a wholly owned subsidiary of the Limited, a retail firm also based in Columbus. Express recently became the first in its market to launch a website, setting up a virtual store in IBM's World Avenue, an electronic mall.

"The legal approach we've taken is to treat this just like a catalog operation," explains Express vice president Les Duncan. "Take the issue of who pays duties and customs charges on orders outside the country. We highlight the customer's responsibilities along with ours on the order screen. Customers know that we pay the shipping, and they're responsible for duties, customs and local taxes, just as they are with a catalog order."

Another legal issue with serious ramifications for Internet marketers involves the maintenance, storage and retrieval of digital information. Attorney Wright points out that some companies have not fully considered the importance of archiving and accessing their digital files, an oversight that can come back to haunt them if they're audited by the IRS or state tax officials.

"You have to maintain and store digital records for seven years or longer, as required for accounting and tax purposes," he advises. "So you must have very disciplined programs for managing your records."

Some companies, Wright says, confuse good records management with good systems management. "Records management involves a lot more than having the right systems in place," he notes. "It also requires disciplined policies, procedures and programs for handling data."

The third legal area—the issue of trademarks and domain names—must be addressed head-on by senior managers as well as attorneys.

"Companies have to register their domain names early," attorney Sutin warns. "The Internet takes names on a first-come, first-served basis. And there can only be one domain name, as opposed to trademarks, which can be used by different companies for different goods and services."

Airgas, a supplier of industrial gas products, is one company looking to preserve its place in cyberspace. "We're scrambling to register every name we might use down the line," reveals Rich Bradley, the electronic commerce manager for the Radnor, Pa.-based firm. "There's no protection in the area of domain names, so we have to do whatever we can to protect ourselves."

Airgas launched a website last August to sell protective clothing, gloves and other safety products. It formed a new division called Airgas Direct Industrial to market that line, and plans to register multiple variations of that name—ADI, Direct Industrial, etc.

But Airgas missed the boat when it acquired IPCO Safety, a telemarketing company based in Bristol, Pa. A printing company named IPCO had already registered "ipco.com."

"The trademark problem is our biggest headache," concludes Bradley. "If a customer clicks on an address and gets another company, it's bad for our business."

The biggest legal worry at Dakota Electric Supply, a Fargo, N.D.-based full-line electrical distributor, is making sure company logos and names are correct.

"Some of the manufacturers we work with are very particular about how we display their logos, so we've got to be very careful that our website has all the correct sizes, fonts and colors," explains Arne Breikjern, marketing and training coordinator.

Overall, attorney Sutin sees international sales as the major legal battleground in the field of Internet commerce, given the technology's inherent lack of borders.

"One problem involves the inconsistencies in bank secrecy laws in different countries, which inhibit the free flow of credit information," he reports. "Another is the lack of a coordinated effort to reach agreement on standards for electronic documents. And then there's the ongoing debate about various forms of encryption."

While these issues are outside management's daily purview, Sutin insists that Internet players can influence the global debate by participating in periodic Commerce Department hearings and lobbying their Congressional representatives.

For now, however, many U.S. companies have all they can do to handle their domestic business without worrying about the international market.

"There are tariff and VAT [value-added tax] issues that will eventually demand our attention," admits Rick Fernandes, executive vice president of CUC International, a Stamford, Conn.-based mass marketer of discount home shopping, dining, travel and other services. "But, since most of our content is currently only available in the United States, those issues will have to wait."

 **Article Review Form at end of book.**

WiseGuide Wrap-Up

Although the issues discussed in this section have social, legal, ethical, and moral dimensions, marketers show interest because of the effect they have on consumers. Consumers have become very possessive of information about themselves, and rightly so.

Personal information will become a commodity that marketers will use incentives to get. However, extreme protection of personal information may very well hinder marketing on the Internet. The reluctance consumers show toward online buying and otherwise taking part in online marketing resembles the hesitation they showed when checkout scanners first came to use not too long ago. Sellers had to overcome the fear that scanners might read a price too high to make that technology acceptable. Luckily, that was a simple challenge.

R.E.A.L. Sites

This list provides a print preview of typical **coursewise** R.E.A.L. sites. There are over 100 such sites at the **courselinks**™ site. The danger in printing URLs is that web sites can change overnight. As we went to press, these sites were functional using the URLs provided. If you come across one that isn't, please let us know via email to: webmaster@coursewise.com. Use your Passport to access the most current list of R.E.A.L. sites at the **courselinks**™ site.

Site name: Filtering Information on the Internet

URL: http://www.sciam.com/0397issue/0397resnick.html

Why is it R.E.A.L.? Scientific American examines the efforts to filter information on the Internet to curb the potential problems of exposure to unwanted content.

Key topics: Filtering techniques, filtering software, electronic labeling, trust and trusted systems

---

Site name: Customary Law & Power in Internet Communities

URL: http://www.ascusc.org/jcmc/vol2/issue1/custom.html

Why is it R.E.A.L.? Studies the virtual communities and "virtual law" as the members attempt to bring order to their communities.

Key topics: Cybercommunities, MUDs (Multi-User Dungeons/Domains), MOOs (MUD-Object Oriented), Usenet, self-regulation

---

Site name: A Separate Jurisdiction for Cyberspace?

URL: http://www.ascusc.org/jcmc/vol2/issue1/juris.html

Why is it R.E.A.L.? Raises the question whether the Internet needs a separate jurisdiction and discusses the need for such separation.

Key topics: Applying law to technology, Internet communities, national borders (or lack of them), international law, copyright issues unique to the Internet, real-world and virtual-world principles of law

---

section

6

Web technology as a tool for presenting large amounts of information poses several usability challenges to Web site developers. Many sites suffer from clutter, confusion, slow rendering, and other design flaws that mar their usefulness. The few readings in this section will offer some ways to deal with these challenges. A critical reading of these articles will help you understand:

• The nature of HTML as the engine that drives the Web.

• The differences between traditional media and the Web as a communication medium.

• The challenges of the Web that need to be considered when designing Web sites.

Site Design

When Tim Berners-Lee conceived the World Wide Web (WWW, Web, or sometimes W3) in 1989, he did not envision people "designing" Web sites or even writing HTML documents. His vision encompassed the world of human knowledge seamlessly linked using hypermedia. The concept would allow unstructured exploration of information hosted on any number of servers. The hypertext transfer protocol (HTTP) would facilitate the communication between the user and the information provider.

That simple idea grew rapidly and with so many enhancements that it probably surprised even Tim Berners-Lee. With the extraordinary growth of the World Wide Web, the shortcomings of the original markup language, HTML, became evident. As Mosaic, the first multiplatform graphical user interface Web browser, awakened the masses all over the world, the potential of the Web showed the tip of its iceberg. Many rushed to create their Web sites, and the feeling of euphoria and liberation spread like wild fire.

Web sites and servers started coming online with variety of content, and the idea of a "home page" entered the language. The notion that anyone could publish content that looked far better than other available methods then emerged as a liberating idea. However, the HTML had serious restrictions in the way it could control the layout of Web documents. Pushing the envelope, Netscape added its own "extensions" to the standard HTML when it released version two of its browser. Among others, one of the most popular elements introduced was the new tables capability. Web developers and designers quickly started using tables to exercise added control on the layout, and the second generation of Web sites emerged.

The second-generation sites contained highly designed pages, extensive graphics, and highly controlled layouts. Although these made the sites look very attractive, the pages became too big for the available bandwidth, and users started getting frustrated with the slow rendering of pages. The steward of the Web standards, the World Wide Web Consortium, began developing the new generation of HTML standards and integrating many "extensions" into it.

The relative ease with which anyone could publish information and the increased desire to be on the Web grew the amount of available information on the Web. Suddenly the problem was reversed. The question changed from "how can we find more information?" to "how can we sift through information?" Webcasting, or push technology, emerged as a possible solution to this problem. According to the vision of push technology developers, users would subscribe to the content they wanted, and it would be delivered to their computer using one of the competing push technologies, one developed by Netscape and the other by Microsoft. Despite the initial excitement and plenty of hype, push technology is still developing. Only time will tell whether users really want content delivered to them on selected channels resembling television with flexible programming.

Questions

1. What are the main limitations of HTML in its current form? Why do these limitations pose a challenge to designing marketing-oriented Web sites?

2. Find information about the evolution of HTML from its initial release to the current standard. What has been added to the standards along the way and why?

3. Find some examples of well-designed marketing Web sites and poorly designed ones. Outline the points that make them good or poor Web sites. Can you write guidelines for yourself to follow, based on your observations?

Untangling the Web

Surfing the World Wide Web is increasingly frustrating. As the Web ages and its girth expands, two problems are more and more likely to thwart eager seekers of useful information. One is the increasing chance of encountering the annoying geek-speak "404 Not Found" that pops up and brings a hunt to a halt, signalling that the website being sought is defunct or has moved, and no one has bothered to leave a note saying where it has gone. Such "broken links" are on the rise as old websites are abandoned or moved to different computers.

Worse than this by far is the volume of junk retrieved when panning for gold with one of the Web's search engines. A computer searching the Web's 320m pages (and counting) can reach at best no more than a third of them. Moreover, being unable to distinguish between (potato) chip, (micro) chip and (Mr Fred) Chip, search engines haul back every reference they find regardless of whether or not it makes sense. Add to this the fact that the current way of presenting and transmitting data over the Web, the HyperText Markup Language (HTML), is increasingly outdated,

and the World Wide Web looks more like the World Wide Mess.

Electronic Esperanto

In hope of straightening out these tangles, the World Wide Web Consortium, the Web's governing body, has recently released a new standard for creating Web pages. It claims that the new programming lingo, called Extensible Markup Language (XML for short) will abolish most of the agonies and restrictions imposed by HTML, and thereby make the problems of broken links and junk easier to solve.

HTML has contributed enormously to making the Web accessible to ordinary people: it is simple and compact. But as Web pages burgeon with ever more complex designs and fancy features to show information, writers of HTML are starting to feel as if they are trying to do calculus with an abacus. Meanwhile, to make some of the new features work, rival makers of browsing software (such as Netscape and Microsoft) have adopted different standards, making life still more hellish for those who design and maintain websites. Over the past

few years, therefore, it has become clear that a more flexible and powerful way of presenting data on the Web is needed if Internet business is to compete with business by mail order. Hence the hope placed in XML.

XML is not an improved version of HTML, but a simplified dialect of the mother of all document-defining languages, the definitive but labyrinthine Standard Generalised Markup Language (SGML). SGML was pioneered by IBM in the 1960s and is still used as the global standard in the aerospace industry as well as by chip makers and other manufacturers for managing their technical documents. XML is not as powerful as SGML, but it is much easier to use.

At first glance, a Web page written in XML looks just like one in HTML. Both use "tags" at the beginning and end of the various components on a page (for instance, H1 for the biggest headline, P for paragraph, IMG for image, and so on). But here the similarity ends. Whereas HTML has a set lexicon of about 90 tags, XML has an infinite one: authors of XML documents can invent their own tags. The tag names, and what they mean, are left for the author to define depending on the subject matter.

This sounds splendid—but it presents a problem for browsers such as Netscape Navigator and Internet Explorer, which will need somehow to interpret all of these new tags. Thus each XML document must be provided with an appendix, known as the Document Type Definition (DTD), a kind of glossary containing information of the nature of the document's content, the tags used for various elements, as well as a listing of where in the document the tags occur and how they fit together.

Creating such an appendix can be arduous. But they will not always need to be built from scratch. Because XML is a stripped-down version of its mother tongue, the thousands of DTD appendices already written for SGML can be used seamlessly with XML. And if an XML document is built conforming to certain predefined features, it may not need a DTD at all. Such a "well-formed" document is sim-

ply read by a browser in a particular way, much as an HTML document is read now.

XML ought to help with broken links and junk. It will have a far more sophisticated way of defining "hypertext links" (the words underlined in blue on Web pages today), which should make it easier to keep connections between different Web pages current. And because it allows more detail to be included in documents, searching for specific topics should become more accurate, avoiding many of the accidental mismatches. Navigating through websites should become more sophisticated too. Future browsers could have Up and Down buttons as well as Back and Forward ones, allowing users to dig down into data "nested" inside other data.

XML will also allow Web designers, if they are clever enough, to present data in many new ways. For example, they could easily provide different views of the same data—such as an instruction manual that grows ever more detailed as the user learns

more. Or think of the savings a media group could make by not having to reformat a master XML document when publishing it as a book or CD-ROM, instead of as a set of Web pages.

But the biggest role that XML is expected to play is in integrating the way that existing paper documents—invoices, loan applications, contracts, insurance claims, you name it—are exchanged between organisations around the world. Imagine what the world would be like if one company's computer system could automatically read any other organisation's documents—and make complete sense of them? This is the goal that the technique known as Electronic Data Interchange has struggled, unsuccessfully, to achieve for years. Though efforts have barely begun, there is a chance that XML could actually make that happen. If it did, business on the Web could run riot.

 **Article Review Form at end of book.**

Fixing Web-Site Usability

How to let visitors to your Web site cut through the document maze.

Lynda Radosevich

Senior Editor Lynda Radosevich specializes in Web-related issues.

Randomly surf the Web, and you will find many amusements and perhaps some interesting facts. But try to find the hard information pertinent to your job and chances are you will end up frustrated.

The fact is, most Web sites stink when it comes to gathering useful information. In a recent usability study of nine highly regarded Web sites, including those of Fidelity Investments, Disney, and travel-services site Travelocity, most of some 70 test users could not find specific information they were instructed to find a majority of the time. Scientists at User Interface Engineering, the North Andover, Mass., think tank that conducted the study, only asked for information that they knew existed on the site.

The lack of usability does not stem from insufficient resources. As Jared Spool, principal investigator at User Interface Engineering notes, bookstores contain more computer books than cookbooks. A large portion of the computer books are on Web design, and most of them agree on Web design fundamentals.

Meanwhile, Forrester Research says that high-profile content sites that cost $893,000 annually to operate in December 1995 cost $3.1 million to operate today and will cost $6.3 million in 2000. The financing and expertise are available.

However, the problem lies in faulty intent and poor testing. More often than not, companies design Web sites with their marketing and business objectives in mind, rather than their customers' needs. And even if they do think of the users, they often base decisions on common-sense design rules and skip usability testing.

As the results readily demonstrate, common sense doesn't work. The Web is unlike any media to have come before it, and the old principles don't apply, experts say.

"There is perception that print and Web are very similar; that good design for print is good design for Web. We found that was not true," says Spool, who also co-authored *Web Site Usability: A Designer's Guide.*

Another explanation for the fact that so many sites are so difficult to use is that the Web's barrier-to-entry is very low. Any company with an Internet account and determination can put up a site easily.

"It's like having 90 percent of radio stations being karaoke," says Steven Nelson, vice president at Clear Ink, in Walnut Creek, Calif., which designed sites for Apple, Oracle, Ascend, and Southern California Gas. "You still get your site, but you have to sort through all the karaoke."

Totally Uncool

Building usable sites, as opposed to "cool" sites, has never been more important. Increasingly companies are counting on the Web to provide customer service, make sales, and manage business and employee relationships. Today, a customer's initial point of contact with a company often is through its Web site. That first impression sticks.

Also, some companies aren't getting their money's worth out of their high-priced Web sites. Disney reportedly spent $10 million on the initial launch of their site (http://www.disney.com), and has since then spent more on the revised versions, Spool says. But Edmunds, which publishes information and magazines for car buyers, spent less than $10,000 on the launch of their site (http://www.edmunds.com) and did it on a weekend. Yet Edmunds' site did as well as Disney's site in usability testing.

"If you have limited resources, which direction would you pick?" Spool asks.

And considering that Web sites are becoming more complex—the average Web site has 6,300 pages, and by the end of next year will have 15,000 pages, Forrester estimates—the need for creating more usable sites becomes even more apparent.

Before understanding how to create usable Web sites, companies must understand what wrong with what is out there.

By now most Web-site architects have heard that large image maps and fussy layouts are out. In fact, a user backlash against first-generation sites' overzealous design has prompted the leading Web design companies and their customers to adopt clean, sparse, simple-to-use layouts. (See http://www.spiralmedia.com and http://www.clearink.com as examples.)

Nonetheless, many seemingly right but actually wrong Web-design principles persist. For instance, in its usability study, User Interface Engineering found that white space, a staple in good print design, hurts a Web site's usability.

Rethinking Design

Other counter-intuitive findings include that users are more successful at following longer, more descriptive text links than shorter, less informative ones; navigational graphics aren't helpful because users explore text links first and don't wait for graphical links to download; users shun nonstop animations; however, they will gladly wait to download informational graphics, such as a picture of a new car model.

Also, convention says that users hate to scroll beyond the "fold" (the bottom of the screen), but the testing found it made no difference whatsoever.

Another revelation will come as an unwelcome bit of news to some Web builders. The sites that employed the increasingly popular "shell" strategy construction—in which programmers create a generic site structure and navigational hierarchy, and others plug in content later—confused users. Shell sites do not work because the links are so generic, users rarely get what they expect, Spool says.

Perhaps the most surprising of User Interface Engineering's findings is that onsite search engines confuse and frustrate users more than they help them.

"If users looking for information do not use a search engine, they're 50 percent more likely to find the information than if they click on the search button," Spool says.

The problem with full-text search engines is that users don't understand how to use them. It's not unusual for a visitor to type in a very broad keyword, such as "travel," which returns a plethora of useless links. Also, search engines do stupid things. When

testers of Smithsonian magazine's site (http:/www.smithsoniamag. si.edu) typed in the word dinosaur into the search engine, the first article returned was about the American steel industry. Still, search engines are extremely popular, and users revolt if they cannot find one, Spool says.

Being Well Connected

These examples point to a key challenge in building a usable Web site, creating good links and navigation mechanisms.

"The tools don't help you create navigation tools on a Web site, but the bigger problem is that the information is not always organized intuitively," says Murray Maloney, technical marketing director at Paris-based tool vendor Grif and a member of the World Wide Web Consortium. "What site designers need to begin to understand is that there are often several different paths that could lead to any given page on a Web site."

The most intuitively usable Web sites are those in which the developers determine what information users are most likely to require and strive to make it readily available.

"A lot of businesses could do well just by saying, what are the top ten things people call us up and ask, and if nothing else, have a site that just answers those top ten questions," says Clear Ink's Nelson.

A couple of tips include the following: From the home page, information should not be more than two clicks of information, and the underlying structure of the code should use metatags that identify key words to search spiders.

Also, developers should keep the download times to a minimum.

"Usability research shows that page download has to be faster than 10 seconds for users to keep their attention on the site," says Jakob Nielsen, an engineer at Sun Microsystems and author of *Designing Excellent Web Sites: Secrets of an Information Architect.*

When it comes to graphics, experts remind designers to adhere to the KISS (keep it simple, stupid) principle.

"You can do a lot with simple design that looks good but doesn't get in the way of finding information," Clear Ink's Nelson says.

Let Mom Test It

Still, no matter how well-conceived a site may be, visitors will rarely use it as anticipated. For that reason, the only way to ensure a site is usable is to test it with users who have nothing to do with creating it, experts say. Unfortunately, Nielsen estimates that only 20 percent of Fortune 1000 companies do so.

"Most Web designs are internally focused, meaning that they aim to please the company's own staff, and especially the executives. Thus, evaluation consists of showing a design to the vice president of marketing, and if he or she likes it, then it's OK," Nielsen says.

Nonetheless, that 20 percent marks an improvement compared with a few years ago, and more companies are wising up to usability testing.

"We may hit 50 percent by the year 2000," Nielsen says.

Before conducting tests, successful Web site developers set up the right environment. When Constantine & Lockwood,

a usability-testing company, in Rowley, Mass., conducts Web-site tests, the process is very structured. They set an agenda, determine beforehand how much of the site will be reviewed, and define usage scenarios, which can be representative cases or special instances. They also divide the inspection into phases, starting at the home page.

"Ask for the users initial reaction, because you only get to have an initial reaction once," says Larry Constantine, principal consultant at Constantine & Lockwood.

Garbage Detection

Demonstrating their technique in a session at the October Web Design & Development Conference '97, in Washington, Constantine and his partner Lucy Lockwood instructed attendees to shout "garbage" every time they noted a design defect in a test site. Defects could include links that sent users down the wrong path, blinking graphics, cryptic menu bars, etc. After overcoming their initial shyness, the attendees turned mean, shouting "garbage" liberally and loudly. By the end of the session, the testers had a long list of defects to consider.

To encourage users to speak up, Lockwood and Constantine prohibit Web-site builders from explaining or justifying their design.

"The reviewer needs to protect the user, because usually when the user doesn't get something the designers and programmers jump in to explain," Lockwood says. "Then the user feels stupid and shuts up."

Also, Lockwood believes the users are not the final authority, and testers should not make promises.

In setting up a test environment, companies also strive to recreate the technical environment of the typical user. For instance, if users have 28.8Kbps connections, so should the testers.

Finally, experts warn companies not to confuse market research with usability testing. Market research determines what it will take to make people buy something, but typically it does not address whether they will be able to use the product, Nielsen says.

"Normally [usability testing is] not necessary: If you are testing a new potato chip, then everybody knows how to move the chip from the bag into their mouth," Nielsen says.

But interactive systems such as the Web are another matter altogether. When Sun was working this fall on a redesign of its home page, site creators tested six designs with six users, leading to a specific design direction. They then tested three prototypes of different variations of the direction that was chosen, completed another redesign and testing of a single design, and tested the final version with five users. The redesigned home page will be launched around press time, Nielsen says.

Content Control

Testing helps the developer create sites that are easy to navigate, but if the information isn't relevant and up-to-date, the site's usability is shot. But companies often place their emphasis on the initial development and launching of the site, and forget to allocate enough attention, time, or money to the ongoing maintenance, says Clear Ink's Nelson.

"It's like buying a car, spending all money on the car

and not having any money left over for gasoline, oil, or car washes," Nelson says.

For instance, KGO, a California radio station, boasts on its Web site (http://www.kgoam810.com) of its up-to-the-minute news. Yet in early November, the home page flashed the word "September."

In addition to keeping information timely, companies can make sites more usable by providing personalized content. Amazon.com, in competing with Barnes & Noble, offers agents who recommend books based on what a user has bought recently and on what other people who liked a chosen book liked in addition to it.

K2 Design, in New York, uses a "cookie trail" tracking mechanism to follow users' navigation path and display the pages they have visited first when they come back to the site, says John Balestrieri, vice president and director of technology at K2.

Also, technological considerations and limitations also strongly affect Web-site usability. For instance, the visitors' browsers and PC platforms are different, and a site can look quite different to diverse users.

To manage that diversity, Clear Ink designs each site to work with the peculiarities of multiple browsers.

"Netscape and IE [Microsoft Internet Explorer] support different sound-embedding tags, so we'll design the page to support either," Clear Ink's Nelson says.

Another technological consideration is the use of frames, which despite their ability to improve navigation increasingly are becoming a no-no. The reason is that for every frame and every object embedded in a frame, a browser must make an additional HTTP call, adding to the download time of a page. Keeping page download time to a minimum is key—K2 tries to keep a page

between 30K and 40K including everything—so frames are out.

"I thought frames were really cool when they first came out, but I hardly use them for anything now," says K2's Balestrieri.

Because the Web is so new, and so fast-changing, Web site creators within corporations and the design firms they use can easily get distracted by cool technologies and their own need to hype themselves. But that does not fool most users, who visit sites to gather useful information, so judicious use of design elements and new technologies, along with rigorous testing is paramount.

"'Because I can' is no longer a good reason for doing something," Balestrieri says.

 **Article Review Form at end of book.**

A Way Out of the Web Maze

It's called Webcasting, and it promises to deliver the info you want, straight to your PC.

Amy Cortese

With Robert D. Hof in San Mateo, Calif., and bureau reports

Since the World Wide Web burst into the mainstream two years ago, it has seized the popular imagination with a vengeance. The number of Web sites has exploded as companies and individuals have jumped eagerly into cyberspace. Today, hundreds of thousands of sites offer everything from government documents to financial data to pure whimsy. Internet terminology—Web page, hyperlink, anything.com—are part of the everyday lexicon. And being wired has become a measure of status among Gen-Xers and business leaders alike.

The Web is hip. The Web is way cool. And increasingly, the Web is way frustrating.

The Web, it seems, is a victim of its success. The volume of information on it is staggering, and search engines and other devices bring littler order to the chaos. "It's a little like taking a farm boy from the Midwest, putting him in the middle of Manhattan, and telling him to go have the time of his life," says Ariel Sella, an Internet software entrepreneur. Then there are those endless waits to see Web pages. These days, when you log on, don't forget to bring a book.

The noise and congestion is making it hard for Web sites to attract visitors—and keep them coming back. Without steady traffic, Web sites have a hard time selling advertising, which, despite meager sales today, remains the most promising way to make money. As reality sets in, dozens of sites are scaling back or shutting down. At this rate, the Web could collapse under its own weight.

Even the Web's biggest promoters are sounding the alarm. "The Net for the first time is causing information overload," says Marc Andreessen, who helped write the Navigator browser at Netscape Communications Corp. Adds Eric Schmidt, chief technologist at Sun Microsystems Inc.: "Manually searching the Web is not a sustainable model, long term."

So, software entrepreneurs are borrowing from another medium—TV—to take the work out of the Web. "People want their computers to be as easy as their television," says Kim Polese, former Java product manager at Sun and now chief executive of Marimba Inc., a Palo Alto (Calif.) software startup. "They want just a few channels that they can turn to."

Computers won't get as simple as TVs anytime soon. But a new crop of programs will cut through Web clutter for you by using the same principle as broadcasting. Instead of having to spend hours scouring the Web, news, entertainment, and other Web fare is delivered automatically to your desktop. These new software programs also can deliver rich visual images and animation that approach TV quality.

Internet-style broadcasting has some unique advantages, too. TV features one-size-fits-millions programming. On the Net, digital programming can be targeted to a particular group or individual. It can even be delivered to your pager or cell phone. That ability to "narrowcast" is transforming the Net into a personal broadcast system. "The combination of broadcast and personalization is really a new world," says Schmidt.

And it comes with a whole new lexicon. Companies such as Marimba call their programs "tuners" and "transmitters." Information is organized into "channels," and "push delivery" gets it out to "viewers." Such familiar concepts promise to tame the Web, enhance corporate communication, spur digital commerce, and provide one more jolt to the software Establishment.

Welcome to the world of Webcasting. "Just as the browser opened the door to the Internet, 'push' will bring another fundamental way of communicating to the Net," says Christopher R. Hassett, chief executive of Webcasting pioneer PointCast Inc. Adds J. Neil Weintraut, a partner with 21st Century Venture Partners: "It makes the Web relevant to the masses."

The new Net software is not just for couch potatoes, either. Companies such as Amoco and Fruit of the Loom are pushing industry news and other data to employees' desktops. They're also setting up in-house channels on their own networks, or intranets, to make sure employees get the latest announcements and corporate communiques. And because any digital information can be Webcast, the new approach is a natural for distributing software programs, applets, and updates— saving time and money. "This kind of push technology is going to be a big thing," says William Stewart, co-chairman of the Chicago Board of Trade's Internet Advisory Committee, which is looking at push delivery to reach its 4,000 members.

Hot Buttons

As with any new technological shift, Webcasting is creating fresh opportunities for software and media entrepreneurs. The ferment has already produced dozens of PointCast challengers,

from Marimba to BackWeb Technologies to IFusion Com. They're all taking different tacks. But one of them could hit on the right formula and become the next Internet powerhouse.

Or maybe not. Both Microsoft Corp. and Netscape are scurrying to bring out later this year their own software to display Webcasting information on your desktop. When they do, your PC screen might consist of half a dozen channel buttons: one for news, one for company information, one or two for entertainment, and—someday—a "productivity" channel that you'll switch to when you need spreadsheets and word processing programs. "It fundamentally changes the whole concept of software," says Weintraut. The line between software programs and content begins to blur.

For such a fundamental innovation, Webcasting is almost deceptively simple. In most cases, it works like this: When you register for a service, you specify the channels you want and the specific topics you're interested in. You also choose how often you would like updates, which can arrive continuously and seamlessly on corporate networks.

Behind the scenes, Webcasting is more complex. Software programs diligently monitor Web sites and other information sources on your behalf. Upon finding news of interest to you, most will send an alert that pops up on your screen or scrolls across a ticker. When you click for more details, you might be launched to the Web site.

Other Webcasting programs, including PointCast, take the liberty of sending full articles, Web pages, and animations to your PC. You may not realize it, but when you pause to look at a Web

page, which leaves the line free, these Webcasting programs grab the line and start downloading files onto your hard drive. When you click on a sports score for more detail, there's no World Wide Wait: The full story and a video clip can appear on your screen instantly.

Push delivery is as old as E-mail. But PointCast took things one step further. Hassett and his brother, Greg, launched their first product in 1992. Journalist, a custom news service for Compu-Serve Inc. and Prodigy Services Co. members, was difficult to use, though, and never caught on. By early 1995, when the Web took off, the brothers tried again. This time, they would pump out continuously updated information and, in a novel twist, display it on a screen saver when a PC was idle. Flying toasters gave way to scrolling news headlines, stock quotes, and weather updates.

"Different"

PointCast released a test version of its software last February and a finished version in May. By early fall, a million people had downloaded it. Today, PointCast has more than 1 million regular viewers— mostly within businesses—and some 15,000 people register for the service each day. At 30 million to 50 million viewer hours a month, the PointCast Network is comparable to a midsize TV network. "I see push creating almost a second Internet," says Halsey Minor, CEO of CNET Inc., a Web news service. "The model is really different."

Indeed, Webcasting offers the best hope yet to build a business on the Net through advertising and delivering customized content that people might finally pay for. "We're huge believers," says Time Inc. New Media General Manager Bruce Judson. The Internet is already a direct-marketer's dream. Now, instead of waiting for Web surfers to stumble onto their sites and banner ads, marketers can send animated ads directly to the desktops of target customers. Retailers such as Lands' End Inc. and Virtual Vineyards are dabbling with such in-your-face methods to notify subscribers of promotions and even send them order forms. Merchants can approach live sales prospects and not just couch potatoes. "It's not about cost per thousand, but cost per lead," says J.G. Sandom, director of Ogilvy & Mather Worldwide Inc.'s Interactive business.

How do they identify leads? Webcasters have a unique ability to track viewers' actions. They do that two ways. First, when you sign up for a Web service, you're asked to give some basic demographic information along with your interests. Then, once the receiver software is downloaded onto your PC, Webcasters can track when you tune in and what you click on for more detail. That provides a level of accountability that TV and print can't touch.

PointCast offers still more: access to the corporate market. "It's the first medium to ever reach people at work in a meaningful way," says John Nardone, director of media and research services at Modem Media, an interactive ad agency in Westport, Conn. "You can literally say, 'We had 3,000 people from Microsoft looking at your ad yesterday,'" crows Nardone.

Missteps

For these reasons, Webcasting could quickly grab a sizable chunk of the Internet economy. By 2000, Webcasting and related push technology will generate a third of the $14 billion in Net advertising, subscriptions, and retail revenues, projects Yankee Group Inc.

If Webcasters aren't careful, though, they could spark a backlash. "There's a fine line between adding value and the consumer feeling that you're being intrusive," warns Evan Neufeld, an analyst with market researcher Jupiter Communications Inc. People are already inundated with junk mail and now junk E-mail. Webcasting, if misused, could become one more avenue for unwanted solicitations and irrelevant material. "It's bad enough to pull garbage, but you don't want it pushed," says Joe Firmage, CEO of USWeb Corp., a Web-site builder.

There are potentially more serious problems. Webcasting programs can tie up networks and load up hard drives. Most of the programs do regular garbage collection, deleting ads and files from your PC after a certain amount of time has elapsed. But dangers still lurk. A lot of programs, including PointCast, automatically download the latest versions of their software; when you're ready to update, it's already on your PC. That saves you time, but there's a downside: "If it's buggy, you've just hosed a million people," says Sun's Schmidt.

These concerns resonate with corporate managers. PointCast's early missteps don't help assuage their fears. When the PointCast software came out last February, it quickly spread throughout corporations. Before long, some sites had thousands of people running PointCast—and soaking up as much as 30% of network capacity. Companies began banning it.

Last November, PointCast came out with a fix. With a new program called I-Server, companies can have PointCast content sent once, then rebroadcast it to employees. That cuts down on Net traffic going through the corporate security firewall. Another plus: Companies can set up their own channels to broadcast internal news. So far, Hassett says, more than 1,000 orders have been placed for the $1,000 package.

Still, companies remain wary. Hewlett-Packard Co., for one, discourages the use of PointCast, although it isn't banned outright. Robert R. Walker, HP's chief information officer, says push programs can help cut through information clutter, but for now, the benefits don't outweigh the risks. "We don't view this as a panacea," he says.

Potential problems are eclipsed for now by an all-too-familiar burst of Netmania, with startups galore. At this early stage, there is plenty of opportunity—and money. "The venture-capital community is fully engaged and fully lathered," says Andreessen. Some $80 million in venture funding has been lined up by just five startups, according to Venture-One Corp. Some investors can't wait to harvest some profits.

The startups are all over the map, both in terms of technology and business model. PointCast provides a collection of brand-name channels in a one-stop service—sort of a Webcast version of America Online. PointCast reformats the content, and the company's giant broadcast center handles the transmission. Unlike AOL, the PointCast Network is free. It make its money by selling ads on its network, which has four dozen advertisers, and shares ad revenues from its partners' channels. So far, the PointCast Network is delivering. After Pfizer Inc. started promoting an allergy site and its Zyrtec drug on PointCast last August, "traffic on our site increased tenfold," says Mark L. Linver, an information technology director at Pfizer.

A number of upstarts spot a chink in PointCast's model. They figure that, just as with Web sites, companies are going to want to offer their content directly to customers. BackWeb Technologies, IFusion, Marimba, and others offer software tools that let any company create its own channel. They also offer more flexibility than PointCast. Marimba's Castanet software, for example, allows software programs to be linked to content. That makes it possible for subscribers to play a game on an entertainment channel or analyze a stock portfolio on a financial channel. And IFusion has an edge in delivering sophisticated multimedia.

Companies are embracing the idea of do-it-yourself channels. General Motors and ZDNet have BackWeb channels. And The Wall Street Journal Interactive Edition is testing one for subscribers to its Personal Edition. When news stories are updated, a tiny front page containing headlines will appear on their screen. "It's kind of like being paged," says Tom Baker, business director for the Interactive Edition, which has increased its paying subscriber base to 70,000 from 30,000.

In Korea, Samsung Group's New Media Group is preparing to launch a series of information and entertainment channels for the Korean market, using software from IFusion. And The Weather Channel is experimenting with Webcasting software

from IFusion, BackWeb, and NET-delivery. "Push technology allows us to be more proactive," explains Kathleen Daly, director of new business development for The Weather Channel.

Weather, sports, and news are all obvious applications for Webcasting. The less obvious possibilities are only starting to open up. Rent Net's Web site provides constantly updated apartment-rental listings and relocation help for 1,000 cities. IFusion's ArrIve software will run a new Rent Net channel that will alert people to listings that meet their specific criteria. Subscribers can then look at floor plans and do 3-D virtual walk-throughs. "It brings the information right to you," says Rent Net Vice-President Jed Katz.

For all the activity, the hottest market right now for push programs is not Web sites but corporate intranets. It makes sense. Business professionals rely on up-to-date information, and they typically have high-speed, full-time connections to the Net. "It helps raise the corporate I.Q.," says Patrick Flynn, vice-president for systems development at Fruit of the Loom, which has PointCast installed on 250 employees' desks.

Focus

After spending last year putting up intranets, corporations are finding that they are becoming as cluttered as the public Web. By setting up their own channels, they can make sure that important company news and announcements get out to employees. NationsBank, for example, is developing a system it calls NationsCast, using software from Wayfarer Communications. It will broadcast corporate news, product information, and the bank's

stock price (a keen interest since the bank recently granted employee stock options) to 23,000 headquarters staff. Mitch Hadley, vice-president of NationsBank's Strategic Technology Group, says someday such technology could even be used to push information to customers at kiosks or ATMs.

What's more, these systems can be tied to corporate databases and programmed to Webcast alerts automatically. Ben & Jerry's Homemade Inc. is evaluating Wayfarer's software for a system that would alert managers when the company's perishable inventories drop below a certain level. Companies are just beginning to explore the possibilities. "We're drinking from a fire hose," says Kelsey Selander, vice-president for marketing at BackWeb.

The consumer market may be slower to develop. But that isn't stopping companies from targeting news and entertainment junkies. Berkeley Systems has turned its famous flying toaster screen saver into a PointCast-like service called After Dark Online. It culls information from such sources as Sports Illustrated and The Wall Street Journal Interactive (for paid subscribers) and displays it on the screen saver. Cambridge (Mass.)-based My Way Inc. has launched a service that will deliver personalized Web fare and Web site reviews to home users it figures are too busy to surf.

This spring, Paul Allen's Software Corp. will begin testing a PointCast competitor called Starwave Direct. It will pull together content from various Web sites the company has set up, including ESPNET SportsZone and Mr. Showbiz, along with personal-finance information and news, probably from ABC.

The Web Gets Pushy

1. A person downloads Webcasting software. She is asked to fill out a profile specifying what type of information she'd like to receive—for example weather, computer industry news, and selected stock prices.

2. The profile is submitted to the Webcasting service and stored on a database.

3. Special software programs then search a pool of content—in most cases a selection of content "channels" and Web sites. The software retrieves the requested information and sends it out.

Who's Who in Webcasting

AOL:

Its 8 million members will be able to have AOL and Web content sent to them automatically when the online service launches Driveway this spring.

Backweb:

Sells software tools so content providers and corporations can create their own Webcast channels.

Berkeley Systems:

The screen-saver veteran is getting into Webcasting with After Dark Online, which delivers content from Sports Illustrated and others to consumers.

IFusion:

This startup has a service similar to PointCast, but it can handle more TV-like animation and video.

Marimba:

Founded by former members of Sun's Java development team, Marimba's Castanet software can send programs and applets along with content.

Microsoft:

The company will make its foray into Webcasting midyear with a new version of Windows merged with the Internet Explorer browser and organized into channels.

Netscape:

Today, Netscape E-mails articles to users of its browser with In-Box Direct. In the spring, it will come out with Constellation, a browser and user interface that will display Webcast content.

PointCast:

The Webcasting pioneer. Content from partners, including CNN, The New York Times, and Wired magazine is displayed, along with ads, on a screen saver.

Wayfarer:

Its software is intended for use by companies that want to Webcast corporate information over their intranets.

Battle Royal

The competition is jolting established players into action. This spring, AOL's 8 million members will get their first taste of Webcasting. AOL plans to add a feature called Driveway that will periodically go out and fetch AOL content, Web pages, and E-mail based on members' preferences and download it onto their PCs. By letting members view information offline, AOL could ease the network jams that have plagued its service.

AOL, PointCast, Starwave, Microsoft—any one could become a media powerhouse of the emerging Internet broadcast medium. And they'll have plenty of competition as the distinctions between traditional media disappear in this digital melting pot. "What matters is having viewers' eyeballs," says Weintraut.

Ultimately, this is a battle for the desktop, and the two companies with the most to lose—Microsoft and Netscape—are quickly trying to rope it all in. As Webcasting transforms the way we consume business and entertainment information and even software, controlling the delivery platform will be even more critical. So in the coming year, the two rivals will each try to define what the desktop of the future will look like.

Netscape will be first out. This spring, the company will introduce Constellation, a software interface written in Sun's Java language and designed to run on top of any desktop operating system. Netscape hopes Constellation will become the main way people view information, whether it is stored on their PC, on a Web site, or Webcast to their screen.

Microsoft will make its move this summer, with a version of Windows that folds in the Internet Explorer browser and will display Webcast information in windows. Microsoft's name for the technology, Active Desktop, says a lot about the shape of things to come: The new Windows will be organized into half a dozen or more channels—including one for Microsoft's MSN and others featuring brand names such as PointCast.

The two giants have similar visions for how the Net will merge with the desktop, but their agendas diverge sharply. Microsoft wants to pull the Web into Windows and all of its software. Netscape is trying to break its rival's hammerlock by creating software that will work on any PC or gadget. To do so, it's enlisting the help of Marimba. The company's Castanet software will be included in Constellation so it will be able to store Java applets.

That could help accelerate the move toward software components delivered off the Net—and it could put Microsoft at a disadvantage. Companies such as Lotus Development Corp. and Corel Corp. are creating software applets that could be distributed that way.

There's nothing to stop Microsoft from doing the same. But for now, its big sellers, such as Microsoft Office, are way too big for that kind of delivery. And the Net is moving so fast that both companies are scrambling. "You're catching us right in the eye of the tornado. A lot of this hasn't been decided yet," says Brad Chase, vice-president in Microsoft's Application & Internet Client Group. Either way, the battle promises to keep viewers riveted to their seats. So don't touch that mouse.

 **Article Review Form at end of book.**

WiseGuide Wrap-Up

The process of pushing the HTML envelope has been going on at a rapid rate, and no end is in sight. Browser wars continue, sometimes frustrating and other times benefiting the users. The technologies behind the Web have improved very rapidly and will likely continue to do so for some time. Every new version of a Web browser will likely bring new capabilities and make the medium richer. The advances in communications technology promise a greater bandwidth that will allow users to handle the richer environment and growing content. In the not too distant future, users will watch full-length movies on demand as part of a Web site's offering, among other activities that are highly information-centric.

R.E.A.L. Sites

This list provides a print preview of typical **coursewise** R.E.A.L. sites. There are over 100 such sites at the **courselinks**™ site. The danger in printing URLs is that web sites can change overnight. As we went to press, these sites were functional using the URLs provided. If you come across one that isn't, please let us know via email to: webmaster @coursewise.com. Use your Passport to access the most current list of R.E.A.L. sites at the **courselinks**™ site.

Site name: World Wide Web Consortium

URL: http://www.w3.org/

Why is it R.E.A.L.? The World Wide Web Consortium oversees the HTML standards and houses a wealth of information about HTML and related technologies.

Key topics: World Wide Web, HTML, cascading style sheets, the development of the Web, past and current HTML standards, and related advice

Site name: Netscape Web Building

URL: http://home.netscape.com/computing/webbuilder/index.html

Why is it R.E.A.L.? This section of Netscape Web is full of tips, tricks, and general assistance on Web site design.

Key topics: HTML, Web design and design aids, JavaScript, design elements, graphics

Site name: Site Builder Network Workshop

URL: http://www.microsoft.com/workshop/

Why is it R.E.A.L.? Microsoft offers extensive help to Web developers, as well as materials for them to use.

Key topics: Web design, HTML, Jscript, VBScript, Active-X, design components, graphics, samples pages

Site name: Creating Killer Web Sites

URL: http://www.killersites.com/

Why is it R.E.A.L.? One of the design gurus on the Net shares his design philosophy. Although the site is designed to supplement the book with the same name, there is still plenty to learn from the site.

Key topics: Web design, HTML tags, design tips, graphic design for the Web, Web design tools

section

7

Learning Objective

- Embrace change and the challenge to be an agent of change.

Looking Ahead

WiseGuide Intro

The future has no introduction. Therefore, this section contains only one reading. This solitary reading acts more as a reminder of the importance of technology's future and the difficulty of predicting it than a foretelling of what is ahead. What was "ahead" then has become the past. Written in 1997, this reading is now a way for us to look back and contemplate what the future was in 1997 and what the future will be in years to come.

Question

1. Assess the accuracy of the vision presented in the article. Do you see them as predictions of technology in 1998? Where did the author come close and where did she not to the reality of 1998?

The Top 10 Trends to Watch in 1998

Laurie Freeman

As marketers head into 1998, several hot trends are shaping up that will affect the business-to-business arena.

To get an idea of what to expect, Business Marketing talked to a variety of players for their perspectives on what will emerge as key areas. Here's a look at the 10 hottest trends that top b-to-b marketers will focus on in 1998.

1. Online Customization

While 1997 was the year the Internet was widely embraced by b-to-b marketers, 1998 looks to be the year when marketers hone their online skills, presenting customized offerings.

"As people get comfortable, they spend less time surfing for information; time becomes a precious commodity and they want only the specific information they want without having to dig for it every time," says Greg Smith, strategic resources director, Darwin Digital, a New York interactive marketing agency.

"Customizing (using push technology) helps achieve that goal."

Getting online customers directly to the Web page and information they want instead of starting out on a home page is a priority for marketers.

"Online customization also means giving customers the ability to access a manufacturer's database via the Web site and bring up specifications, designs and pricing," says Andy Howarth, president, Snickelways Interactive, a New York Web consultancy that specializes in b-to-b applications.

2. Electronic Commerce

In 1996, marketers dipped their toes into the online sales waters. In 1997, a second generation of applications that use the Web as a front end to conduct business took off. In 1998, e-commerce tools will continue to evolve to allow complete transactions, including payment, online.

"We are going to conduct more and more business electronically," says Mr. Smith of Darwin Digital. "This is the decision time. Either get in now or

watch the competition take over your business."

Mark Silber, VP-executive creative director of Grey Interactive, New York, handles the Dell Computer Corp. Web site. The site already handles about $3 million in sales per day and allows online payment.

While Mr. Silber hesitates to project what will happen in '98, he says, "I think it's a snowball that will continue to grow because it makes so much sense on so many levels, particularly for companies like Dell that have a direct relationship with their customers. This is as close to a no-brainer as you can get in the business world."

3. Web Design Maturation

As a tool, b-to-b Web sites are undergoing multiple redesigns, becoming more functional and featuring more complete offerings.

"We're learning more and more about what customers want, how they use the Web sites, how they make their choices, and that rapid understanding quickly leads to better Web site design," says Darwin's Mr. Smith.

Specialization will drive Web site design and features in 1998, says Snickelways' Mr. Howarth. But he says it will be at least five years until companies routinely conduct transactions online.

4. Globalization

In 1998, globalization will no longer be an option, but simply a fact of doing business.

"This is not a new frontier anymore," says Clay Timon, chairman, Landor Associates, a San Francisco brand consultancy. "It's an expectation of business today that the marketplace is the entire world, and it's standard operating procedure that companies are thinking of the global market as part of the overall marketing plan."

Mature U.S. markets have forced businesses to go overseas, while the Internet makes global marketing possible, even easy.

"Today, people don't even ask where the supplier is or where the warehouses are," says Gary Stibel, principal of New England Consulting Group, a Westport, Conn., brand marketing consultancy. "You log on, you bring all the alternatives up and you make a business decision based upon facts presented and you proceed."

5. Loyalty Marketing

Call it relationship marketing, customer retention or frequency marketing, it's all loyalty marketing—the process of better understanding customers to make them lifelong brand and company devotees.

"Marketers today are beginning to think about what else

their customers want from a brand," says Watts Wacker, resident futurist of SRI Consulting, Westport, Conn. "Customers want more from their purchases, something that shows them that the brand values them as its customer," he says.

For many b-to-b marketers, this means redefining the entire sales process. Rather than sticking with a hit-and-run strategy, where sales reps concentrate on making the sale, the focus should be on the aftersale period.

6. Database Integration

This story has the makings of a modern day myth. A big Midwestern company, with hundreds of products and hundreds of salespeople for each product, sent reps into the field without tracking who was handling what. One customer, tired of the endless parade of Company X sales reps, took pictures of each one and sent them to company headquarters saying, "I don't care which one you send. Just send one."

In 1998, more companies will look to database integration to deal with their version of this problem.

Says John Ruf, a consultant with the New England Consulting Group, "By creating a data warehouse, accessibility to various types of data enables executives, from customer service to sales reps, to make decisions faster and with the most current information possible."

But the question is control.

"People are very protective of their data," says Daniel Boone, VP-direct marketing, Saatchi & Saatchi Business Communications, Rochester, N.Y. "Salespeople have cultivated those relationships and feel proprietary toward them; people in distribu-

tion and inventory control also have established relationships that they have a great deal vested in. When someone comes in to integrate all the data systems they have, they feel threatened."

Still, more companies will work to overcome that problem since the payback can be huge.

7. Consumerization

The idea that everyone, ultimately, is a consumer is gaining ground in b-to-b marketing. Numerous companies, many of which previously spend their entire ad budgets in trade magazines, have moved into consumer media, particularly TV. More and more marketers are treating business prospects as individuals.

"It's continuation of the trend of business-to-business marketers being interested in the ad disciplines used by packaged goods companies," says Chet Kane, president of Kane Bortree & Associates, a New York brand image and marketing consultancy.

Whether the end user is a business professional or consumer, Mr. Kane says, "People (who make buying decisions) think about how they're going to fulfill a particular need or desire. They don't think in terms of categories, market segments and niches, but that is how too many companies insist on marketing to them."

8. Emotion in Advertising

Along with a slide toward consumerization in marketing, more use of emotion—good, sad or bad—will crop up in advertising.

"Emotion is intended to open up the people who hold the corporate purse strings," says

Ann Hayden, executive creative director, Saatchi & Saatchi Business Communications. "It's all about having a human being relate to another human being. It's finally being recognized that big purchase decisions are more than a rational decision; people make really important decisions based on the way they feel and think."

While advertisers must be careful not to offend their audience, emotion is "a way to make you relate very quickly to a product or service," says Ms. Hayden. "It's a shortcut."

9. Shifting Research Models

The demand for faster information and research is inspiring more companies to make their immense information resources available online.

A survey by the Council of American Survey Research Organizations, Port Jefferson, N.Y., earlier this year showed that two-thirds of large companies plan more Internet-based and Internet-aided research. Dun & Bradstreet Corp., Murray Hill, N.J., for one, allows subscribers to tap into its Million Dollar Database online.

Still, though the Internet certainly can be a valuable asset to accessing information, many business executives stop short of hailing it as a substitute for other market research. What is more troublesome as 1998 arrives, industry executives say, is the growing use of research as a crutch.

"Because there is so much information and research now out there, companies are using research, any research, to validate bad strategies," says Mr. Stibel of New England Consulting. "It's getting to the point where business managers are incapable of making a decision without having a research study."

10. Brand Emphasis

There is a growing consensus that brands are a greater asset in b-to-b than previously thought.

"What we're seeing now is companies have really squeezed every cost saving they can out of their organizations, whether by restructuring, spinning off, offloading, that the only way to continue growing the bottom line is to really dramatically grow the top line," says Landor's Mr. Timon. "So companies are looking at what they have that allows them to increase their share and that's the strength of their brands, the few things that can truly give them differentiation in their category."

Component advertising, such as Intel's "Intel Inside" campaign for microprocessor chips, E.I. du Pont de Nemours & Co.'s print ads for its patented technologies and BASF's "We don't make many of the products you buy, but we make many of the products you buy better," run in consumer and b-to-b media.

"It's the branding of the corporate franchise, making it appeal to both consumers, as in the b-to-b customer (who buys the components), and the end user of the product," Mr. Timon says. "Equally importantly, there is a message to the investing market" that a company name is the source of product value.

"The bottom line for companies today," he says, "is that people care about brands."

 Article Review Form at end of book.

WiseGuide Wrap-Up

In this extraordinary dynamic technology age, we can expect the following:

- "Change" will be with us, and the rate of change will accelerate.

- If someone comes up with a new idea, it is highly likely that somebody has a working prototype.

- The speed with which the ideas turn into reality will become a strategic strength.

- The new way of looking at the future will be as a series of short runs.

- Most long-term forecasts will likely be wrong.

Think about it.

R.E.A.L. Sites

This list provides a print preview of typical **coursewise** R.E.A.L. sites. There are over 100 such sites at the **courselinks™** site. The danger in printing URLs is that web sites can change overnight. As we went to press, these sites were functional using the URLs provided. If you come across one that isn't, please let us know via email to: webmaster@coursewise.com. Use your Passport to access the most current list of R.E.A.L. sites at the **courselinks™** site.

Site name: World Wide Web Consortium
URL: http://www.w3.org/
Why is it R.E.A.L.? The World Wide Web Consortium tackles some policy, technology, and society issues. Various sections offer descriptions of the projects underway.
Key topics: Web standards, technology policy, social impact of the Internet

Site name: Electronic Frontiers Foundation
URL: http://www.eff.org/
Why is it R.E.A.L.? Electronic Frontiers Foundation addresses issues that may affect the legal, ethical, and regulatory directions that affect the Internet and activities on it.
Key topics: legal, ethical, and regulatory issues; intellectual property; privacy; social dimensions of the Internet

Index

Note: A reference in boldface type indicates authorship of the reading that begins on that page.

"Push" technology
  online marketing and, 12
  original vision of, 139
  problems with, 101–2, 149
  and Webcasting models, 147–52

R

Race, of Web users, 53
Radosevich, Lynda, **143**
Record-keeping, for online commerce, 137
RelevantKnowledge, 117–19
Rent Net, 150
Request-based model, 1
Retailing, Internet's impact on, 4–5, 115–16, 122–24
Robert Waxman Camera, 78
Ruby, Dan, **113**
Rules-based matching, 55, 56–57

S

"Sandbox" security approach, 133
Screen savers, and push technology, 148, 150
Scrip, 38–39
Search tools
  onsite, 144
  shortcomings of, 141, 144
  and Web advertising, 85–86
Secure electronic transaction (SET), 25–26, 40
Secure sockets layer (SSL), 25
Security
  and online fraud, 130–33
  of online sales, 12, 25–27, 42, 79, 84
  of smart cards, 34–35
Security Store, 78
Seigniorage, 32
Self-regulation, 129
Selling Wine Without Bottles, 22
Seminerio, Maria, **98**
A Separate Jurisdiction for Cyberspace?, 138
Service providers (ISPs), ratings of, 94–95
Sex products. *See* Pornography
Shell sites, 144
Singleton, Solveig, **127**
SkyMall Inc., 93
Smart cards
  development of, 12, 30–32
  potential problems with, 34–35
Snap Online
  CNET participation in, 16, 17–18
  services of, 90
Sniffing, 26
Spam, 98, 99–100, 101–2
Sponsorships, 49, 86
Spoofing, 26
SportsLine USA, 88, 108
Staffing, for new ventures, 14–15
Standardized generalized markup language (SGML), 141, 142
Starwave, 108
Starwave Direct, 150
Stock market information, 3–4

Storytelling, online, 19
Subscription fees, 49, 103–4
Sun Microsystems, home page design, 145
Sweepstakes, 71–75

T

Targeted e-mail, 99–100
Tax fraud, 35–36
Taylor, William C., **71**
Technology, and branding, 110
Telephone scams, 130–31
Television
  as model for Web, 147
  and online services, 18–19
  promoting Web sites on, 108
Testing, of Web sites, 143–46
Top 25 Web sites, 117–19
Toyota, 9, 88
Trade Compass, 96
Trademarks, protecting, 137
Trade Show Central, 27
Traffic, measuring, 63, 117–19
Training, Web-based, 81, 111–12
Transaction processing
  future of, 155
  growth of, 96–97
  for online banking systems, 26–27, 79
  security of, 12 (*see also* Security)
Travel, online services, 4, 11, 82
Travel agencies, Internet's impact on, 4, 11
Trojan horses, 26, 130–32, 133
Trust, building, 12, 23

U

United States government, role in digital cash debate, 32–33, 34, 37
United States Government Electronic Commerce Policy, 125
Usability, of Web sites, 143–46
Usenet groups, 48
User fees, resistance to, 87, 92
User Interface Engineering, 143, 144
UUnet Technologies Inc., 94, 95

V

Value webs, 67
Virtual auctions, 10
Virtual Vineyards, 7, 8, 25
Viruses, 26
Visa International, 30–31, 88

W

Walker, Christy, **93**
Wallace, Sanford, 98, 99–100
Wall Street Index, 27
Wall Street Journal Interactive Edition, 150
Wal-Mart, 122
Wayfarer, 150, 151
Web21, 118

Web advertising
  effect of online communities on, 48–49
  growth of, 5–6, 20, 85–90
  measuring, 90
  quality of, 87
  revenues from, 6, 7, 89–90
  strategies for, 19–21
  and Webcasting, 148–49
  See also Advertising; Online marketing
Web auctions, 10, 61–62, 120–21
Web-based businesses
  evolution of, 113–14
  strategies for, 8–13, 66–68
Web browsers. *See* Browser software
Webcasting, 139, 147–52
Web marketing. *See* Online marketing
Web site design
  and community-building, 10
  evolution of, 139
  future of, 155–56
  high-quality approach to, 9
  usability issues, 143–46
Web sites
  average size of, 144
  determining top 25, 117–19
  early commercial approaches, 113
  maintaining, 107, 145–46
WebTV, 18
Web users
  classifying, 58–60
  demographics of, 50, 53, 58–60
  in European homes, 116
  growing numbers of, 86
  habits of, 51–52
  tracking, 149
The WELL, 48, 49
Wetzel, Rebecca, **94**
White space, 144
Whoosh effect, 67
Wine, online sales of, 7, 8, 25
Woodruff, David, **115**
Wooley, Scott, **120**
World Avenue, 78
World Wide Web
  audience growth for, 86
  common uses of, 51–52, 53, 58–60
  difficulties of using, 141–42, 147
  ethics and (*see* Ethics)
  evolution of business on, 113–14
  legal issues of (*see* Legal issues)
  measuring traffic on, 117–19
  as news medium, 19
  privacy vs. free speech on, 127–29
World Wide Web Consortium, 153, 158
Wreden, Nick, **76**

Y

Yahoo, 17, 18
You Don't Know Jack, 87–88
Yoyodyne Entertainment, 71

Z

Ziff-Davis, 88

Putting it in *Perspectives*
-Review Form-

Your name:_____   Date: _____

Reading title: _____

Summarize: Provide a one-sentence summary of this reading. _____

_____

_____

_____

Follow the Thinking: How does the author back the main premise of the reading? Are the facts/opinions appropriately supported by research or available data? Is the author's thinking logical?

_____

_____

_____

_____

_____

Develop a Context (answer one or both questions): How does this reading contrast or compliment your professor's lecture treatment of the subject matter? How does this reading compare to your textbook's coverage?

_____

_____

_____

_____

_____

Question Authority: Explain why you agree/disagree with the author's main premise.

_____

_____

_____

_____

_____

_____

COPY ME! Copy this form as needed. This form is also available at http://www.coursewise.com
Click on: *Perspectives*.